Achieving Competence, Success and Excellence in Teaching

Mark Brundrett and
Peter Silcock

ROUTLEDGE / FALMER
Taylor & Francis Group

London and New York

First published 2002 by RoutledgeFalmer
11 New Fetter Lane, London EC4P 4EE

Simultaneously published in the USA and Canada
by RoutledgeFalmer
29 West 35th Street, New York, NY 10001

RoutledgeFalmer is an imprint of the Taylor & Francis Group

© 2002 Mark Brundrett and Peter Silcock

This book is a true co-construction. Authors' names are ordered on the book's cover alphabetically, and for no other reason.

Typeset in Bembo by BC Typesetting, Bristol
Printed and bound in Great Britain by
TJ International Ltd, Padstow, Cornwall

British Library Cataloguing in Publication Data
A catalogue record for this book is available from the British Library

Library of Congress Cataloging in Publication Data
A catalog record for this book has been requested

ISBN 0–415–24068–9 (pbk)
      0–415–24067–0 (hbk)

Contents

Preface

Teaching: a profession on the move

At present, teachers in England and Wales are experiencing changes to their jobs and status more rapid than any most will remember. They can still (just about) claim to belong to the same profession. But they are increasingly grouped differently in terms of their performance. Those with 'advanced' skills, those who have cleared performance thresholds to win more pay, those on a 'fast track to promotion' work alongside others who have no privileged status. They are appraised via a range of criterion-based systems (including Ofsted inspection). They are publicly accountable to parents, peers and school governors. They are separated via targets and league-tables into those who match up to expectation and those who do not. They may be counselled on their shortcomings by 'performance managers'. The policy of 'outsourcing' as a way of turning around failing schools and local education authorities accelerates, so some teachers are, now, being guided by those whose educational credentials may be professionally dubious.

Such 'reforms' (most introduced by the present government during its previous term of office) are all based on a belief that good teaching is a single, unitary process, to be agreed by practitioners, inspectors, appraisers, parents, governors, performance managers, private consultants and contractors or whoever. Despite inconsistencies built into the various assessment and appraisal systems presently used, reformers seem to take for granted that there are, to hand, sure-fire ways of separating the good from the bad, the advanced from the less advanced, those who satisfy expectation from those who do not. This assumption is named in the ensuing text, 'the myth of the formula'. It is believed false. A *single* cohesive blueprint for checking any teacher's performance, to which most professionals agree and which can be applied justly, cannot be devised. Educational and social scientific theory has always supported divergent models of good practice arising in settings which make comparative assessments between teachers and schools problematic. It is not that we cannot tell good from bad teaching. But we cannot do so easily, or in ways agreed by everyone, for reasons this book makes plain.

Unfortunately, at the moment, the academic world of English education rather resembles the character in the film *One Flew Over the Cuckoo's Nest* who has frontal cerebral lobes surgically removed to rid him of his violent, antisocial behaviour, but in the process loses his zest for life. The ideological blood-letting which used to hamper progress has vanished. But so has our trust in the theories which triggered it. This has resulted in there being few solid alternatives published, over recent years, to the radical changes being wrought to teaching – though many innovations are based on dubious justifications (where these are known). Many writers have dissented to various 'reforms' and continue to dissent. Few strike as hard as they might at these, by showing what could take their place.

This book discusses a way of prescribing quality teaching different from that underwriting present-day legislation. It does so partly to set the record straight about uncertainties involved in judging what is competent, successful and excellent teaching, but mainly to show that we can deal with such uncertainties better than we once could. It is perfectly possible to write about good teaching without being doctrinaire. It is also possible to admit that competing value-systems give birth to competing models of good practice while, at the same time, promoting one of them (i.e. 'partnership approaches'). There is an important difference between recommending a model of good teaching and prescribing it for everyone. Schools are never served well by regulatory systems which, while purporting to raise standards, actually remove from teachers that choice of approach which is at the heart of their professionalism.

Mark Brundrett and Peter Silcock, July 2001

1 The study of teaching

Introduction

We can, already, recognise competent, successful and excellent teaching. Prospective schoolteachers who satisfy a range of standards set by the Teacher Training Agency (TTA 1997b) are competent. Good and excellent teachers divide from the satisfactory via common 'Office for Standards in Education' criteria (Ofsted 1995): all school inspectors judge poor, acceptable and first-rate teaching using the same framework. Lately, the Department for Education and Employment (DfEE) has named six areas for excellence meant to guide the assessment of Advanced Skills Teaching (Sutton *et al.* 2000). These are: 'achieving results; subject knowledge; lesson planning; motivating pupils and maintaining discipline; assessment and evaluation; supporting and advising colleagues' (Sutton *et al.* 2000: 418–419). So the TTA, Ofsted and DfEE, together, give us reliable ways of sorting out what is and is not quality teaching.

But standard guides, alone, do not deal with classroom specifics. Even the most detailed frameworks (e.g. Hay McBer 2000) have to be applied to particular circumstances by professionals themselves. Elements of practice that school inspectors are trained to inspect (planning, relationships, methods, work-setting, pace and subject knowledge) span broad classes and combinations of skill. Nothing is assumed about the precise content of lesson objectives, pupil–teacher relationships and strategies likely to work, what makes a lesson well paced or betrays how deeply into subjects teachers should reach. Inspectors – like all others who find their judgements prey to the unforeseen and unpredictable – accept that there are many ways to teach well. Teachers are paid to bring about learning in pupils, and factors that ease or impair learning are legion, since children enter schools with widely varying capabilities and ambitions, born from culturally and economically diverse backgrounds.

Admittedly, good teachers keep a weather eye open for anything likely to affect pupil learning. This fact preserves the utility of TTA criteria. For it is teachers who must '*ensure* effective teaching of whole classes, and of groups and individuals within the whole-class setting, so that teaching objectives are met' (TTA 1997b: para. 2f, italics added). Teachers have to take whatever steps are needed to safeguard their success. Yet, on the face of it, no amount of 'taking into account' of pupil attitude and capability will 'ensure' that teaching objectives are met, where 'ensure' means more than teachers doing their best. No action, however informed or sophisticated, can oblige learners to behave in ways contrary to their own inclinations, even if major factors affecting teaching-learning circumstances are known. Strictly speaking, teaching and learning are independent processes. One human being's behaviour does not cause improvements in another in an unmediated fashion (except at primitive levels where 'laws' of conditioning prevail), for each human being is sovereign in his or her own mental domain. We would not wish it otherwise. We will still insist that teachers do their best to ensure learning. But doing one's best is a world away from ensuring effective teaching. And this realisation forces us towards two connected conclusions.

First, we must honestly square up to the limited control teachers have over some central conditions for learning, owed to pupil and school-specific factors. No less urgently, we should check out these conditions in terms of the known ways of dealing with them. Saying that a teacher's capacity for ensuring learning is limited does not deny it altogether. It is to be hoped that the more we know about the limits of pedagogy the more we can strengthen its influence within those limits. And if it should prove that learners' readiness to learn *is* the one essential ingredient of teaching success, we might give more regard to methodologies which duly respect it – even though such methodologies are not presently *in vogue*. English educational policies are preoccupied with sharpening teacher performance through legislated measures linked to an assessment-led accountability (see Broadfoot 2000). This fixation on remedying teacher shortcomings may have distracted us from helping the same teachers respond intelligently to demands arising from pupils themselves – apart from any duties practitioners might have to the teaching of subjects, hitting exam targets or whatever.

It is a truism that changing times lead to changing expectations. But changes in expectations should not mean always starting from scratch. There is no virtue in dismissing teaching approaches still found in classrooms just because they are out of tune with the latest thinking. It may be that truly innovative techniques, arising from new rationales for learning and intellectual development, work because they extend or develop teachers' existing thinking rather than contradicting it. What will aid us to a grasp of the nature of good and excellent teaching is an in-depth look at the way teachers actually teach – *without prejudice*. And we might look hardest at what can be done to give credence both to our public expectations of schools and to the challenges arising just because they deal with other (usually immature) human beings who have minds and needs of their own.

Three approaches to the study of teaching

As introduced, we must resist the temptation to short-cut theorising about practice by moving too quickly to actual recommendations (especially where theories have been overlooked by legislation). We may not need to disinter old quarrels about incompatible positions, since recent thinking has brought us to a point where we know why *some* positions might remain incompatible yet might not stop us reaching conclusions about practice. If we stick to basics – the interactions between teachers and pupils *vis-à-vis* school subjects found in all school settings – there are only three general ways teachers can approach their task. And it is these easily stated ways which guard strongholds of competing professional ideals (their obviousness witnesses to their abiding effects).

First, teachers can work through some form of top-down imposition. Second, they can shrink from imposition in order to sanction learners' own viewpoints. Third, they can structure a collaborative system which makes a 'middle way' between imposition and learner-centredness. In so far as third way options dominate modern thinking, there is devil in the detail of what these might actually mean. There are strong and weak forms of imposition, middle-of-the-road and extreme types of 'progressivism'. So to seek stable midway points between the two begs questions of definition and practicality. But, staying with generalities *pro tem*, the three options introduced are (paradigmatically) a teacher or subject-centred approach; a learner-centred approach; and a partnership approach (compromising between teacher and learner-demands).

An easy way to compare each of these is by isolating teacher and learner decision-making as 'processes', while making learning and other desirable outcomes a 'product', as follows (see also Silcock 1993a).

(a) Teacher/subject-centred or: *Process* $\rightarrow$ *product*

(b) Pupil-centred or: *Process* $\rightarrow$ *process* $\rightarrow$ *product*

(c) Partnership approaches or: *Process product process*

With the first paradigm, a teaching process outputs directly into a learning product; and in so far as intermediaries affect success it is thought in teachers' remit to deal with these. With the second, it is selected intermediaries, notably the skills, attitudes and commitments of pupils themselves, which give results (learning outcomes): these have the decisive role in the pedagogic equation. So it is on these which teachers must concentrate. With the third, pupil and teacher-actions are integral to a system where each functions optimally in tandem with the other. Two agencies work effectively because they work together. What is promised by insulating the paradigms from each other is that each will faithfully deliver *particular* outcomes. It may not be a question of whether there is one sort of 'quality' teaching, but what, exactly, each promises to any teacher pursuing excellence.

As a preliminary to closer study, it is worth exploring this possibility for each paradigm in turn.

An introduction to teacher-centred approaches

What seems inviting about the process–product paradigm is its stand on a 'zero tolerance' for educational failure. If teachers can really dictate outcomes, the highest fence in the educational stakes is cleared at a bound, at least in principle. An uncluttered 'cause–effect' connection is banked on by anyone believing that standardising curricula is critical to raising standards, given that this belief practically equates clarity of task with curricular delivery. Once teachers know exactly what is expected of them they have success in their sights. Should they, still, fail, they can rightly be regarded as chief culprits for their own failure. Such teachers can be dismissed, admonished or retrained.

A likely flaw in what is the simplest possible pedagogic formula has already been mentioned. It is not that teachers cannot manage pupils' learning at all, just that it is hard to see how they can ever be sure they will succeed. The premise that one group of human beings (teachers) 'manages' the minds and actions of another (pupils) must always be qualified, for it makes all of us potential arbiters of other people's actions and decisions while remaining uncertain arbiters of our own. Yet this 'performance management' formula is seldom questioned by those outside professional circles. Parents often take for granted that any difficulties raised by pupils' intransigence can be ironed out somehow (as Winch 1998 says). They believe (rightly, in Winch's view) that there are practical solutions for all such problems. Of course, to say this belief is not always true, doesn't mean it isn't usually true (Winch and Gingell 1996). Such qualified approval might confirm the first paradigm as one well suited to present-day schools.

But no one would or could argue that today's schools never fail their pupils. Each year, a number of students complete formal schooling with few qualifications; some can neither read nor write at even minimal levels (Pring 1986). Although this failure of educational policy may have other causes than unrealistic expectations of teachers, it does leave open the possibility that unreasonable expectation is a main cause.

An introduction to learner-centred approaches

Kelly (1989), following Stenhouse (1975), has done much to popularise the idea that teachers neither can nor should 'deliver' a set curriculum but are better occupied teaching students how to access curricula for themselves. Core learning processes are outputs we should want, not specified 'content' which, in any case, few are likely to agree about (Kelly 1995). Importantly, such proposals do not diminish the school or teacher's role. For although pupils are treated as agents for their own learning, mediating or facilitating that agency is in the remit of teachers. 'Contextualising' learning or teaching for independence replaces knowledge transmission or performance-management as role-definitions. So if learners fail we can, still, name the teacher as culpable. We can still condemn uncertain empowerment strategies, poorly resourced workplaces, or whatever.

However, prescriptions inferred from the 'process' model are rather tenuously linked to teacher-action and learning outcomes. The paradigm makes requirements for setting and achieving objectives differ between pupils; and there are real uncertainties for teachers working informally in knowing exactly what does count as a successful outcome. If it is in the dispensation of learners, what might we believe indisputably are criteria for teaching effectiveness? Do these lie in the attitudes fostered in learners or in their actual achievements? And does it matter what those achievements are? Or should pupil-empowerment itself become our teaching goal, disregarding the content of what ultimately is learned? To give to learners decision-making powers may overburden them, no matter that they have been educationally enfranchised. Critics (e.g. Alexander 1992) see as bedrock the requirement of a modern educational system that types of learning are non-negotiable (e.g. literacy and numeracy skills); and to offload responsibilities onto learners – albeit creditably armed with positive attitudes and personally useful skills – is to bypass the decisions which matter most. Moreover, to opt for strategies that hit desired targets indirectly, creates a more hazardous set-up than that created by the process-product ideal. Teachers, knowing they will be held accountable if they fail, may find a thoroughly learner-centred curriculum just too risky to contemplate.

Raising such objections does not damn altogether process-based teaching. It encourages us to limit known difficulties while retaining inherent strengths. What commends the classic 'learner-centred' paradigm is its full hearted acceptance of the socio-psychological and ethical deficits earned by teachers exerting top-down control over pupil learning. By not glossing over these, it helps us see where further progress might be made. For, to press on towards the third paradigm, one might speculate that it is reasonable for us to concede some basic misgivings about controlled curricular delivery while, still, insisting pupils meet agreed targets. Surely, all we need do is more carefully demarcate teaching and learning roles? If learning is something learners have to do for themselves this does not mean they do so in an academic vacuum: their capacity and appetite for learning must, somewhere, benefit directly from pedagogic skill. A properly 'dual-referenced' rationale, once written, will guide both teachers and learners towards common goals in practically useful ways. If plainly stated, it should set down rules not to be ignored without doing injury to the paradigm itself.

An introduction to partnership (dual-referenced) approaches

It seems sensible to think that educational outcomes are won by interchanges between curricular partners with complementary roles. School teaching and school learning are conceptually bound together, so they must interrelate practically too. And although partnership work takes for granted that teaching skill alone cannot deliver quality outcomes, it gives just as much credence to doubts about 'empowered' pupils hitting learning targets consistently enough to satisfy parents or politicians. Its rationale condemns both classic paradigms. What, purportedly, it does not do is fudge the issue of whether it is teachers or pupils who matter most to educational success, for it refuses to come down on one side or the other. No matter how autonomous a pupil is, the fact a state-financed regime exists means due note is taken of publicly agreed aims and the rule-governed way in which schools operate. Similarly, no matter how charismatic or skilled a teacher, internal pressures on learners (from social and psychological sources) with which the learners themselves have to cope are respected. The onus on realising curricular aims, therefore, moves from teachers or pupils alone and becomes the responsibility of both, though not always in equivalent measure in all circumstances.

It is common enough in schools for teachers to collaborate with each other, with parents and (in a rather different sense) with pupils. Leaving aside for the moment merits of types of collaborative work *per se*, the partnership approach outstrips the practical benefits of collaboration to become a major paradigm of good practice (or a 'new' professionalism: Hargreaves 1994; Quicke 1998). At a level of personal achievement, pupils fashion their mental worlds and learning skills through their own agency. But (at least in institutional settings) they do so within shared, culturally rich frameworks (resourced especially by teachers and parents) powerfully affecting what they do. This paradigm (related to a socio-cognitive process called *co-construction*) finds an implacable dualism at the heart of schooling, counterpointing the roles of learners with teachers, then extending their relationships to include important others, in a complex though comprehensible pedagogic enterprise.

What knowledge we have of the approach suggests it might be a break-through in teaching methodology (Silcock 1999). Because it is unremit-tingly co-operative (learning is always 'co'-constructed), it invites a bipartisan form of teaching not simply to satisfy the whims of a teacher or the variable demands of circumstance but as a modus operandi. It imposes dyadic controls, rule operations, curricular decision-making and so on. Its binding, contractual nature gives parity to participants by rule: within true partnerships, constraints of rule and relationship affect both agents. It isn't only that learners are constrained by what teachers do, teachers are just as bound by learner-actions and demands.

Unfortunately, deciding that teaching and learning are bound together makes sense only if one can pin down precise terms in which they are and convincingly illustrate benefits. Otherwise, contentions become merely fatuous, reducing to the self-evident fact that teachers and learners must both engage in any organised teaching situation. One suspects that teachers opt sometimes for top-down management and sometimes for learner empowerment because a degree of single-mindedness guarantees results of some sort. There are obvious dangers in trying to achieve too much at once. In the end, we might decide to deal with the currently fashionable topic of what makes for excellent teaching just by reasserting the profoundly variable nature of teaching. Satisfaction might be limited to showing how the different paradigms constrain teachers trying to teach competently, successfully or reach excellence. Model-specific rather than general factors may unite them. This has to depend on what we are looking for when we look for quality of teaching or level of success.

Different standards of teaching

The interplay between generic and contextual factors

Competent teachers are not always successful, and teachers can enjoy success despite their lack of skill. But this does not by itself make teaching a random or irregular craft. Nor does it make generic skills irrelevant. Reasoning in this way would be defeatist in the extreme. It is a fair supposition that those who are effective in classrooms will be largely competent, while those who approach excellence will to a high degree teach effectively. So there is likely to be a linear progression from teaching competence to excellence.

What potentially confuses any analysis of this progression is the fact that to assess teaching as poor, good or excellent is already to assume values taken from the perspective we are trying to judge. We find ourselves pinning our hopes on selected strategies because behind our selection lie those very values sanctioning it (if I believe excellent teaching is that which delivers exam results, I do so because I already value exams). Circularity seems unavoidable. The best we might manage is to take this fact itself part of the equation – that is, admit that teaching quality will always have linear, generic and contextual (value-oriented) features. We just need to decide which dominate in any judgements about teaching we happen to make.

If there is a rule that teaching assessment always invokes multilevel judgements (some of which will be pre-set by value-assumptions behind the exercise), it will stay true even with reference to a nationally imposed curriculum. This rule (assuming it is true) weakens the position of anyone wishing to standardise teaching and assessment methods. Given that one has to partial out the influence of contextual factors, we are left, when defining competent teaching (for example), with generic skills and linear progression. Yet the generality of skill-lists we are left with enormously limits their application. Though there will always be some merit to stating them, at least at the level of initial training, dangers can follow from doing so given that context-specific determinants are likely to count more in many settings than the generic. Whether such hazards are confined purely to the study of competent teaching, or whether they appear just as strongly in studies of teaching success and excellence remains to be seen.

Competence

Competence represents, on one interpretation, a base-line for teaching effectiveness. A competent teacher is someone who retains and exercises proven skills through sustained effort. Any higher levels of skill will add to these building-blocks of professionalism (sometimes called 'competencies': see Chapter 7). But teaching isn't a job like carpentry or plumbing with very specific and well-defined outputs. It is notable for its diversity of task, and the culturally cherished yet often contested nature of the intellectual, social, emotional and physical gains awarded by it. Given that teaching skills have to be applied in almost as many settings as life presents, there is awesome variability in what the job asks for. It is worth returning briefly to the TTA's list of 'standards' (TTA 1997b). Some of these ask for procedural rather than pedagogic skills, some bring intellectual capabilities into play (such as perception), some emotional attitudes (such as perseverance), some stress relationships, pragmatic skills, empathy and so on (Hayes 1997).

On this count, what we need are not so much lists giving all capabilities parity in training, suggesting that once acquired in the normal course they are sufficient to ensure teaching competence. What we need, more, is some inkling of what skills work best in the special circumstances of various types of classroom, how far these will alter through circumstance, and how they will alter. That is, to know what makes for competent teaching we need to know how common tasks give its procedural, cognitive, social and affective capabilities their special character (cf. Reynolds 1999). Put most simply: before we can list teaching competencies, we have to make a better shot at listing the challenges of modern classrooms. If we start with generic skills, we risk getting sidetracked into trying to fit all of them to all tasks, and then having very little insight into the particular ways in which they apply.

Former Chief Inspector of Schools Chris Woodhead's approval of large-scale, direct teaching methods (Ofsted 1996) fitted comfortably with his premise that teachers should focus on delivering the National Curriculum. That was the touchstone of their professional duties. Yet when we start elsewhere – perhaps with an experiential form of values-education preparing learners for 'life-long' learning or for 'citizenship' (Starkey 2000) – we might take a very different stance. Teachers of citizenship must at a premium work persuasively to help pupils commit themselves to virtuous, responsible, value-driven ways of life (Silcock and Duncan 2001). Questions of teaching competence are inextricably bound up with questions about aims. And eclectic competency statements (or statements of standards: TTA 1997b) not only avoid value issues, but also can be taken to imply that such issues need not be considered at all.

Success

Competence doesn't guarantee success even when teaching skills are matched to a school or classroom culture. Though a learner's home-spun values may be close to those of a classroom, no child is perfectly primed for school life, for it is in the nature of education to induct children from private and personal worlds to the academic and professional. The induction of people into a new way of life requires a degree of compliance no one should ever guarantee. This is to be realistic not defeatist. And there can be profound social reasons for the really tough problems teachers face in keeping pupils on track for certain types of goal. Value-conflicts can put learners' personal attitudes well out of line with those of a school, returning us to questions of priority. They also reveal the existence of social and political regimes within the wider society opposed to the educational, reminding us that it is partly the potency of these which inspire some people's quest for innovative and 'alternative' modes of teaching.

One might think that where pupil and teacher values are totally at variance, no educational policies can work. So any thoughts about teaching success must confront not only arguments about values but the rights of different groups to assert their own. Almost certainly, in any one society (such as English society at the beginning of a third millennium) there will be moral, academic and industrial pressures from stakeholder groups, unavoidable for teachers as for politicians. If a society ever becomes wholly materialist, perhaps placing consumerism and wealth creation above moral virtues such as honesty, prudence and diligence, the job of teaching by any standard becomes practically impossible. One might think such a situation already exists in inner-city areas where people's aspirations are not in the least like those aimed at by public institutions. How far this is true and can be tolerated, and how far it can be changed, are issues following hard on the heels of those introduced.

Excellence

If excellence transcends competence and success, it must build on both to a degree. For that reason alone, we can immediately decide that there can be no single model of excellent or quality teaching, just as there can be no single model of competence. In Muriel Spark's (1965) book *The Prime of Miss Jean Brodie,* the pygmalion-like control Jean Brodie has over her girls' lives is owed to her romantic and somewhat eccentric ideals. By contrast, the American educator Carl Rogers (1983) tries to eliminate as far as he can his own effects on students, wishing them to tread their own routes to success. Any accounts of excellent teaching have to show how the teaching embodies values the teaching seeks to fulfil.

Principles explaining excellence are intimately close to those explaining competence and success, though, by nature, the degree to which pedagogy embraces fundamental values will be at an optimum with excellence. Other determinants – such as teaching charisma, a narrative gift, the more personal integration of skills into a style – will play a part relative to dominant values, and the point of studying excellence in its own right is to give due weight to these matters. This doesn't alter the salient fact. A general condition for excellence has to be the tailoring of capabilities to valued aims. The ideal of teaching excellence held by those who prioritise knowledge delivery is of a different order to that of teachers who idealise learner autonomy or think both sorts of value really do engage each other. For the latter, where it is expected that conflicts arise as a matter of course between personal and imposed values, negotiation and collaboration will figure as values in their own right. A supremely successful teacher will be one whose convincing presentation of any discipline-based case does not at the same time destroy the force of a pupil's. This may mean a teacher following competing aims at different times – perhaps keeping to strict procedural rules when pursuing academic truths while, later, falling back on different strategies to engage in imaginative problem-solving. We might suppose that this is to rule out of court the brilliant raconteur or the warm, nurturing person who allows even the youngest to bloom precociously. But all that is suggested is that skills are assessed within and not outside the value-context which prioritises them.

There are other approaches to excellence in teaching to set against the value-centred. Management consultants Hay McBer (2000) have given us a list of qualities needed by newly qualified and advanced skill teachers and by those applying to cross the government's new performance threshold (see Sutton *et al.* 2000). These consultants took from discussions with large numbers of teachers and pupils incidents and actions having positive (excellent) classroom outcomes. There is much that is worthwhile in any survey of teacher views. Yet taxonomies share the weaknesses found in the other lists of competency statements introduced. There are innumerable ways to show excellence in teaching, as there will be in any profession which works in a range of environments. Simply to report what teachers themselves say misses the need to couple what is said to the (usually hidden) reasons why such views are held. It isn't just physical and human settings that decide excellence (a taxonomy can perhaps cope with that fact), it is the value systems held by practitioners and clients alike *vis-à-vis* such settings.

Just as we cannot decide what is competent or successful teaching just by looking at what practitioners do, so we cannot decide what excellent teaching is just by talking to teachers or to pupils. We have first to agree our expectations of those who teach; and that is never going to be straightforward. At the moment, aims built into the way the 2000 English/Welsh National Curriculum is assessed (via league-tables and so on) set performance-standards for all practitioners. If politicians are serious about raising standards, they have to take equally seriously the fact that not only will there be people aspiring to different standards, but also there will be those who cannot fulfil the most highly rated, traditional ideals. Types of competence, success and excellence to be discussed, are those thought most likely to work with children raised in all households, with backgrounds, attitudes, ambitions and capabilities typically found in the United Kingdom. A number of these deviate more and more from a traditional British stereotype. They are discussed in detail and without reservation below.

Summary: the book's argument

Three major teaching paradigms are studied, alongside their rationales, as routes to competence, success and excellence. These are set against a backdrop of changing socio-economic and political demands, and are thoroughly tested against this background as well as against each other. Mainly, it isn't intended to devalue any model beyond clarifying its strengths and weaknesses. For one thing, suitable educational journeys for some learners may not be towards popular destinations, but towards places they can actually reach. What we *can* say is that entrenched, market-driven policies enforcing, for example, the training of 'measurable' generic skills, cry out for rigorous appraisal. One suspects, from time to time, government policies for raising educational standards do assume that there is no viable option but that which legislates for all. To give credence to this as to other possibilities, generic models will be studied alongside those that would, if followed, undermine them. But it will also match 'partnership' models point for point to the requirements of modern western societies, believing that these models open up novel ventures in theory.

The book is planned as follows. Chapter 2 lists first principles of good practice before testing out the resulting general approach against likely criticisms, especially those related to disputes about values and value-conflicts. Chapters 3–5 discuss teaching theories or models as reservoirs of professional knowledge and skill, setting out what teachers must do to reach high standards regarding each one. Chapter 6 is a practical guide to 'co-constructive' teaching, based on premises stated in Chapter 5. Chapters 7–9 bring together main conditions for competent, successful and excellent teaching, showing especially how 'partnership' teaching can and in practical terms fulfil these. Chapter 10 reviews and summarises the book's central case. While harmonising important themes arising in the educational literature during recent years, writers set out a detailed, practical and theoretical guide to good educational practice justified in terms of present-day school conditions. Competing possibilities are compared so as to isolate what each has to offer, without overly stigmatising any, or stirring together incompatible ideas into a fairly meaningless brew.

2 What is good teaching?

First principles and counter-arguments

Introduction: two types of teaching

From time to time, all of us who live within communities become teachers. Directly or indirectly, we teach friends, children, siblings, acquaintances, strangers who need our help, whatever situations demand. And although we will differ in how seriously we take our pedagogic roles, through practice and – sometimes – through necessity, we will develop talents for communication, relationship, empathy, tolerance and so on which mediate the process of passing on knowledge and skills to others. We will become good, mediocre or poor teachers. But we will be teachers of a sort.

Professional teaching can be judged a special case of that informal teaching which becomes a passing brief for most of us. For although professional teachers must presumably bank on the same human talents for helping and informing others resorted to in less formal settings, they will also adapt these talents to larger, more diverse cohorts of students. Over time, complexities of preparing different sorts of learners for their future lives modifies skills otherwise acquired naturally, making professional teaching both similar to and distinct from lay teaching in the way skills are refined and deployed. This conclusion reminds us of how context constrains teaching; but it also reminds us of how long-term intention affects skill, since the reason why we ask professional teachers to work in institutions like schools has to include the special purposes such institutions have.

Arguably, it is the special purposes of professional teaching which entail its having to be organised within institutions so it can be systematically programmed and linked directly to its goals. This is a fairly obvious conclusion to reach, as the product of any sort of teaching must, somehow, call into existence suitable processes. If I teach a friend how to use a woodwork tool, I must have in mind how that tool can be used skilfully.

I will know what will count as a good outcome relative to my friend's starting point, which will, in turn, help me realise how to proceed. These considerations both tell me what to do and how to judge success. However, professional teachers have a much broader remit, transcending the immediate and the situational. What are learned in schools are more than useful skills and capabilities; they correspond to those fundamentals a society believes of value for all (Peters 1966; Pring 1995a; Reid 1998; Wilson 2000b). Such value-related goals oblige teachers to have some fair idea of how an educated person thinks and behaves, so that this conception can condition short-term objectives and related actions.

In particular, it will always entail judgements about what makes for a good learner (whether children, adolescents, students or adults) linked to the educational ideal. Good teachers know what good learners are, and their work usually feeds from this knowledge, in so far as it also fits with more basic conceptions. Such a superimposing of the short onto the long term (knowing what features of learners will, ultimately, define them as educated people) allows teachers to respect basic values while dealing with daily chores. That is why (being accountable for what they do) teachers must sometimes take soundings from longer-term aims so as to be sure they are guiding learners in the right directions. Even if they do so rarely, such soundings will – when they are taken – forcibly impose themselves on events as arbiters of all pedagogic decisions.

To summarise: the starting point for any professionals deciding how to teach has to be their fashioning of concepts of teaching and learning within broader educational ideals (seeing how learners think, act, achieve en route to their becoming educated – in the light of some view about what *that* means). These interrelated concepts mastermind pedagogy, within educational institutions, framing it as a potentially sophisticated theoretical as well as practical business. They do so because ideal conceptions (of child and adult learners) quickly bring into play academic theories to back up the more practically focused theories or models of teaching which, according to Biggs (2001) all institutions as well as teachers should follow if they are to be successful. Whether teachers refer much to long-term goals or give thought to attendant academic questions is another issue. But teachers must *at some stage* confront their own ideals, if only as implicit justifications for those 'espoused theories' which any institution uses to advertise its educational wares (Boyer 1990, cited Biggs 2001).

The educational ideal

As argued, thoughts about what it means to be educated rely on value-judgements about how human beings learn and develop (Wilson 2000b clarifies this: ch. 1). But these can split sharply into judgements about process and product. In the end, few people will dispute that educated people should live happy fulfilled lives, with personally satisfying jobs and appreciating 'worthwhile' activities. Often, it isn't what we mean by the 'good life' which causes disputes as how pupils best gain entry to it. Asking, for example, 'how much freedom youngsters need in schools for them to graduate as the rational autonomous adults everyone admires' raises a host of further questions needing practical as well as theoretical answers. Teachers needn't ponder over such questions interminably; but they must take account of them simply because there are points in teaching where we cannot decide practicalities without at least nodding towards such preconceptions.

Theorising around ideals (of adults and young learners) is the price we pay for seeking to educate rather than, just, teach. It is easy to agree on ways of teaching someone to dress, eat politely or use a computer correctly. It is much harder to be sure about how best to educate someone for whatever we think is the right way to live. We might agree on generalities (like the need to be literate, grasp moral issues and so forth). But we will debate at length whether teaching others to read, write and behave in one way rather than another is guaranteed to help them use their skills within the life-styles and attitudes we dignify as cultured or educated. Admitting this not only reinforces the role of values and ideals, but also affects decisions about how long-term ends are to be delivered. Different methods must be linked to different ideal conceptions – otherwise, how could we ever realise our ideals? Generic skills, for example (of communication, relationship etc.) interact with ideal notions of learners, since it is these latter which guide the *deployment* of communication skills, sympathetic relationships, and all the many and various decisions teachers need to make.

Together, a concept of education and practical principles underpinning it are the stock-in-trade of professional teaching. Which is not to say that every teacher *must* regularly think through first principles if he or she is to be a professional educator. The temptation to give little thought to eventual outcomes may prove irresistable when one is teaching a 'national' curriculum (such as in England and Wales) meant to satisfy all citizens, which therefore serves many different sorts of values. Yet to strive at different times towards very different kinds of outcome – as the English/Welsh National Curriculum manifestly does – must oblige teachers to glimpse something of the types of teaching and learning standard curricula assume and whether it is possible, realistically, to arrange for all of them. Teachers can make such judgements only by comparing their professional know-how (first principles) with a rationale embodied in the national curriculum concerned.

First principles of good teaching

It is useful to restate the above as rules or first principles, generating the knowledge, skills and capabilities which, as said, are professional teachers' stock-in-trade.

First, teachers need concepts of teaching and learning fitted to their educational 'ideal' (how learners are expected to reach valued ends: see Wilson 2000b). Their overall concept of education will shore up some 'espoused theory' (Biggs 2001) or 'model of good practice' which advertises a school's central mission, its intentions for its pupils. Teacher-centred, learner-centred and democratic options were introduced as our best known paradigms. Although teachers can teach well (i.e. using generic skills pragmatically) without such conceptions, they will not be teaching professionally, as that has been defined. Educational concepts of the sort discussed relate to teachers' long-term values and to public beliefs about how human beings develop and change.

Second, because a general ideal implies criteria for anyone conforming to it, such assumptions are teased out as practical principles guiding a teacher's deployment of skills. These assumptions are vulnerable to theoretical, empirically based argument.

Third, procedural rules can be stated as governing the way teachers cope with mundane chores as well as use complex skills (though they may not be learned formally as procedural rules, as will be discussed later). Classroom strategies, methods, etc. are not exclusive to paradigms; it is the way these are integrated and deployed which determines ends, and this deployment can be described in terms of procedures. To re-stress, it isn't suggested teachers, themselves, need consciously keep to such rules, for their methods always alter with different kinds of pupils (e.g. those with special educational needs (SEN), of different ages, for different backgrounds etc.) and to academic subjects. But these altered methods must conform, somehow, to procedures linked to longer-term conceptions, since if they did not it would be impossible to judge how far they were likely to be successful.

Fourth, generic skills (of relationship, communication, tolerance and empathy, of administration and organisation, etc.) become professional (educationally speaking) when guided by procedural rules linked to long-term aims. What separates good from bad teaching is not just whether the teaching is skilled or not, but whether skills are suitably or unsuitably deployed in service of justifiable ends. In sum, the means-ends behaviours which have been described are the theories of teaching or models of good practice which all teachers need to work systematically and purposefully and which educational studies illuminate (Wilson 2000b: ch. 3).

Objections to first principles generating theories of good teaching

A number of objections might be made to the principles stated above, some of which have already received comment. It is worth classifying these before considering them.

First, whether one likes it or not, in England and Wales ongoing educational 'reforms' have pre-empted some basic decisions teachers would otherwise take about their work and there might seem little point in mulling over circumstances one cannot change. Adhering to legislated demands has itself become a major occupation and hard-pressed practitioners might well find theorising about the longer term takes from them precious time. Second, even if teachers should occasionally refer to long-term notions, we might still wonder whether these need consideration if they are seldom consciously acknowledged in classrooms. Surely they stay as implicit, affecting very little, while the practical business of teaching proceeds? Third, accepting that teachers should and do refer to teaching models, we might query why only three have been chosen from a potentially much larger number, given that we cannot fix any one as superior to the others except by invoking situation. Fourth, drawing criteria for quality teaching from the same listed principles might be judged dubious, and probably too complex to be practically useful. Others have come up with other criteria (usually of a simpler sort).

Dealing with the above objections goes beyond justifying any single approach. It justifies the use of theoretical models, *per se*. It also lets us probe not only variants of good practice (e.g. in terms of competence, success and excellence), but also variants of bad practice, which may prove hard to discern in that they often masquerade as instances of good teaching.

First objection: **should** *teachers use theories of good practice?*

Standard curricula seem to remove from teachers the need to refer to their own educational values since these are predetermined. Yet, as it happens, the aims and values of the English/Welsh National Curriculum have only recently been spelled out by the Qualifications and Curriculum Authority (QCA 2000). This fact sits somewhat strangely with above proposals about the key role of values in education. For value-driven conceptions of what it means to be educated would normally precede any listing of curricular content, rather than statements of content being decided first with statements of value added later. The point is, without such an ordering of events, there is always likely to be a mismatch between curricula and their own values. The idea of starting with some concept of education is that it will limit later decisions. To have no limitation set when devising a curriculum invites a free-for-all among interested parties. Exactly the same problems would arise for a religious group agreeing its forms of worship and ritual before clarifying the nature of its god; or for a political party settling on practical policies before admitting its political ideology. Where values are left in abeyance, vested interests win out according to the strength of their representation rather than according to how far their proposals are likely to produce desired outcomes.

Indeed, the uncertain value-commitments of political 'reformers' designing the United Kingdom's Education Act 1988 probably explains why early critics homed in on reformers' intentions as much as on the reforms themselves (Chitty 1992). Some noted a prevailing consumerist attitude to education and learning (Whitty 1990) while others worried about the 'professional vacuum' left by rather sketchy values' statement which did exist, thinking it could easily open the door to indoctrinators (Brighouse and Moon 1990). In the event, the QCA's (2000) overview of values and purposes was based on a consensus reached within its own Values Forum (see Haydon 1998; Marenbon 1998; Talbot and Tate 1997). Broad aims for the school curriculum were made to echo those embodied in section 351 of the Education Act 1996. They are as follows.

'[The] school curriculum should aim to provide opportunities for all pupils to learn and to achieve' and 'the school curriculum should aim to promote pupils' spiritual, moral, social, and cultural development and prepare all pupils for the opportunities, responsibilities and experiences of life' (QCA 2000: 2–5). These aims correspond to values concerned with 'the self', 'relationships', 'society' and 'the environment'. The preamble to the statement wisely acknowledges that it is not exhaustive. For instance, it avoids being swayed by religious beliefs or teachings. The statement is nonetheless an attempt to reach general agreement on 'universalisable' values (QCA 2000: 4) to which all educational stakeholders as well as teachers can agree.

Recalling first principles, what the QCA statement does not do (and is not meant to do) is resolve ongoing conflicts about what it means to become educated. Exactly to avoid such conflicts, it puts together a list of 'middle-level' rules (Marenbon 1998: 16ff; Standish 1997) which side-step questions about whether, for example, anyone can at the same time systematically prepare pupils for citizenship, for personal fulfilment and for jobs. Additionally, even if one treats the QCA list as a set of ideals to which all teachers can subscribe, their task remains hampered by a National Curriculum still heavy with subject-based teaching. Turner-Bisset (2000) cites the influential government white paper *Excellence in Schools* (DfEE 1997) as advising that 'excellent' schools must press beyond improving literacy and numeracy towards 'a broad, flexible and motivating education recognising the different talents of all children and delivers excellence for everyone' (DfEE 1997, cited Turner-Bisset 2000: 4). Agreeing with Alexander (1998), she suggests that National Curricular orders themselves remain too inflexible to achieve both the instrumental skills required for a modern society and the 'broad, motivating education' delivering excellence for everyone.

In sum, if they adequately tell us what the National Curriculum seeks to achieve, value-statements are insufficiently detailed to give guidance on teaching aims at a curricular level. In so far as they are interpreted as accepting broadly agreed priorities most school missions recognise, they highlight the shortcomings of the revised National Curriculum. In other words, it is, still, for teachers to expand on and interpret both National Curricular values and National Curricular programmes, in ways they can manage. Concepts of education served by the English/ Welsh National Curriculum do not give teachers the value-framework they need to teach the National Curriculum's own content. Statements about the importance of self, relationships with others, society and the family are applicable to almost any ideal. That is, they contain no implications for our deciding how educational insights might actually develop in young people (and how learners might therefore be taught).

Of course, any diet of programmes laid out for a whole nation, satisfying no single set of interests, is bound to tie itself to generalities. Yet the QCA statement is, theoretically, the linchpin for everything else. And, practically speaking, teachers do need such guidance. The enormous scope of a national curriculum is such that teachers cannot, simply, teach it as it stands. They must interpret it according to other criteria – and the only criteria intellectually sturdy enough to bear such a burden are those locked into established conceptions of what it means to become educated (promoted in later chapters).

Second objection: do teachers use theories of good practice (even if they should)?

Noting the shortcomings of a standard curriculum does not by itself mean that teachers will detect such shortcomings and behave in more virtuous ways. Anyone watching skilled teachers at work in an English primary or secondary school might not notice any rules operating apart from their general compliance with National Curricular orders. At first sight, teachers dealing with day-to-day chores appear pragmatic rather than formulaic, following personal rules-of-thumb they have concocted from their own unique experiences. Their actions and decisions do not seem to follow any 'theory' at all, moment-to-moment problem-solving being the only sure sign of professionalism on offer.

Schon (1983, 1987) describes what is happening here. He suggests professionals use implicit or 'tacit' theories (Polanyi 1967) rather then formal blueprints while dealing with tasks, trusting in an 'artful competence' to get them through their business rather than technical skill. Tacit theories are not prescriptions so much as routines which teachers fall back on unthinkingly – fleeting, inner dialogues which throw up tentative, promising gambits to try out with ever-changing problems (Schon 1983; Van Manen 1995). Yet personal or tacit theories – being specific and practically focused – need not contradict general rules. Even unique practices can correspond to and become justified by abstract theories (in the end, they must be so justified: see Korthagen and Kessels 1999).

What we might conjecture is that, because they are professionals (i.e. not engaged purely in trial-and-error work) teachers' practices will come to conform to general theories of good teaching, over time, as natural outcomes of their work. We might concur with Korthagen and Kessels (1999) that they must do so. Teachers certainly 'think on their feet' as Schon and others have it (Labercane *et al.* 1998; Van Manen 1995). But to reduce teaching *wholly* to an intuitive grasp of unique events – using something called 'tact' (Van Manen 1995: 42, discussed in Labercane *et al.* 1998) – overlooks what might be thought the 'bigger picture'. Teaching routines – to be routines – must follow agreed plans, and these will, somewhere, service short-term and, ultimately, longer-term goals. It is unthinkable that approaches to classroom organisation, assessment, equal opportunities, the teaching of standard subjects aren't at some level programmed and agreed by groups in ways which fit a common rationale. These approaches will approximate to more abstract conceptions of teaching which will, accordingly, require theoretical justification.

Usefully, Schon helps us see how professionals come to devise their programmes pragmatically, and so gives us clues as to how teaching models arise *as models* in the first place, and so helps sanction their study. Although Schon's (1987) speculations on professional training cover person-to-person coaching and situational learning, he does not believe anyone copies mentors indiscriminately. Student-teachers interpret for their own purposes, i.e. in a 'social constructivist' manner (Schon 1987: ch. 3; see also Korthagen and Kessels 1999). Novices improve through reflecting on actions in the light of real outcomes. What this makes plain is that to succeed teachers cannot work *only* pragmatically or through observation but will (i.e. for sake of collaboration) fashion their own kinds of explanatory concepts to share. They will have a discourse to use with other groups to whom they are accountable (parents, governors, inspectors, other professionals, school managers, etc.). They need not openly rely on an abstract model for their terms of reference. But it is pointed that the three models to be discussed *do* regularise strategies and techniques teachers use because their structural elements (teacher and pupil relationships and responsibilities) present themselves in all teachers' experiences. They unerringly give teachers options typically needed for routine tasks.

To be precise, as teachers organise schemes, plan strategies, record and assess, they are faced with doing so in a top-down pre-decided way, of allowing pupils substantial freedom of choice, or of seeking to establish a democratic consensus on ways forward. To keep faith with their values, they will tailor-make and continuously revise rules and procedures. They need not study formal accounts (like the ones in this book), though by means of such accounts they might most easily revise and refine (in terms of coherence, systematicity, and so forth) whatever approach they take. Nor will this be true only for teachers. It is hard to see how those who inspect or advise teachers can do so except via some underlying belief system generated by a teaching model (Silcock and Wyness 1998).

On such grounds, theorising about pedagogy becomes in the end not an imperative for the sake of accountability, it becomes the only sure way a teacher can get past mere competence. Shulman's 'missing paradigm' – knowing how teachers *do* decide what and how to teach (discussed by Fang 1996) – must, somehow, be equivalent to strategic policies which can be refined within coherent systems. The fact that over recent years rich and complex ideas (such as 'learner-centred') have been replaced by technical descriptions of curricular schemes or practices, has not led to the redundancy of the former, which imply unavoidable issues of pedagogy. But it has led to an impoverishment of our educational vocabulary so impeding what teachers do (Fielding 1999; Frowe 2001), imposing hidden values and – some think – dubious theoretical models on classrooms (Fielding 1999 discusses 'performativity').

Obviously, no one believes that teachers learn just by reading books. The rather strange research finding of Preece (1994), that teachers' pedagogical knowledge correlates negatively with competence – i.e. that teachers versed in theory are less rather than more likely to teach well – must, somehow, hinge on their dislodging theories from what is being theorised about. Fault for the practice–theory mismatch lies not with theorising itself (otherwise we end up in quagmires of amateurism) but with the idea of anyone memorising strategies purely as a discourse rather than actually learning how to use them (see also Chapters 7 and 9). Teacher-education courses are regularly pilloried for purveying theory divorced from practice (Ben-Peretz 1995; Korthagen and Kessels 1999; Zeichner and Tabachnick 1981). This fact smiles on various types of school-based teacher education, school–college collaborations, and post-technocratic models of continuing teacher development. But we don't have to believe teacher educators must *of necessity* teach theories in isolation from the practicalities they are meant to serve (see Chapter 7).

Now, suggesting that teachers find systematic solutions for repeated problems does not mean they gradually work out highly sophisticated blueprints. Teachers have a professional taste for any tricks of methodology known to be usually effective and their theories will embrace these. What *is* argued is that for teachers to succeed consistently, they have little choice but to act consistently; and it is such consistency which in the end builds approximations to ideal models (whether teachers themselves favour such models or not). Good teaching approximates to a professional ideal for reasons born from consistencies of purpose. For instance: it is probably true that most teachers use 'behaviour-management' techniques to keep order and guarantee pupils' physical well-being. But how far they resort to hard-line conditioning at other times depends on how far they are dedicated to the swift, correct response to questions and easily testable educational outcomes (see Chapter 3). It will depend on their favoured theory of teaching. It need not vary according to a familiarity with Behaviourist psychology – though it might do so.

Similarly, although primary school teachers are eclectic in their choice of methods when teaching reading, as Stahl (1999) discovers, this does not mean either that they all teach literacy in the same way (notwithstanding any 'national literacy strategy') or that their methods do not become comprehensible in more general terms. Teachers align eclectic methods to purposes differing between teachers. Some might think enskilling pupils as readers and writers is basic. Others might wish mostly to inspire that enjoyment of literature which will or should govern skills' development. Those who do not pick their way between aims must, still, conjecture on how gaining one sort facilitates or hinders the other. These issues are issues of belief and priority, not of empirical fact, and are unavoidable in that the very act of having to choose between methods invokes them. All teachers are pragmatic up to a point: but to adopt pragmatism *consciously* as a standard (i.e. to believe that 'goodness of fit' is itself a teaching philosophy) is to condemn oneself forever to mediocrity. Anyone who does that cannot at the same time strive full-heartedly towards goals built into publicly appraised professional models.

We will find, later, that formal theories linked to each model (serving more general concepts of education) are in almost all cases tried and tested. Undoubtedly, behavioural conditioning works (Chapter 3). 'Rogerian' self-concept theory tells us something worth knowing about pupil attitudes and various types of 'constructivism' approximate to how people construe circumstances and improve their minds (Chapter 4). And the point about placing these explanations within abstract models is that they then mark out the *best* routes (the best we know that is) to valued goals. To adopt one approach is to increase the likelihood of achieving one set of goals *at the expense of another* (see later chapters for substantiation). Teaching is complex. Yet in so far as educational theory is reliable, we do know how to reach some ends. And it has to be that the consistent use of reliable strategies within coherent models is the reliable way to attain these. This is exactly what is meant by subscribing to a 'model of good practice'. It is also to define (by contrast) a 'model of bad practice' in that it follows from what has been said that bad teaching is exactly that approach where actions taken are not clearly linked to valued goals (consciously or unwittingly only heeding pragmatics). Teachers may avoid ideological commitment, believing they can realise all worthwhile aims, without prioritising. But this is itself a commitment (to all possibilities) which risks achieving very little because it attempts too much.

So models of good practice are born in the two ways given. They are shaped by discrete values and discrete bodies of theory, both of which are embedded in known conceptions of what it means to be educated. And it is concluded that teachers often do use models described here, albeit personally transformed in the way Schon (1983), Korthagen and Kessels (1999) and Van Manen (1995) suppose. What we can be emphatic about is that teachers *should* refer to one or other model. To bypass or totally cut out models of pedagogy (perhaps surrendering to bureaucratic chores) is to court bad practices. It is one thing to avoid conflicts between groups with different ideals (i.e. to believe naively that one's own model is the *only* one which is worthwhile). It is another to believe either such ideals don't matter or (more usually these days) that one can have all of them equally. One way of pinning down how teaching theories work within schools is to see them as a ways of ordering priorities. It is hardly credible that teachers will never use techniques found by reference to published models. But they will use some techniques more than others according to their professional values.

Third objection: are there only three models, and, if there are, which is best?

There are certainly more than three teaching paradigms and one might subdivide main types endlessly into different versions. Where a theoretical boundary is drawn is probably irrelevant to how well teachers actually teach. What matters is that any one approach gets support from self-consistent theories surrounding known goals. This is why value-neutral theories (in terms of aims), such as 'reflective practice' and 'teacher-researcher' approaches, popular with teacher-educators (see Barrett *et al.* 1992; Hargreaves 1994) are denied model-status since their very value-neutrality disqualifies them. One would expect skilled teachers of any sort to be reflective and to research their effectiveness. Even dubious practices such as indoctrination benefit from systematically reflective and enquiring attitudes. Reflective practice and teacher-research tell us what all teachers must do to teach with reasonable competence – a realisation which explains not only the widespread popularity of these ideas but the widely differing definitions and usage of concepts such as reflective teaching (see Humphreys and Susak 2000).

They are 'models of practice' more than models of good or effective practice, which is why the idea of 'reflective teaching' especially has become vague and over-inclusive (Coldron and Smith 1999; Humphreys and Susak 2000). Despite its potentially subversive role (Hargreaves 1994), the most pragmatic types fix professional action within situations, so can easily be harnessed to teaching dominant ideologies (Chapter 3). For example, Coldron and Smith (1999) find that key policy documents published in the UK over recent years demand reflective teaching to ensure standardisation. In short, reflection is a paragon courted by all who admire good teaching. 'Reflective practice' and 'teacher-research' mark general strands of skill and belief woven into all models, rather than dividing them.

Three paradigms of professional teaching are allied to three philosophies of human behaviour. Anyone who studies human beings sooner or later meets up with them. This suggests another reason why teachers will find them intuitively familiar, just because they will daily choose to deal with practicalities in one way rather than another, and these practicalities cluster around fundamentals which make teaching the sort of job it is. For example, Hajnicz (1998) writes about the two 'subjectivities' (adults' and pupils' perspectives) which place different planes of teacher-action under differing priorities. Pupils' interests tend to be short term, teachers' long term. To stop this priority-opposition crippling classroom policies, Hajnicz recommends twin-task schedules whereby adults' decisions always complement rather than contradict those of pupils. In her opinion, teachers will only unfailingly avoid conflicts by not cutting across pupils' own choices of activity, task and so on – i.e. keeping out of their subjective territory. Her reasoning will be familiar. Although Hajnicz does not entertain outright pupil dominance, she edges near to that learner-centred paradigm (as defined in Chapter 4). By avoiding conflict – pretty much at all costs – she diverges from democratic (co-constructive) teaching which *invites* a divergence of view on tasks in order to reach novel syntheses (see Chapters 5 and 6).

Moore (2000), by contrast, thinks that an inviolable part of teaching is helping pupils deal with tough public issues they will inevitably encounter as world citizens. He condemns the two classic stances (teacher and learner-centred) for being neutral towards such issues, leading us towards what are called, here, partnership models, which do meet them head on. His point is that teaching which tries to be uncontentious and stay within boundaries of safe argument bypasses exactly modern-day issues which education exists to address. Even learner-centred approaches find socio-political change hard to grapple with except where it impinges directly on pupils' own lives and locales. To an extent, this is why partnership models flourish. Modern egalitarian movements have tended to replace notions of equity bought by individual freedoms (a libertarian ideal: see Hargreaves 1996) with more interdependent sorts founded in communitarian values. It is not suggested that the two visions are wholly opposed, but they are different enough to support separate teaching models.

The three main models have long pedigrees. They are found to represent three avenues to conceptual change. With the teacher-centred (more traditional) model, people opt for tried and tested ways of resolving their dilemmas and contradictory perceptions. With the learner-centred, people win new insights through their pursuing more narrowly sighted ambitions. With the democratic/partnership model, people advance through reconciling and negotiating disparate views. All three modes of conceptual change are underwritten by substantial theories, and relate to distinct epistemologies (see Chapter 6). One might suppose the latter supersedes the learner-centred in contexts where group conflicts are likely; or that personal idealism is fitted for homogeneous milieus where group differences are minimised. But we should recall that the only value-criteria we can use to make comparisons already generate the parent models themselves.

Though one might be judged superior to another in its relevance to prevailing conditions, there are dangers involved in suggesting that a wider context should decide how schools operate. For this could just as well legitimise a repressive society making schools repressive. We might not want to sanction repressive schools. The fact is that models of good teaching reflect familiar pictures of human development, of society, of citizenship, of conceptual change, and so on, which tells us that under-lying values and conceptions of what it is to be human are themselves fundamentals. We cannot get behind them to point out how one is inherently better than another.

We can be open-minded about what the adopting of a model leads to in terms of educated citizens or communities. And we can point to the greater likelihood of one model rather than another working with any pupil-groups. Transmission approaches to teaching often give worth to 'high culture' which most pupils find hard to appreciate (Pring 1986). In other words, they tend to be 'elitist' in their curricular content (though they might not be elitist in intent: Gingell and Brandon 2000). Learner-centred and democratic ways of teaching avoid elitism. This does not mean egalitarian intentions are invariably fulfilled, simply because of our relative lack of understanding of how to design successful learner-centred or democratic systems (it is this uncertainty about means which is arguably the achilles heel of such approaches). Nevertheless, such warning against undue optimism shouldn't detract from what is probably the central point here, that teaching models will recommend themselves to different societies at different times, just because how societies see themselves tends to change. Modern preoccupations with knowledge and skills' transfer leads us into some prioritising of partnership ways of teaching (Chapters 6 to 9). This interim conclusion returns us to issues of why, and how, competent, successful and excellent teaching can be differentiated, within any approach.

Fourth objection: why 'competence', 'success' and 'excellence'?

As argued, to assess levels of good practice, we need to know the features of a model which best define it, then infer from it suitable teacher-attitudes, judgements about pupil learning and knowledge, prioritised skills and techniques, forms of assessment and so forth. We need to see how the integration and deployment of skills, strategies and so on might unerringly erect hierarchies of standards. These two exercises occupy the rest of this book. What is seldom attempted is the putting together of 'rounded' models of teaching integrating distinct theories. Only when we do so, can we see how capabilities are best integrated within any one model. This opens doors for possible judgements about what makes for quality in a model's application, simply because it explains why different sorts of competent application are possible.

What was stressed is that a contemporary obsession for uncovering generic building bricks for 'excellence' and 'effectiveness' easily misleads us into citing such qualities as responsible for the effectiveness of any teaching performance. Actually, the point of dividing 'lay' from 'professional' teaching was to explain how the latter alters the former within institutional contexts and in pursuit of specified ideals (concepts of what it means to become educated via suitably focused learning). This fact makes criteria for quality teaching relative to a set of more general indicators as well as to a set of socio-physical circumstances. And it allows differentiations to be made in the way we deal with standards of good practice themselves.

This justifies a decision to separate standards of competence from those of success and excellence. Teaching may well be high quality relative to a general model yet fail in particular circumstances. Conversely, it may be well suited to a socio-cultural setting yet be poorly matched to an agreed ideal. This chapter inserted such possibilities into its first principles, automatically setting up problems for anyone seeking to assess or appraise teaching outside of socio-cultural contexts and without due regard to particular classes of aims. General and specific circumstances always constrain each other, so each will outweigh the other in importance depending on perspective taken, leading to different ways of judging the same teaching.

Nowhere is this possibility more obvious than in the assessment of teaching relative to standard curricula. Although the English/Welsh National Curriculum's value-statements were shown to leave open how these are to be interpreted, it has been hinted that a heavy, prescriptive curriculum lends itself to some interpretations more than others. One cannot, just, compare models of teaching in the absence of considerations of how these will work in various circumstances. One might argue that standard curricula are, themselves, enormous handicaps to any sort of professional teaching geared to specific problems thrown up by specific contexts. But where one exists (and looks set to keep existing), it would be perverse to ignore the implications for classroom practitioners. Consequently, as part of a next stage of discussion, as well as determining their features, the strengths and weaknesses of teaching models relative to modern conditions will be listed. This stage precedes the notionally more contentious business of actually prescribing how teachers can reach the competence, success and excellence they all seek.

3 Models of good practice 1
Teacher-centred approaches

Introduction: theorising about teaching

First principles of good practice were summarised (Chapter 2) as the working out from educational ideals of how to deploy skills and techniques, choose content, modes of assessment and so on. At a minimum, teachers try systematically to fulfil their own views on what it is to be an educated citizen in a good society. Their individual and/or shared 'visions' inspires their professional roles. And the fact that there are competing ways of fulfilling or characterising educational ideals (e.g. of how to teach effective learners to be effective citizens) means that many considerations will present themselves, from time to time, dedicated to confirming a position taken by teachers or changing it. These will be practical, political, ethical and academic.

If teachers commit themselves to some educational concepts or other, theorists will latch onto this commitment as justification for the closest possibly study of its theoretical implications. To repeat an obvious point, it isn't that teachers flounder unless they grasp educational theory. It is just that theoretical (research-based) debate is the only way we know for predicting what may happen or not happen when one decision (about educational curricula, say) is taken rather than another. Because human interactions occur on so many levels (physical, social, psychological and so on), it is very difficult to observe these cause–effect relationships happening in schools and colleges, whereas it is not only possible but also pretty certain that hidden outcomes, by-products, unnoticed side-effects will accompany any one brand of teaching. Educational theories exist to predict such side-effects as well as confirm mainline expectations.

So how competent, successful and excellent teachers really are can be determined only by applying theoretical concepts to what they do. It follows that if they are *knowingly* to teach well, their best chances of doing so must come via a study of the main theoretical rationales for the particular approach they take. Such rationales, with their associated terms and justifications, should be standard educational fare, giving us our most reliable means of assessing and appraising central initiatives and policies. So in this and the following two chapters, main reasons for settling on an approach to teaching (for realising some educational ideal or vision) are discussed prior to a statement of strengths and weaknesses (relative to twenty-first-century conditions) and principles of practice defining it. Studying theoretical formulations of the three main teaching paradigms clears the ground for a more detailed look at perhaps the most promising of these (for reasons to be discussed) – a partnership approach.

Teacher–centred approaches

Teacher-centred approaches begin with that 'classical' educational ideal (Lawton 1973; Silcock 1999) which commends one group (e.g. knowledgeable adults) prescribing for another (e.g. children and adolescents). Teaching tends to work through exacting from pupils conformity and obedience (i.e. to what is prescribed). Adults may admire this approach for reasons connected with their own commitment to 'traditional' values, or because they find its implications for teaching policy and practice are sound. Those who reject it may do so because they believe individual learners should have a deciding role in their own education or because they doubt whether a 'transmission' model of teaching can actually work. That is, while accepting they are accountable in general for what pupils learn, teachers invariably differ in how far they believe they can (or should) decide what pupils actually do (Wilson 1999).

Skilled teachers can think it possible and proper to take learners, step by step, down educational highways well signed by others, whatever learners themselves may think about the matter. Government agencies, intent on channelling school outputs into industry and the labour market, and politicians who wish to make electorally prudent promises to parents, may agree with them. From politicians' point of view, legislation constrains teachers in ways it cannot constrain learners. If teachers really do manage pupil progress, the secret of taking charge of educational outputs has to be that of taking charge of teacher decision-making through legislative and other means. At present, a modernisation of the UK's teaching profession (DfEE 1998; Merson 2000; Thompson 1999) gives teeth to national and local-management policies for implementing 'reforms' expected to raise standards.

Nationally, an Office for Standards in Education (Ofsted) inspectorate, a Teacher Training Agency and the Qualifications and Curriculum

Authority shape what happens at managerial level in schools, while teachers get more down-to-earth guidance from the strict application of performance criteria. Locally, school staff are answerable to governing bodies with growing interventionist powers, while teachers' careers are increasingly bound up with performance standards. Those ready for 'fast track' promotion or to have 'advanced' status are hived off from those who are not (Sutton *et al.* 2000). Where necessary, 'performance managers' advise teachers or headteachers on strategies for improvement (Marsden 2000; Smithers and Robinson 2000; Sutton *et al.* 2000; Thompson 1999).

The point is that such a plethora of top-down policies is not, merely, politically expedient. It makes sense in the light of beliefs about what teachers can do once we burden them with chief responsibility for outcomes. A natural line of influence drops down from political legislation through performance-management of teachers to the learners themselves who, one might suppose, respond readily to whatever is asked of them. And although the common-sense and (for many) very desirable hypothesis that the 'process-product' paradigm applies in a fairly unqualified way to schools does not have unqualified theoretical approval, there is a literature supporting it. Explanatory arguments and social-scientific insights tell us not only how far top-down rationales are reliable (if they are) but also what makes them reliable – i.e. what gives one set of human beings (teachers) managerial/pedagogic powers over another (pupils). However, related theories merit perusal. It may be that predictions we make about schools and classrooms are correct only where adults are careful to act in certain sorts of ways, or only with regard to very limited types of learning.

Relevant theories are grouped in four ways, according to whether the process-product link happens in direct or indirect manner (extrinsic/intrinsic). There are direct behaviour-management strategies (a) and techniques founded in empirical research (b). There are acculturation techniques (c) and moment-to-moment, pragmatic interactions teachers have with pupils, in the light of a personally fashioned, professional knowledge (d). Although each of the bodies of literature called into service appoints different roles to teachers and learners, what unites them is a pedagogic wish to hit known targets and fulfil legislated conditions. A further reason for selecting these four versions of teacher-centredness is that they complement each other. Behavioural (a), academic (b), socio-cultural (c) and personal (d) dimensions combine into a plausibly rounded version of quality practice.

(a) Extrinsic design 1: teaching as performance-management

Those who approve of targets and benchmarks (pupils reaching achievement 'levels' by a certain age; teachers reaching performance thresholds) will be impelled, at some stage in their thinking, to reappraise conditioning techniques worked out almost a century ago by behaviourist psychologists such as Thorndyke and B.F. Skinner (Gross 1992). Behaviourists' 'laws' make all learning heir to reinforcement (positive and negative). Reward, repetition and exercise are grist to every performance-manager's mill – especially as recommendations are simple enough. Over time, and provided behaviourist rules are followed unswervingly, rewarding wanted actions and ignoring the unwanted will increase the wanted and eliminate the unwanted. And the rules themselves are few. Apart from keeping faith with reinforcement schedules, teachers must write curricular aims as behaviours which can be learned or eliminated. This harvesting of behavioural objectives from curricula adequately satisfies performance-benchmarking, provided the latter align with the scheduled programmes of learned actions. What a behaviourist would frown on are teaching through intuition and hunches, personal explorations of curricular backwaters and side-issues, or digressions into the creative and adventurous. For targeted-learning, pupils must chain responses that can be reproduced sufficiently well to satisfy some form of criterion-referenced assessment.

Such well-monitored systems will work in so far as teachers stick to their own plans and resist faint-hearted sympathy for pupils difficult to condition and provided they can stand the scrupulous attention which has to be given to personalised timetables. They must also believe that chained human actions do in some sense correlate with those deeper level cognitive and affective gains education implies. Not everyone believes they do. Davis (1999), Fielding (1999), Frowe (2001), Kelly (1989), Pollard (1999), Stenhouse (1975) and White (1999) warn in their different ways that behavioural performance relates tenuously to in-depth comprehension and long-term attitudes, and may even be inhibiting rather than causal in effecting long-term gains. Davis (1999) thinks systematic instruction in closely defined skills (e.g. the 'thin procedures' taught in national literacy and numeracy strategies) works against the 'richly textured' knowledge we really want for our children. Knowledge, he writes, becomes conceptually rich and capable of transfer and application within exactly those informal circumstances a strict programming towards prescribed goals prohibits (see also Chapter 9). White (1999) agrees.

But educationists are not blind to the fact that managing pupil responses can bring *some* universally prized skills in sight for all (such as those required to ensure health and safety in schools). Through operant conditioning (where actions anticipate likely future rewards rather than recall past successes) students can be taught to condition themselves; though if they are sufficiently self-aware to do so one might wonder whether strict target-setting is actually needed at all. Certainly, implementing performance-management programmes is not out of keeping with present-day expectations that teachers must answer for educational success or failure. Uncomfortable side-issues about the fostering of 'materialist' values, the practicality of ignoring (negatively reinforcing) all unwanted actions and arranging complex reinforcement programmes for pupils whose lives are only temporarily under teachers' sway may, nonetheless, be fatally inhibiting for many.

Doubtless, whatever learning-culture a school opts for, the routine rewarding and exercising of skills will figure somewhere, if only because an ever tighter screwing of curricular policies into performance moulds will have knock-on effects for pupils. From one viewpoint, this may be no bad thing, recognising that we do have a weighty psychological literature to set parameters for us. We know quite exactly what targets we can and cannot guarantee through performance-management. Significantly, behaviourism has been virtually abandoned by academic psychologists at a theoretical level, not because it has become unreliable, but because its further exploration is near exhausted: there is simply nowhere else for behaviourist theory to go. We are probably as sure as we ever will be as to how far a performance technology really can mint for us another human being's mind and actions.

In any case, there are subtler and more sophisticated ways of prescribing for others.

(b) Extrinsic design 2: teaching through prescription (technical rationalism)

Technical rationalism is the philosophy that we can tailor means to ends through trial and error or experimentation. Behavioural conditioning in schools is a technical-rationalist enterprise, and, although it isn't the only one, it does cue us for essentials. For one thing, behaviourist literature models very well the theory–practice bond which gives approval to technical-rationalist programmes. That is, not only should these programmes tell us how to hit specified targets, but also we should know why their techniques work. Otherwise, we might misread what is their most potent ingredient and implement flawed policies (behaviourism 'works' because humans cannot adapt to environmental contingencies without responding predictably to reinforcements, which makes the different ways people find activities rewarding and unrewarding significant). It follows that technical rationalism relies on good quality, explanatory research to open doors to optimum performance.

Precepts for teaching reliant on what is sometimes called 'effectiveness' research begin to meet some such specifications. By definition they tell us what teachers should do to teach effectively. This is why part of the present government's 'modernising' ambitions is its insistence that headteachers have an up-to-date understanding of what makes for an effective school and an effective teacher (DfEE 1998; Merson 2000; Thompson 1999). And there is no shortage of people trying to satisfy demand. A cursory look at the research literature finds 'effectiveness' studies aplenty (e.g. Caldwell and Spinks 1988; Mortimore *et al.* 1988; Reid *et al.* 1989; Reynolds 1992; Reynolds and Farrell 1996; Sammons *et al.* 1995; Sanday 1990; Scheerens 1992; see also Chapter 8). Researchers have struggled since the late 1970s to find out what marks out the best schools from the mediocre. It is fair to comment, after mountains of paper, oceans of ink and millions of hours (not to mention money) spent in the search, that if we cannot now tell good from bad teaching and good from bad schools, we probably never will. And, on the face of it, we can.

We know that school headteachers should be good leaders; that deputies and class teachers should be 'involved' in school decisions. Teachers should be skilled and should teach consistently within structured lessons. Curricular content should not be too diverse. Programmes should be well managed and clearly written, with coherently linked aims. Pupil esteem matters. Clarity of vision matters. Staff knowledge, motivation, commitment, teamwork, communication and involvement are not optional extras. Homework is a good idea, provided it isn't too demanding. Lists of effectiveness factors span professional skills and curricula and spill over into connected, resonant areas such as a 'positive climate' and 'parental involvement' (Mortimore *et al.* 1988). Researchers have stoically visited every corner of school life (and sometimes out-of-school life) to discover what might contribute to a successful performance (usually – though not always – based on test results).

Yet on consulting our checklist of what counts as a viable technical rationalist theory, and looking for *why* one form of organisation, relationship, strategy works and others do not (we must correctly interpret research findings) we find that research projects give little credence to any parent theory or rationale. This weakness is conceded by researchers themselves (Goldstein and Woodhouse 2000). So our surety about them is often owed to two very different sorts of criteria. First, there are the statistically reliable techniques researchers use to draw our attention to one sort of practice rather than another. Second, there are our own expectations of schools and teachers, giving us that 'seat of the pants' feel that what is proposed makes sense, in the light of what we know about schools. In educational studies (as in the social sciences generally) we often trust our own intuitions when evaluating research into human learning since all of us have had some experience of acquiring new skills. When educational systems are set up, politicians and their advisers are usually guided by these broad expectations prior to seeking confirmation in large-scale technical-rationalist research.

And effectiveness research does confirm many of our expectations. It does so because, when we check why these expectations exist in the first place, we find they are already built into the way we organise institutional settings. Educational systems demand, *as a matter of course,* that school and teacher processes work in particular ways. Headteachers must be good leaders because we have made them 'heads' (i.e. leaders); teachers must work towards clear goals in a systematic, involved manner because that is pretty much how we think about teaching. Western education channels the roles of teachers in set ways and to identify those ways is to identify the criteria by which (by definition) they will work. For teachers to teach they must – to a degree anyhow – know what they are to teach, realise the goals they seek to hit, be motivated, purposeful and committed to these things. Curricula, being designed as means–end structures, have to be treated as means–end structures if they are to work. Sometimes, teachers might succeed despite being poorly motivated, having ill-defined purposes, not linking means to ends clearly and so on, but we would never prescribe such routes to success – not only because empirical research reveals their weaknesses but also because they contradict our built-in expectations.

A supporter of effectiveness studies might object that this is not the point; researchers arrive at different priorities for what are, naturally enough, structurally part of teaching or schools (otherwise why test for them?). But competing ranges of priorities may still accord with the assumptions the researchers begin with. Goldstein and Woodhouse (2000: 360) are worried by 'a notable lack in the current literature of serious attempts to expose the underlying assumptions that the research is making . . . existing assumptions need to be exposed and questioned'. They cite research projects which draw causal conclusions (about what makes for effective teaching) on the basis of little evidence, gathered in circumstances where initial assumptions were almost bound to be confirmed. They are particularly concerned at the cosy relationship they find exists between effectiveness research projects and government policy-makers (discussed further in Chapter 8).

It is, admittedly, impossible to remove value-related assumptions or expectations from research. The danger is to ignore them, or believe they masquerade as limiting criteria. For example, teachers these days commonly believe in 'high expectations' of pupil attainment and the need to ask 'challenging questions' which have been given research status (Galton 1995; Mortimore *et al.* 1988). In fact, such beliefs, in themselves, make the qualifiers 'high' and 'challenging' into value-judgements, spelling out what teachers must do (we see both as desirable). Unfortunately, because research has already confirmed these expectations, no standards are assumed by which we might assess them. Relative to what standard is a high expectation? Relative to what degree of difficulty is a challenging question? Without our knowing what a normative standard of question difficulty is, we cannot even start to detect an appropriately high or challenging question, though we instinctively sense these are desirable. We have no option but to judge by the extent to which the expectations and questions actually do lead to pupil learning, and soon realise that pupils differ in what they find challenging and we must modify expectations accordingly.

Teachers can only glean from their own know-how what an appropriately high expectation or appropriately challenging question might be. It is their professional judgements rather than the authority of research findings which decides what they do. One might conclude (as Davis 1998 does; also Schon 1983, 1987) that as a matter of principle only teachers are in a position to decide on methods, and that professional judgements must overrule technical prescription. To repeat what is salient: effectiveness criteria draw to our attention features of schools and classrooms to which teachers must attend – and these will usually be implicit in what we normally expect from teachers, schools and classrooms.

Researchers are well aware of the limitations of their research and have lately sought to look harder at teaching in so-called natural settings. 'School improvement' research is partly an offshoot from the 'effectiveness' movement (Duncan 1999; Goldstein and Woodhouse 2000), checking how school context constrains effectiveness in varying circumstances: it has an admirable strategic dimension (Fullan 1991). Such constraint is often calibrated as the 'value-added' progress schools make because of their unique qualities. Context-specific diagnoses of performance disclose that a bare assessment using surface criteria (such as examination league-tables) may divert us from inroads that teachers have made into the tough problems facing them (Duncan 1999). Because 'school improvement' research prescribes for individual schools rather than schools in general, it can be seen as complementing rather than following technical rationalist paradigms, though sometimes researchers do seek the elusive principle which might make a difference to all schools. Duncan comments, wryly, that 'in this [i.e. school improvement] field . . . certain overused words are in the ascendancy – "vision", "collegiality", "innovation" and "empowerment" for example' (Duncan 1999: 35), deciding that (as with effectiveness research) this rhetoric does no more than clarify what we already know.

But she goes on to admit that school improvers do cut their way into the fabric of school life and tangle with the messy business of intervening in real problems and policies. When they do, they may decide that raising teaching standards is possible only for the people who are directly engaged with them (Van Velzen *et al.* 1985). It has become a presumption of school improvement that potential change-elements must – to effect change – inhere within a school's culture. This presumption casts something of a shadow over the whole technical rationalist enterprise in making the sticking points for improvement school-specific, not generalised difficulties to be met by wider legislation. These sticking points may amount to no more than teachers listening to what effectiveness researchers tell them (even self-evident findings are not always recognised as such). But they are usually less transparent than that. School improvement researchers can find themselves taking actions which conform to no particular blueprint, but are decided by circumstances arising during the period they work in institutions.

The same doubts about technical-rationalism surface when we study other ways politicians have tried either to measure or improve school and teacher performance. Fielding's (1999) attack on target-setting echoes that of Davis (1998) on prescriptive teaching and assessment. The now familiar SMART acronym (specific, measurable, attainable, relevant, time-related: see Fielding 1999: 278) directing us to a highly successful way of raising test scores, clarifies the school enterprise. But in so far as test scores come to signify school success they make more basic kinds of success (the realisation of broader aims) that much less likely. If schoolwork is about hitting specific, attainable targets in a measurable manner, it is not about hitting non-specific targets in ways hard to measure.

Moreover, technical-rationalism is not always successful, even within its own terms of producing standard, reliable ways of assessing performance. Regarding teaching itself, for example, Smithers and Robinson (2000) review four recent UK reforms meant to calibrate teaching skill so as to reward the best teachers – a 'threshold' system of performance-related pay; a performance-management scheme; fast track promotion and a new advanced skills grade. They discern that each scheme relies on quite different assessment-criteria encouraging commentators to conclude 'the government has no clear concept of what constitutes a good teacher' (Mansell and Kelly 2000: 3).

The difficulties that politicians have coming up with coherent performance-assessment criteria makes us look hard at any centrally imposed methods of teacher improvement, including the UK Ofsted school-inspection system. For practical reasons, connected with what they do, school inspectors are backed by criteria for good practice general enough to be linked structurally to every school's role (Chapter 1), impelling school managers – in any event – to respond to inspection findings with a plan for improvement. This formula for change (whatever the status of the criteria themselves) would appear, if not foolproof, as one likely to lead to an improved situation more often than not. What early follow-up studies reveal of the way school staff develop plans rooted in inspection findings is that few actually follow these through to the end (Gray and Wilcox 1995). Ignorance of what needs to be improved cannot be cited as culprit for a school's lack of progress, for school staff know from Ofsted (and usually accept: Gray and Wilcox 1995) what their schools must do to move forward. The fault presumably lies more within the culture of teaching itself. Later research may contradict the earlier findings (see Chapter 9). Yet if it should still prove that teachers resist change because they resist any meddling with their own professional beliefs and values, widespread professional improvement might ask for a degree of consciousness-raising which intervention strategies (via Ofsted or any technical rationalist policy) cannot manage. It could be that a more profound policy for school improvement rests with more radical strategies bent towards altering either the culture or the professional beliefs of teachers as a whole (or both).

(c) Intrinsic design 1: teaching as 'acculturation'

Principles of human development are a bottom-line for teachers. Assuming we know what they are, they limit what we can and cannot expect from human beings at distinct points in their life-cyles. And powerful socio-cultural axioms see teaching as a form of acculturation, whereby pupils are initiated into cultural routines and conceptual systems, often covertly (Gingell and Brandon 2000; Lyle 2000; Pollard 1999; Smith and Standish 1997). Such principles come (in British education) from selections from the translated writings of Vygotsky (1962, 1978) by neo-Vygotskians (such as Bruner 1990; Mercer 1991). They arise from the insight that human minds grow through 'internalising'

(Vygotsky 1978) or 'appropriating' (Rogoff 1990) what other human minds organise for them, showing why one social group (such as children) becomes like another (such as adults). A tendency for social groups to reproduce their own life-styles and priorities happens because of the human propensity to *interpret* events (Bruner 1995a). Even the most idio-syncratic and personal experiences are grasped via culturally forged tools. Put another way, we never live our lives in isolation from others, even in infancy, but take meanings from experience in culturally prefigured ways. We learn via the symbolisms (mainly languages) cultures make possible. Since cultures are ways of life of particular groups, inhabiting different space–time locales, this means we can only learn in culturally validated ways within social settings.

Inspired by socio-cultural insights, Bruner proclaimed a 'contextual' revolution in our understanding of mind in 1990 (discussed in Liverto-Sempio and Marchetti 1997), which others have translated into terms relative to schools (e.g. Driver *et al.* 1994; Lyle 2000; Pollard 1999). As Driver *et al.* (1994) say, school learning must, at some level, be a process of 'acculturation' (also Gingell and Brandon 2000; Smith and Standish 1997), since it is subject-discourses which are to be learned. And discourses are socially fabricated languages, altering and expanding only according to well-known and agreed conventions (e.g. peer-referenced debate). Teachers may not have sure-fire techniques they can apply to classrooms. But, at least, they can master the languages they have to teach, knowing that education requires their pupils similarly mastering the language of subjects taught.

On this view, teaching is the use of those explanatory (often simplified) forms of discourse which teachers need to introduce students to other (subject) discourses. Such a version of teaching is sometimes called 'social constructivist' (Mercer 1991; Wells 1986); though some types of social constructivism give a more independent role to learners (Driver *et al.* 1994; see also Chapter 5). Whatever terminology we use, accultur-alist teaching is one that leaves both teachers and learners participating in group-related transactions from which neither can exit. In short, it isn't so much that teachers 'transmit' a culture directly as that underlying any form of teaching which is socially organised are cultural templates. These are to be found in the symbolically built structures of academic subjects, which any one school will embed within its own culture to a greater or lesser degree.

Schools usually seek to bind all staff to the same values, modes of discourse, agreed rituals and ceremonies, and in doing so will self-consciously adopt acculturation strategies. High-profile public and pri-vate educational institutions often signal the culturally specific nature of their academic success through rituals, ceremonies and prized symbols (school uniforms, speech days, award ceremonies), involving parents and distinguished representatives of a wider society. Acculturalist theories of human cognitive development (Pollard 1999 has a mainstream account) suggests that schools will knowingly or unknowingly 'transmit' culturally valid ways of dealing with knowledge, and the point is not so much whether this happens at all as how thoroughly 'cultures' are, in the event, transmitted.

Schools and teachers certainly vary in the extent to which they consciously engage in acculturation. Some individuals and groups may not (for whatever reason) willingly collude, and may even suggest (as Burtonwood 1996 does) that such a process is akin to indoctrination, and should be resisted. Also, by its nature, socio-culturalism takes little account of psychological evidence for the effect on adaption of individual personality. However, socio-cultural argument can be judged as superior to the behaviourist, educationally speaking, in showing how children learn prized higher-order skills, such as critical thinking and moral judgement. These skills are learned as by-products of daily transactions with the (grounded) specifics of situations. Socio-culturalist theorising critiques technical rationalism (see Pollard 1999) through its insistence on the dominance of culture context not technical intervention. It also constrains and complements top-down educational policies by showing exactly how national or cultural traditions can dictate educational processes and, therefore, outcomes (Broadhead *et al.* 2000).

What is queried, then, is not the success of acculturation but how deterministic it really is and whether there are drawbacks linked to conceiving mental growth as always culturally grounded. For it is one thing to admit we are all prey to acculturation, it is quite another to say that everyone imbibes cultural experience with little option in the matter. Constructivists (Chapter 4) and some social constructivists (Chapter 5) explain how individuals do intervene in their own acculturation. For mainstream socio-culturalists (e.g. Wertsch 1991), individualism is, itself, socially constructed. What is at stake is whether socio-cultural theory can underwrite forms of direct teaching which have some form of cultural transmission as its aims. For the moment, we might prudently hold fire on how far learners can – at least in theory – resist acculturation policies, if they wish to do so.

One reason we might think such a move wise is the vulnerability of acculturation to contingencies of circumstance. If it were really our best shot at explaining educational success, anyone's efforts to take charge of his or her own progress are severely compromised, since learners succeed, by and large, through colluding with what is prepared for them by others. This ideal of learners and teachers as 'apprentices' (Rogoff 1990) contains a conception of knowledge as ever more irretrievably locked inside public discourses. These discourses are unlocked by those possessing the right cultural key who, in that sense, have the qualification to become an educational elite (they manipulate the system which creates them). It is not an ideal shared by everyone.

(d) Intrinsic design 2: reflection–in–action

A rather more dynamic view of teachers and learners' cultural participation in shared practices arises from the 'reflective teacher' movement. It is immediately important to recall Chapter 2's argument that reflective practice is not, itself, parent to a single teaching model, although Schon's (1983, 1987) influential proposals concerning reflective practice do reject technical rationalism and versions take that rejection as an impetus for their own rationales. Hargreaves (1994) looks at it in this way. Referring to a survey reporting the grip the 'reflective practitioner' model has on postgraduate initial teacher training (Barrett *et al.* 1992), he finds its popularity owed to its legitimising in trainees the 'promotion . . . of a highly critical approach to the practices observed during the practicum' (Hargreaves 1994: 431). He is saying that 'reflective practice' is used by teacher-educators to subvert the current status quo, rather than as a specific teaching model in its own right. Yet Hargreaves dubs the reflective practitioner ideal as 'not inherently incompatible' with 'post-technocratic' teaching models where teachers' professional development continues after training within classrooms in terms of given curricula. In fact, 'the opposite may be true' (1994: 431).

As Hargreaves judges, reflective practice in Schon's analysis can be construed as one way (perhaps that most expected to work) for any group of teachers working to hit curricular targets (whether set by them or for them). We can go further. It may be markedly suited to those who accept rather than reject the status quo. Somewhat ironically (given that reflective practice is seen by many as an antidote to prescription), Schon contends that the professional meanings that teachers 'construct' are dominated by context (as with acculturation), rather than any tendency to stand aside from context in order to be critical of it. His point is that teachers draw on a range of social and personal as well as school experiences to sustain them each day and these experiences come to structure their professionalism, being exploited often unthinkingly. This situation usually works to a teacher's advantage. Almost non-stop interactions with pupils require a sensitised capacity for interrelating and communicating. Little time is left for (say) checking classroom situations against formal research findings, in a technical rationalist manner. Teaching, as a form of 'artful competence' (Schon 1983: 19), applies transitory rationales or 'theories of the moment' to passing situations. In other words, a skilled professional is someone applying his or her embedded skills freely to tasks. Berlak and Berlak (1981), too, uncover teaching skill from the layers of experience teachers accumulate through daily resolving classroom dilemmas, unpredictable because always unique.

What partly saves us from the acculturation trap is Schon's stipulation that 'reflection' is the means for professionals revising and reconstructing their own pragmatic experiences, though how far they do this is reliant on whom they meet and what happens to them. The reflective teacher ideal avoids technical rationalism by advising that school and classroom uncertainties make technical skills not in themselves a good bet for dealing with events. Rather, teachers are better developing 'practical intelligence' (Carr 1989, 1995) or reflection-in-action (Schon 1983). Such capabilities (also dilemma-resolution: Berlak and Berlak 1981) pin down process-dimensions of teaching whereby professionals respond speedily and sensitively to fluctuating problems which formal theories cannot help with. The situational instability of post-modern societies erects social and physical barriers to anyone trying to teach in pre-programmed ways.

Only, being situational, practical intelligence and 'reflection in action' have the critical weakness of being hard to alter to fit non-situational factors – until, that is, practitioners begin to reflect upon or about action. Affected by post-modern flux and alienated from any universal guidelines, teachers are prey to whatever situational influences do obtain. Though they can 'converse' with situations (Schon 1983: ch. 3), it may only be through critically evaluating situations from outside the situations themselves, that they can overcome the hazards circumstances may always erect. The best indoctrinators, as well as the best teachers, will probably be 'reflective practitioners' in the sense of being able to adapt skilfully to situational demands. Schon (1987) writes fairly pessimistically about programmes of training and professional development: the only way forward for teachers appears to be the hard graft of wrestling with job-specifics. Yet one thing we know for certain is that day-by-day experience *per se* isn't enough to guarantee quality practice: otherwise length of service would equate with teaching excellence. We know it doesn't. We also know that no one can programme experiences precisely for anyone else (though in-service courses may attempt to simulate typical instances), and we certainly cannot alter past experiences so as to change present behaviour.

Somehow or other, the intrinsic structure of teaching practice has to become vulnerable to extrinsic design. Put another way, reflection-in-action has to integrate with reflection-on-action and reflection-about-action. This realisation (see Griffiths and Tann 1991) has generated proposals for improving teaching effectiveness based on elaborating or integrating differently designed reflective practitioner models (e.g. Griffiths and Tann 1992; Pollard 1997; Zeichner and Liston 1987). But it does not override the point (implicit in Hargreaves's 1994 discussion) that teachers who wish to win success within a centrally devised framework will do so more effectively through a form of collaborative 'reflection' than through unthinking compliance.

Competence, success, excellence: designing quality teacher–centred practices

A teaching model protects itself by incorporating theories in such a way that criticisms can be dealt with by the right theory. Because teaching is multifaceted, we cannot expect any one account to deal with even the most common dilemmas. What we can expect from a self-consistent model is that some argument lodged within it will provide a suitable shield to ward off any dangerously critical arrow.

What have been laid out are those behavioural, cognitive, socio-political and personal dimensions of teaching believed to justify and protect a top-down teacher-centred approach. Anyone wishing to short-cut towards known goals will try, at some time, to manage learner-performance through response-habituation, apply researched techniques in standard ways, weave important messages into the fabric of a school or classroom culture, and reflect daily on events which ultimately make the formalities of such teaching second nature. Teachers vary in their taste for one strategy or another. But to be consistent, they will hardly undermine the whole enterprise by omitting to apply principles derived from any theory closely tied up with its aims.

For example: teachers who systematically regulate pupil behaviour through rewards, repetition and benchmarking will soon see the sense of also regulating pupil attitudes and values through systematically promoting specialised discourse and rituals. They will manage a school and classroom culture as carefully as they manage reward schedules. Similarly, for the very reason that teachers consent to curricular transmission, they will just as much fall victims to acculturation as learners, whether they are 'reflective' or not. The best teacher-centred practitioners, while routinely resolving practical dilemmas will keep track of broader aims, and (one suggests) not shrink from altering features of context. Those who see reflection as a primary catalyst for change and improvement, even as a vehicle for critiquing teacher–centred systems show how teachers can escape context-specificity for a world of more stable truths and, perhaps, more widely approved values (e.g. see Griffiths and Tann's 1992 developmental theory).

Competence in the teaching of set curricula is achieved through behaviour management, technical skills, cultural regulation and self-consciously reflective manipulations of context. Success should follow from the managerial techniques outlined, used in situations benign to them. That is, competence leads to success where there are no inhibiting factors. Or, put more directly, teacher-centred competence heralds success where it is ideologically matched to the belief-systems operating within and upon schools. Excellence will, in turn, be harboured in the actions of those capable of the most thorough and comprehensive application of controlling techniques, allowing a maximum number of pupils to assimilate lessons prepared for them. This is true because we recognise an excellent teacher, delivering set curricula, via the summative assessments put in place for that very purpose. Successful delivery of given standards is measurable via league-tables of pupil performance and Ofsted comparisons, simply because standards are 'given' and thus crack the whip of performance. The higher they rise in league-tables the more 'excellent' schools are likely to be judged. Controlling pupils' performance in assessed work is the *raison d'être* of teacher-centred strategies. To repeat: standards of teaching quality are implicit in the rationales for the various teacher-centred approaches themselves. This doesn't mean that they cannot be questioned in their own terms (initially in ways seeking to improve the model), and such a questioning might hint at more basic flaws.

Before itemising the strengths and weaknesses of teacher-centred approaches, it is worth summarising the above discussion in terms of the basic principles of practice already worked out. These are constituted by a long-term aim (ideal conception) and associated principles of practice or procedure.

Summarising first principles

The educational ideal

Teachers often believe that learners must value what educated citizens already value. Learners must stride forward within a tradition venerating the status of past and present achievements. No equally worthwhile options are admitted. When guided by standard curricula, schools there-fore teach the content of that curriculum as necessary knowledge – this being publicly venerated. Model learners are welcomed into a main-stream culture which it is their duty to take forward. A recent defence of this position (Gingell and Brandon 2000) proclaims 'high culture' as the brightest educational beacon guiding the school enterprise.

Associated principles

First, learners are relatively ignorant and unskilled 'apprentices' to more knowledgeable elders. Their role is to submit to tuition and discipline until they are initiated into that desired educational status marked by exam certification, professional qualification and so on.

Second, targets can be set because aims are clear enough for goals to be made finite and measurable. Curricular prescriptions hang on the tails of assessment. Learning programmes are linked to whatever test results pick out as needing attention.

Third, teachers variously manage pupils' learning and behaviour to ensure pupils hit prescribed targets. Competent top-down teaching deploys conditioning or technical rationalist skills, respecting socio-cultural principles, in a reflective, humanitarian manner. Success and excellence are judged according to prescribed assessment criteria decided by teachers and teacher-advisers.

Notable strengths and weaknesses of working in a teacher–centred manner

Strengths

This approach is – by definition – managed by 'experts' qualified to write and administer educational curricula. It is therefore straightforwardly evaluated. Goals are fixed, forms of assessment logically related to what is sought, and desirable outcomes plain to all. Its flaws (see next sub-section) are usually related to the cultivating of a sort of passive depen-dency in pupils – not best preparation for 'life-long' learning within a post-modern society. But some writers argue the reverse – that life-long learning demands a knowledge base which has to be taught securely (Rossbach 2000). What is also often forgotten is that children do not only attend school. For many, a rich home life adequately compensates them for the rigours of schools. Schools – for some – are, simply, places where they acquire those qualifications needed for them to take a respected place in a pre-ordered society. 'Passively' acquired knowledge is precisely what they want, as this is assimilated to already actively constructed concepts then applied fruitfully, as desired. Learners whose autonomy and breadth of experience is guaranteed at home may be able to resist, reject or modify knowledge presented to them (assuming teaching methods fall short of indoctrination), in ways personally suited to their own ambitions and life-styles.

By the same token, top-down management may suit older pupils and adults who have established a base of autonomy during their earlier education (perhaps in primary school). Lectures – still the staple of higher education institutions – are obvious instances of 'top down' teaching. University tutors assume that adult students selected for advanced courses are cognitively ready to process lecture material in service of higher-order problem-solving. The strengths of top-down approaches, therefore, are fixed in terms of control, pre-determined quality and appropriateness for some pupils at some points in their lives.

Weaknesses

Harmful side-effects can follow from relentless adult domination. If we are preparing students for independent roles in a fluid society, the best way may not be to make old wisdom the main texts we work from – even where students can already think for themselves and, therefore, reject as well as accept what is taught. Some learners thrive when encountering pre-tailored curricula (see above). Others do not. A possibly intransigent difficulty for top-down systems is that they leave no opening for students who find rigours of formal assessment debilitating and damaging to their own feelings of self-worth. Covington (1998) gives many examples of motivational problems met by American students (mostly adolescents) working in the same type of competitive framework as students in contemporary England. The stresses of their having to raise performance to meet given standards can be so emotionally destructive students lose heart and are switched off learning rather than being switched on to it.

Discussions with English primary school pupils find some admitting to test anxiety, while a few are openly rebellious about biases in their standard curricula (Silcock and Wyness 2000; see also Pollard *et al.* 1994; Trigg and Pollard 1998). Even infant age pupils can be disheartened by a constant diet of 'number' and 'writing' judged as right for them by adults, especially if they find work hard (Silcock and Wyness 2000). Studies of schools where teachers meet state-generated criteria such that most (in some cases all) pupils reach expected levels note that these schools probably over-teach assessed areas at the expense of a 'broad and balanced' subject-range (Williams 2000). Largely, pupils do collude in all their studies because they believe their futures depend on it. What Woods (1990) calls a 'socialised instrumentalism' cultivates an unshakable belief that jobs and affluent life-styles are to be bought by an unwavering and uncomplaining diligence (Silcock and Wyness 2000). Such beliefs are common even among 5 year olds (Sherman 1988).

It would seem fair to wonder whether we might not, on balance, prefer our pupils to study for sake of enjoyment rather than for sake of material reward and take cognisance of their own insights into their talents and ambitions. On such a tack, Paechter (1998) reviews evidence that school knowledge, presented by teachers as special and distinct from that familiar to pupils has, somehow, to be 'won' by them through those rituals and triumphs legitimised by the school. Paechter argues that teachers cannot blend school knowledge into 'real life' illustrations within a curriculum because 'it remains possible for the school to take over such knowledge, rendering it powerless and no longer owned, stripping it, in the process, of its connection with its original context' (Paechter 1998: 173). Through its presentation, prioritisation and assessment, school knowledge ceases to be 'real' in any recognisable sense and pupils become alienated from what should be their birthright. Paechter refers to humanist contentions (Rogers 1983) that student-generated work will guarantee students' ownership of what they do. Such options are unavailable within teacher-centred systems where the *raison d'être* is to bypass whatever pupils might wish in favour of teaching what adults have already decided is in pupils' interests.

An advocate of teacher and subject-dominated work can learn from such criticisms and seek to ameliorate the worst effects of top-down coercion by sympathetically helping pupils with difficulties and by leavening hard instruction with relaxed interludes. Research into National Curricular literacy teaching finds that instruction can be mixed with some individual and paired (collaborative) work (Sylva *et al.* 1999). The best teacher-centred practices will probably not be those where teachers expect pupils to submit to acculturation without resistance. It is perfectly possible to maximise the likelihood of children assimilating set curricula without resorting to oppression or threats.

Yet, how far teachers can sugar the pill of testing and targeting – especially in schools anxious not to fall behind in league-tables – is another matter. 'Naming and shaming' procedures are the logical concomitants of persuading 'failing' schools to turn themselves around in a top-down manner. They put pressure on teachers to coerce pupils ever harder towards exactly those values teacher-centred systems exist to promote. Teachers may, successfully, steer their pupils towards test success.

They may even achieve 'excellence', when this is measured through formal assessment. But they may do so at some cost.

That cost has to be paid not only by pupils, but also by their teachers in terms of professional morale and personal satisfaction. The second endemic weakness of teacher–centred approaches is that teachers, themselves, become alienated from curricular processes they implement (for which they then become responsible). Up to a point, teachers always 'interpret' central curricular prescriptions in the light of circumstances and beliefs. But their room for manoeuvre may be limited by increasingly punitive accountability systems. Poor teacher morale and lack of curricular ownership can make acute difficulties for an educational system when curricula are already 'heavy' with content, as happened in the early days of the English/Welsh National Curriculum (Campbell 1993; Silcock 1990). Although teachers have always striven to make the reforms work (Silcock and Wyness 1997), what stays the biggest fly in the National Curricular ointment is the sensitive matter of who owns educational curricula. The hard business of educating the young might be found easier by teachers who have curricular reins in their own hands.

4 Models of good practice 2

Learner-centred approaches

Introduction: first principles and historical background

There are many ways to explain learner-centred teaching and terms such as 'child-centred methods' have a long, chequered history (Chung and Walsh 2000; Kliebard 1995). But however we view its history or conceptual base, all modern followers of this tradition are likely to believe that school-students, both factually and by rights, are agents for their own learning. That is, there are empirical and moral claims at the heart of all learner-centred positions. 'Progressivist' teachers of a spiritual sort (perhaps inspired by Swedenborg or Froebel: Bloomfield 2000; Froebel 1909) or informed by developmental theory (perhaps in Rousseau's work: Darling 1994) delegate both natural rights and practical decision-making powers to pupils (revisiting Wilson's 1999 distinction between teacher-accountability and responsibility). Good practice is no longer invested in teaching activity *per se*. It is intimately tied up with the way teachers guide and delegate rather than 'manage' learner behaviour.

What is 'idealised', then, is the autonomous learner able to shape his or her own destiny over the short and long term. Teachers may 'facilitate' rather in the way a midwife facilitates a baby's birth (Rogers 1983); they may 'empower' students (Kelly 1989) or 'liberate' their natively endowed talents within institutions (Silcock 1999). For Kelly (1989, following Stenhouse 1975), teachers of learner-centred curricula foster learning *processes* (positive attitudes, talents for independent learning, for rescheduling tasks in personally accessible ways and so on) and find performance targets distract from their primary task. This partly explains why, since the late 1960s or so, interventionist governments in the UK have viewed with ill-concealed mistrust the delegating of powers to pupils that ministers believe only teachers should wield. Their top-down policies represent, up to a point, an adverse reaction to advancing notions of pupil autonomy, participation and control.

Academic critics have been even more damning. Some have believed that learner-centred pedagogies are nearly always ineffective (Bennett 1976; Galton 1989, 1995) and that few (if any) teachers actually use them (Galton 1989; Mackenzie 1997; Simon 1981). They are irrelevant to the needs of modern societies, being irretrievably individualistic (Lawton 1989) and outmoded in describing how schools actually work (Moore 2000). Child-centred teachers oppress young children via a specialised discourse (Walkerdine 1992). Their sloganising distracts from the more urgent practicalities of teaching (Alexander 1994), while ideologies of any sort are seen as poorly suited to life in post-modern societies (Mackenzie 1997; Schon 1983; Sugrue 1997: see also Chapter 2). Of those who have defended learner-centred teaching, Kelly (1994a, 1994b, 1995) remains most suspicious of imposed target-setting, especially for the youngest pupils (Blenkin and Kelly 1994). Silcock (1993b, 1996, 1999) condemns critics' reduction of progressivism to a narrow method-ology so as to attack it – to small-group and individually assigned tasks (Galton 1995), teaching 'style' (Bennett 1976), 'discovery methods' (Askew *et al.* 1997), or an over-exclusive 'informality' (Alexander 1994; Mackenzie 1997; Sugrue 1997).

What might be helpful in beating back this avalanche of criticism is to admit that – to be fair to learner-centred teaching as mainstream model – it should never be detached from the values it serves. If teachers wish to hit prescribed targets, it is hardly surprising if methods suited to different purposes (which may of course *involve* hitting prescribed targets) do not completely fit the bill. So success at pupil-centred teaching is unlikely to arrive by someone slavishly following a blueprint, if only because theoretical models are by their nature hypothetical constructs to be modified until they work as we wish. Anyone finding that a teaching approach falls short of its own ideals must modify the approach not abandon the ideals (unless they are proving unworthy for some other reason).

It is true that teachers' and theorists' disapproval of practices may have little to do with their value-orientation. Teachers may find them too complex and indigestible to swallow wholesale (as Galton 1989 specu-lates). This could explain their decline in popularity in English schools (Francis and Grindle 1998; Pollard *et al.* 1994; Silcock and Wyness 1997; Webb 1993), though it would leave mysterious why 'child-centredness' continues to dominate early years teaching (Vartuli 1999; Woodhead 1998). Reputably making English early years teaching the best in the world (Pascal and Bertram 1993), it also flourishes world-wide (Rohrs and Lenhart 1995). In the end, we are obliged to evaluate a mode of teaching on its merits regarding present educational needs, as objectively as we can. The business of educating others (especially children) has too much riding on it for us to be strongly swayed by historical contingencies affecting (for example) the United Kingdom since the late 1980s or so.

Learner-centred approaches must connect with the wide-ranging ways teachers have sought to realise them. And it is useful to cluster these (as with teacher-centred work) around some minimal review of the ways learners can be central to teaching. That is: theories can be grouped to cover main conceptual, cognitive, affective and socio-political parameters. Related areas may well have long pedigrees. For example, a philosophical/historical tradition promoting 'humanistic' ideals gives a good first perspective on the approach (a) because it may well be the longest relevant tradition. Almost as influential, and more up-to-date, psychological assumptions behind learner-centred teaching are 'constructivist' assumptions (b) linked loosely to the Piagetian developmentalism which underpinned the Plowden report's recommendations (Central Advisory Council 1967). Third, the personal/emotional benefits won by learner-centred teaching come into view through the lens of Rogerian person-centred theory (c). Fourth, the pedagogic arm of children's rights' movements have, by nature, to be student-centred, and are regularly seen as such (d).

(a) Humanism: teaching the 'whole' child

Student-centred theories are not always humanistic. But resurgent progressivist campaigns often take their colours from older, humanistic traditions in the social sciences and in philosophy. Rousseau's (1911 [1762]) humanism is, for many, the historic parent to child-centred teaching, though such a belief is often shared by those wishing to tar progressivism with the brush of a naive *laissez-faire* morality, or accuse teachers of young children of a rather precious 'innocence' (Alexander 1994). Rousseau wanted his fictional child Emile to escape the corrupt societies of seventeenth-century France and be educated within a natural setting. Darling's (1994) commentary on Emile defends Rousseau from Dewey's (1916) and Alexander's (1994) indictment that the philosopher believed child development occurred best without adult interference. Darling (1994) points out that Emile did have a tutor, and Emile's tutor led the boy in some directions and not in others. In Rousseau's book, it was the tutor's skill not the natural environment which nurtured the child's curiosity and capabilities. Rousseau's own concept of education can therefore be thought of as one of guided self-discovery, rather than being unduly reliant on 'natural' growth.

Modern humanist philosophy is hard to capture in a few words. The definitive term (humanism) always guards a rationalist refusal of thinkers such as Rousseau, Sartre, Popper, Berlin and Chomsky to make our humanness obey supposedly more basic elements (ethical and/or practical). At some level, all humanists celebrate the integrity of whatever it means to *be* human and deplore reductionism (there are disagreements about what humanness is of course). In modern times, phenomenologist and existentialist projects such as those of Sartre have thrived by opposing religious and scientific (or 'positivist') habits of treating humans as objects of study rather than subjects. They have similarly backed liberal policies against legislation seeming to deny human beings basic rights (e.g. Berlin 1969; Popper 1966).

Educationally speaking, an anti-reductionist stance to learning (that is, a humanist stance) is one where two criteria apply. First, as human beings, learners earn fully fledged rights of participation in their schooling, i.e. with some sort of decision-making powers. Second, they are to be seen as whole persons, in that no part of our humanness can legitimately be detached from other parts in order to subvert it (Biber 1972; cf. the raising of self-esteem where a person's esteem is freed from other dimensions of general welfare). Both criteria assume that learners will monitor and direct their own progress. Typically, child-centred practices are those where teachers treat children as whole individuals (Alexander 1992; Biber 1972; Silcock 1999; Silcock and Wyness 1997), with real curricular responsibilities. So progressivism is a form of humanism, at least in the sense that pupil-centred teachers regard pupil assent as a plank of good practice.

Rationales for a humanist brand of education invariably share distrust for theorising which places mental functioning outside subjective influence. Humanists are sceptical of behaviourist and other materialist philosophies (cf. Chomsky 1959, 2000; Popper and Eccles 1977). Typically, they argue that causal explanations for our actions relying on situational contingencies say little if anything about the conscious decisions we make. One cannot meaningfully be reduced to the other. To illustrate: 'interpretivist' views of mind (Brockmeier 1996; Bruner 1990, 1995a) do not contradict outright the idea that children's thinking and reasoning powers are 'scientifically' caused (perhaps in ways described by Piaget 1954). But they do say that without our interpretations of events in terms made sensible by shared experiences, all human action – including that of neonates – is inconceivable. No matter how old we are, what most matters in our lives are attributes we ascribe to and discover within our-selves. So there is never justification for thinking learners cannot properly have a controlling part in decisions concerning them. The claim that children's voluntariness must inform school-teaching recurs repeatedly in modern learner-centred theories.

(b) Constructivism: learners as agents for their own learning

That explanation for the features and growth of minds called 'constructi-vism' usually gives learners charge of their own affairs. Some versions conform to a near 'Rousseauesque' stereotype of learners being forced to rely on their own resources, with limited potential for benefitting from help (von Glaserfeld 1995). Others give more ground to group influence (see Phillips 1995; see also Chapters 3 and 5). Classic versions derived from Piaget's work (1954) explain human achievements in terms of unique experiences (Driver 1983; Hand and Treagust 1994; Littledyke 1998; von Glaserfeld 1995). Because we all experience the world differently, we all construe it differently. This fact has two entail-ments, educationally speaking.

First of all, if school-pupils bring unique constructs (or in Piaget's 1954 terms, 'schemas') to tasks, teachers must respect the integrity of these, even when pupils misconstrue some mathematical, scientific, literary (or whatever) idea. If learners genuinely believe that – say – a substance alters in shape, volume or mass when it moves in space, this is a construct which can only be modified. It isn't a 'wrong' solution or misperception to be discarded: constructs, or schemas, change and develop, they never conveniently disappear. Second, holes in learners' grasp of their world equate with gaps of experience which, somehow, require 'filling in'. Part of any remediation has to be pupils rectifying their own miscon-ceptions, since, for a teacher (of science, say) just to correct pupils' naive opinions is of little worth if it leaves a learner's more basic pre-conceptions untouched (Driver 1983; Driver and Bell 1986). So it isn't only that all children have their own starting points for learning but that each has personal barriers to overcome.

For constructivists, conceptual change is the integrating of challenging experiences within a growing principled knowledge forever expanding and being modified. This remains true when pupils encounter academic subjects: i.e. in order to understand ideas scientifically, some principles (such as the nature of scientific method) must, truly, come to stand behind what is understood and not simply be reproducible in essays and test answers. It is to safeguard this process, whereby learners properly understand what they learn (their knowledge is structured in some sort of principled manner *vis-à-vis* a subject discipline) which keeps constructivist teachers looking for ways of teaching actively and experientially. Their purpose is to ensure that what is learned becomes integrated with pupils' dominant ways of interpreting their worlds, and is not, just, memorised.

Vygotskians and neo-Vygotskians have revised and expanded constructivist accounts. In their revised versions, to agree that human beings meet the world uniquely does not mean they construe events uniquely. An 'interpretivist' (Brockmeier 1996; Bruner 1990, 1995a; Bruner and Haste 1987) supposes that children exploit unique experiences via common *symbolic* interpretations. It will never be that experiential 'holes' somehow need 'filling in'. Personal experience is an absolute limitation on learning: we can only make sense of anything in terms of the way we encounter it. But a lot can be managed by helping pupils reframe immature notions in ways acceptable to others (working with that sphere of influence that Vygotsky 1978 famously conceived as the 'zone of proximal development'). Unfortunately, Vygotskian and neo-Vygotskian theory is itself split between two camps, one bolstering the social origins of mind (supporting acculturalism: see Chapter 3) the other modifying rather than replacing classic constructivism (Phillips 1995). For one strain of 'social constructivism' (Broadfoot 2000; Driver *et al.* 1994), it is individuals who access those cultures meant to transform them. That is, it is individual pupils who do the work of making sense of school tasks, albeit aided by teachers and peers – perhaps via formative assessments (Black and Wiliam 1998). For others, it is culture-contexts which dominate the lives of individuals. As cultures change, so must the minds and capabilities of the individuals living within and dealing with them (see Chapter 3).

The social constructivist modification of classic constructivism is important. Without it, we might think no teacher can ever really empathise with any learner (Sutherland 1992; see also Chapter 8). Or we might view all teaching as a hit-or-miss business where the best one can hope for is that learners make reasonable stabs at ideas they can seldom comprehensively engage with. Sutherland (1992) notices how pessimistic some classic constructivists are (e.g. Denvir 1985), though few go so far as to deny teachers any decisive influence. All accounts affirm the central problem of teaching as being the relative isolation of learners within their inner worlds. Asking teachers to plumb children's very specific difficulties in order to proffer exactly the right support – via 'scaffolding' techniques or whatever (see Bliss *et al.* 1996) – is asking a lot. No teachers can ever be sure what learners are thinking.

All they can do is steer a pupil through school subjects as best they can. How successful they are will depend, as always, on their professional sensitivity and intuition rather than on any set rules or procedures they can follow. This doesn't mean that much constructivist literature isn't invaluable in explaining central dilemmas of teaching, provided we accept as a premise that the teaching job is more a 'scaffolding' of pupils' in worthwhile directions, rather than being strongly instructional or pedagogic.

(c) Developing the self: the emotional climate of classrooms

Carl Rogers fashioned student-centred learning from his professional expertise in client-centred therapy (1954, 1983) when he found the same principles enlightening both education and psychiatry. In education, as in client-centred counselling, learners come to control their lives by discovering how to rule their own minds. In other words, at the heart of Rogerian theory is a conviction that individual achievements are channelled through self-knowledge. Unique self-concepts figure in all worthwhile education, because permanent changes are personally trans-forming. Moreover, as education has such a powerful impact on how people view themselves, Rogers realised how problematic institution-alised settings must seem to learners. He proposed three main conditions for the positive self-attitudes and associated conceptual change which mark those teaching and learning situations likely to be successful. These he named *congruence, unconditional personal regard* and *self-actualisation* (Rogers 1954, 1957, 1983).

Congruence is the alignment of our self-views with perceptions of how others see us. Whether such alignment happens or not depends on how far the two self-perceptions are compatible. Traditionally, teachers have given little thought to congruence, discerning learners' strengths and weaknesses with an eye on curricular aims rather than learners' mental health. So, sidestepping criticisms to preserve self-worth, some learners virtually abandon their classrooms – psychologically speaking (in some cases literally). The alternative of accepting criticisms as legitimate would invite a self-reproach and guilt that could easily destroy deeper aspirations and motivations. Covington's (1998) plans for retrieving American students' feelings of self-worth (through co-operative game-playing) are soaked in Rogerian theory. For Rogers, the direct path to congruence is via unconditional self-regard – people coming to accept all known self-views, without qualification. But, as implied, students only steer towards unconditional self-regard when their self-worth is not a negotiable issue – i.e. when significant others (such as teachers) unconditionally respect their attitudes, skills, interests and so forth (albeit signalling what changes are needed).

In a context of affirmation and acceptance, learners regulate their aspirations and move on to whatever goals they prize. This personal quest towards a personally-realised future is self-actualisation. Accordingly, there is more to Rogerian teaching than raising and maintaining pupil self-esteem, though self-esteem may be crucial to success (it is an 'effectiveness' indicator: Sammons *et al*. 1995). Self-esteem measures degree of self-liking, and as it happens we may like to be ignorant, destructive and corrupt. Improved or maintained self-worth is implicated in successful teaching, but only when it accompanies self-actualisation in congruent circumstances – i.e. where learner and teacher agree about aims. To guarantee high self-esteem where learners fail and remain contented about their failure is no more than to guarantee complacency. It is self-defeating.

One can see, too, that there is more to teaching in a Rogerian manner than making oneself a conduit for learners' own desires about what and how to learn (Rogers 1983). Teachers must provide banks of physical and emotional resource, and be endlessly resourceful in guiding, advising and keeping esteem levels high. One can see how this policy does obey sound principle, and is likely to foster mutually rewarding relationships between teachers and taught. But one can also see how teachers might respect congruence, self-esteem and personal-actualisation while leading and instructing as well as when facilitating and empowering. Most contemporary thinkers would admit as important the emotional climate of schools and sympathetic teacher–pupil relationships (Hopkins *et al*. 1997), without believing that learners must be in charge as much as Rogers suggests. Even Ofsted includes a school's ethos within its inspection framework (Ofsted 1995). And, again, we might question whether positive learner attitudes are only reliably guaranteed when student curricular decision-making is enfranchised. It is always possible for teachers to believe that a warm trusting relationship with pupils follows from overcoming rather than giving in to learners' whims and fancies.

One reason why Rogers kept to his belief in person-centred work, though, was his conviction that this was the only way to defeat educational failure with any certainty. He never doubted that failure (on a personal or professional level) is destructive of the person concerned and damaging to contexts in which it occurs. And it is hardly controversial to agree with Covington (1998) that many learners are alienated from academic study by their sufferings within a competitive examination system. Rogers' flagship theory for learner-centredness always navigates around the rocks of failure towards the shores of success, when success is defined in terms of fulfilling learners' known aspirations. The central problem for a strict Rogerian is, as said, that most public expectations of schools are not just that learners aim for self-identified goals, but that they achieve goals set for them by others. It is a fair point that modern-day pupils will expect not only to have their own aspirations respected but also to be guided by the value judgements of those already educated. Rogers' work is chock full of practical advice about maintaining healthy, viable self-concepts. Whether the particular student-centred system he advocates is either necessary to fulfil his own criteria for a successful education, or even wholly desirable from a typical learner-viewpoint, is another matter.

(d) Teaching for pupil rights, respecting competence

It is perfectly rational to believe pupils should have rights in schools whether they, themselves, wish it or not. Prior to the abolition of slavery in the United States of America, some slaves confessed that they felt happy and secure. Arguments for human rights do not depend on all human beings becoming aware of their own oppression; they hinge on the soundness of our ethics, of our convictions about how we should all treat each other. If each person is equally deserving of respect, each can expect others to couch that respect within dignified treatment. Although arguments for human rights are hard to formalise non-controversially, it makes sense to suppose that a harmonious and fully inclusive society depends on there being minimally acceptable ways of treating other people, owed to whatever is seen as our common humanity.

International advances were won for children's rights by the United Nations Declaration on the Rights of the Child (Osler and Starkey 1998; Roche 1999) and, in Britain, by the Childrens Act 1989 and Codes of Practice for Children with Special Educational Needs. These rights apply, now, within almost all areas of child welfare and child care (see contributers to Davie *et al.* 1996; John 1996), such that schools where pupils toe a hard-and-fast curricular line do seem out of step. Maybe adult paternalism is entrenched in western educational systems because of the doctrine that economic need demands a trained workforce, and giving in too much to learners themselves will in the end blight a nation's industrial success. International comparisons between test achievements in different countries (e.g. Reynolds and Farrell 1996) raise the spectre of 'informal' teaching hindering industrial progress – much as it was raised by James Callaghan's educational advisers in preparing him for his Ruskin College speech (via the infamous 'Yellow Book':

Chitty 1989). Such distrust of pupil-enfranchisement seems likely to continue keeping them inferior to adults in many walks of life. Some commentators claim that children have replaced women as the main 'invisible' group in our society (Alderson 1999; Roche 1999).

What might, in the end, lead to pupils gaining at least some rights within schools is our changing concept of what it means to *be* a child. The twentieth century marked that great revolution in our modelling of childhood called developmentalism. Giants of developmental psychology, Piaget and Vygotsky, wrote theories which gave children their qualitatively distinct ways of thinking and acting, often binding them to the concrete, enactive and particular (whether for 'natural' or social reasons). Such theories are not, now, judged as wrong so much as insufficiently cognisant of the head-start given to development by innate processes. Late-twentieth-century studies of babies (Konnor 1991; Trevarthan 1992) find that, although experiences constrain intellectual growth developmentally, they do so for contingent reasons (i.e. children have different life experiences to the adult). Young children's learning has features previously thought confined to adults (Lonka *et al.* 2000). *Absolute* differences between child and adult are not as we have believed them to be.

Possibly, determinant structures for all main processing and problem-solving skills featured in adulthood are innate (i.e. they need liberating not implanting: see David 1998). They are hard to detect because – for lack of relevant experience – infants do not apply skills as adults do. Children have to be cared for just because they are not yet versed in the ways of the world (Kelly 1994b); this is important to any assessment of their academic potential. Yet purposive problem-solving which typifies the mature mind cannot be denied to the newborn. It isn't so much that children come slowly to rationality as that inborn processes apply differentially to context as they grow older. In a non-normative sense, newborns act in a thoroughly independent way, recognising that their physical immaturity and lack of experience limit autonomy to bare means–end essentials (Cousins 1996 discusses autonomous infancy).

But it is not factors of circumstance (even of biological circumstance) which should occupy us, since we are all prey to these and to the ravages of experience. What we should turn to are issues of principle. In principle, children are as equipped to cope with childhood scenarios as adults are to cope with adulthood, once we have partialled out the particulars of experience in terms of actual demands made on them. In the end, we have *always* to justify denying decision-making powers to children in terms of those two factors – relevant experience and relevant demands. We cannot deny children powers on the basis of the simple fact that they are children (whatever their age). They are not naive innocents. Nor are they so lacking in rational thought that they easily fall prey to unreason and faulty judgement, though their rationality may inhere only in the most basic practical skills. As those who seek to protect children's rights (cf. Kelly 1994b; Roche 1999) make plain, no one is asking for children to be treated as adults. Only that adults must let pupils take or modify decisions usually made on their behalf, unless we have good reason to believe they cannot sensibly do so (rather than it being the other way around).

Educational 'reforms' in England and Wales since the late 1980s have done nothing to speed on a thorough-going review of children's rights in school, but that is evidently what is required. Some form of learner-centredness waits in the wings to benefit directly from any such review. It is hard to see how pupils can be given rights of participation in schools except via strategies worked at to fit just such circumstances (although these need not be exclusively learner-centred: see Chapter 5). The main question begged remains the critical one of what makes learner-centred teaching successful or not, and it is this to which attention is turned.

Competence, success and excellence in learner-centred teaching

Learner-centred teachers treating pupils as whole individuals are likely to empathise with pupils' unique (if socially mediated) construing of circumstance, sensing that good teaching stands or falls by how well it colludes with pupils' self-evaluations. Such teachers will liberate pupils' independence, seeing young people's rights as unbounded in principle by chronological immaturity (though modified in practice). As with teacher-centred approaches, the conceptual, cognitive, affective and socio-political dimensions of classrooms will together (because they present different classes of problem) define a teaching model. One way of pinpointing a competent (base-level) form of learner-centred teaching, then, is to ask for sufficient attention to be paid to each dimension to integrate them all within a unified policy.

Complications arise as soon as we start to divine what makes learner-centred teaching *succeed* or not, since the guiding criterion must be the achievement of set aims. Manifestly, this is unproblematic where parents and pupils share the values and aspirations of a school. The situation becomes extremely problematic where students' values and aspirations conflict with those of a school and, possibly, those wished for them by their own parents. For one has then to suggest that learner-centred teaching while realising pupils' own rights and aspirations will in such circumstances fail to realise those of others. Sometimes, having one's cake and eating it too is really not an option! Somewhat paradoxically, success for learner-centredness might imply failure to achieve aims sanctioned, for example, by Ofsted (i.e. implicit in National Curricular target-setting).

One way round this impasse for anyone who sees that state legislation simply does not bargain for pupils steering their own ship is to abandon short-term for long-term thinking. Given that a premise of learner-centredness is its liberation of students' mental powers developmentally, this premise allows pupils to grow in ways of managing their own behaviour and capabilities. Teachers can argue that by opening doors for people to a control of their own lives, they are making it possible for pupils to achieve in publicly valued ways, at least in principle. Even if pupils opt out of other social duties (e.g. citizenship responsibilities), teachers can point out that in their opinion their teaching is still the best shot for longer-term success, given that more imposed strategies risk other difficulties. We know that traditional curricula can alienate pupils from schools (see Chapter 3). It is never self-evident that standard fare – no matter how well assembled – presents the safest option. At least, learner-centred teachers can guarantee their pupils will have *some* success, though, as said, that success may not marry to publicly fashionable mores.

It would be tempting to make learner-centred excellence that mode of teaching which did, in fact, give to pupils both autonomy, in terms of their own life-styles and success in traditional forms of testing. But this would misread the true picture. Educational excellence (if the concept is to have consistent meaning) must be that which realises stated values optimally. And the values implicit in learner-centred curricula, are, by definition, geared to helping learners realise their own developing values and certainly not (by nature) any other sort. The Rogerian ideal is that ideal where learners are single-mindedly engaged in 'self-actualisation', not in actualising the wishes and dreams of adults, no matter how virtuous these latter might appear. This means that a mark of excellence in a learner-oriented classroom must be that the talents that learners prize are, in truth, being nurtured and their ambitions are being fulfilled. In the longer term, pupils' life-fulfilments and self-reports would be crucial evidence. Put simply, educational excellence may be impossible to assess except by reference to the expressed views and studied present and future life-styles of pupils themselves. This type of evidence is seldom sought, even by researchers (though see Kershner and Pointon 2000; Rudduck and Flutter 2000; Silcock and Wyness 2000; Woods 1990). Educational assessment has evolved in a rather exclusively 'positivist' not 'humanist' manner, helping us to an extent grasp why it is difficult to assess modern learner-centred teaching.

One would expect a competent learner-centred practitioner to apply skills and express ethically based attitudes called humanistic. This means that the emotional and skill dimensions of teaching support each other: it is hardly credible to suppose that a teacher embracing learner-centredness will believe that children are by nature unqualified to make most decisions for themselves. Such a teacher will respect pupils' own self-evaluations. That is, the effectiveness of learner-centred teaching should show itself not only in relevant performance outcomes (as with any teaching model), but, to accord with its humanistic base, in pupils' expressed views. Excellent learner-centred practitioners have to be those inspiring pupils to a maximum to achieve aspirations and ambitions while, through sensitive facilitation (scaffolding or whatever), monitoring progress towards forms of independence (contextually decided). Their excellence might not be immediately apparent. One cannot imagine how to ascertain the quality of this type of teaching. But over a period, degree of excellence would be discerned through verbal and observational encounters with pupils, supplemented by testing (in so far as 'process' acquisitions can be accurately tested).

The only caveat – which bears repeating – is that a thoroughgoing learner-centred approach will usually fall short in the eyes of those who see it as the job of adults to decide children's future. This will be true not only in broad outline (there would be little disagreement on this), but also in terms of the breadth, depth and detail of curricula. For many, allowing pupils to make curricular choices is never viable. It is simply too risky. Childhood (or adolescent) inexperience will by nature disqualify someone from being the best judge of what is in his or her interests. Today, a learner-centred advocate might reply that (in the absence of any real cut-off), it is hard to see when individuals do inherit the right to decide their own lives, if it is not theirs at birth. Conceivably, one resolution of this dilemma inherent in all educational situations lies in some form of negotiation between teachers and pupils. And it is the process of negotiation which is at the heart of the third model of good practice, to be discussed next.

Summarising first principles

The educational ideal

If educated persons are autonomous adults able to reject as well as accept traditional attitudes and beliefs, it accords with that ideal to model pupils as autonomous learners. Respecting children's independent status is a staging post to responsible citizenship. Whether or not related practices are effective or not may be somewhat irrelevant to the ideal itself. For, to repeat the earlier conclusion, their validity is judged in terms of how effectively they serve stated ends (no methods are prohibited – it is how they are integrated in service of an ideal which might become an issue).

Associated principles

First, learners are agents for their own learning, and classroom curricula must always respect that fact. It isn't that teachers deal with pupils in a *laissez-faire*, subservient manner. They must, simply, act in ways which optimise pupils' qualities, skills and abilities as these are independently applied. This humanistic, 'empowerment' policy respects pupils rights in school (as a matter of course). It benefits not only from a long tradition of humanistic philosophy but also from an equally influential tradition of humanistic psychology.

Second, teaching methods, following constructivist precepts, assume learners actively engage with self-chosen topics in self-chosen ways. They integrate their learning with existing experiences in ways allowing them to apply what they learn to the circumstances of their own lives.

Third, learner-centred teaching is meant to facilitate self-actualisation (as conceived by Rogers: see pp. 56–58). Classroom procedures will at all costs protect pupils' high self-regard while keeping their self-views congruent with their perceptions of how others see them. Feedback to pupils will be positive and improvements achieved through pupils building on existing triumphs (self-actualisation) rather than repairing teacher-identified errors (damaging self-esteem).

Notable strengths and weaknesses of learner–centred approaches

Strengths

The strengths of learner-centredness flow from its ethical and empirical (developmental) rationales.

In one way it is unexceptional, and in another way strange, to treat children and adolescents as human beings with full human rights. It is unexceptional in that the modern habit is to regard all human groups as equally deserving of respect and the ascription of dignity. It is strange in that pupils in schools throughout the world have almost always been powerless – as, they, themselves realise (Buchanan–Barrow and Barrett 1996; Wharton 1997). They are treated as educationally immature humans necessarily of inferior status to adults. The virtue of the learner-centred approach is that it gives pupils their natural human rights while not abandoning the educational enterprise. Progress happens, in ways all can recognise, without classrooms becoming ghettos for the irrational and uncivilised. So this approach remains radical and modern (even post-modern in its refusal to set strict guidelines for curricula), reflecting the fluid uncertainties of contemporary life.

Turning to empirical considerations, one reason why progressivist teachers stay loyal to their ideal is that it respects human developmental theory (it isn't the only approach which does this: see Chapters 5 and 6). Piagetian and Vygotskian accounts have dominated developmentalism for almost a century now and there is no sign of their being displaced. Both traditions see learners as actively engaged with the world in pursuit of advanced conceptual thinking and higher-order skills. Both make us dubious of passive forms of learning. Even 'activities' (games, competitions and so forth) can be queried: the point is that unless activities are self-chosen we have no way of knowing whether or not pupils actually treat the 'activity' passively or not. Learner-oriented teaching is 'developmentally appropriate' (e.g. Fisher 2000). It guarantees quality learning, where this is conceived in developmental terms.

Weaknesses

The weaknesses of the learner-centred paradigm shadow its strengths. Again they can be summarised as ethical and empirical.

Those who cling to what is arguably still the dominant concept of education in England and Wales, the 'liberal rational' version (Peters 1966), may well dispute this chapter's argument for children's educational rights. Peters proposed that children become 'rationally' autonomous through subjection to the study of traditional disciplines (they are not given any choice in the matter). Along with Hirst (Peters and Hirst 1970), he wrote that 'initiation' into these disciplines heralded rational thought and, thereby, delivers children's educational birthright. Despite challenges to this conception (Kelly 1995; Silcock 1999; Silcock and Duncan 2001), it is feasible enough that children's intellectual dependency and immaturity only gradually disappear through their – where necessary – forced 'immersion' in the study of tried-and-tested knowledge.

Empirically speaking, learner-centred theorists tend to overlook the fact that schools are not 'normal' contexts, nor are they the only environments within which learners develop. One can plausibly maintain that rational autonomy is best achieved for some (i.e. those already coping with fairly formal systems) by their voluntarily submitting themselves to study, albeit in potentially 'unnatural' settings. Developmental axioms are not abused by this contention since it is still the case that new learning arises phoenix-like from the old during learners' active engagement with their worlds. It is also worth remembering that to claim children are born autonomous in some basic human sense calls into question any set of theories and practical approaches dedicated to 'teaching for autonomy' (depending what is meant by this).

5 Models of good practice 3
Partnership approaches

Introduction: basic description; first principles

Although teacher and learner-centred paradigms often dominate educational thinking – because each paradigm effectively determines the other – some writers prefer 'third way' alternatives to resorting to a rather stark and over-simple dichotomy. Since these alternatives give formal parity to teachers and learners, they can be called 'partnership' approaches (Ingram and Worral 1993), accepting that teachers and pupils will not normally have parity of authority or influence in all areas. They may be equals in status while making unequal contributions to tasks; or they may have unequal status while retaining complementary roles. So although the term 'partnership' implies some parity of responsibility for outcomes, the partners concerned can tackle their joint enterprise in very different ways.

Generally speaking, a partnership approach will take one of three forms. Teacher and learner-oriented methods may, first, combine *pragmatically*. Sometimes one stance is taken, sometimes another, according to resource, the background and attitude of pupils and so forth. Second, divergent strategies and techniques can be brought together for no other reason than that a teacher has a solid, professional sense of 'what works'. Guided by past successes, teachers may lean towards *eclecticism*. Third, teacher and learner-oriented systems may be given up altogether in favour of strategies relying on teacher–pupil negotiations within a collaborative framework. Negotiated partnerships are, arguably, 'true' partnerships, given that we cannot properly consider one role without considering the other. Decision-making rules agreed democratically govern how the relationship works.

Pragmatic and eclectic strategies rarely enlighten us on how circumstances actually dictate method. Advocates of ideologically neutral approaches hinging on 'goodness of fit' or 'fitness for purpose' (Alexander *et al.* 1992; Gipps and MacGilchrist 1999; Hallam and Ireson 1999) take for granted that a mix of top-down and bottom-up strategies *can* work to achieve aims. Few actually show how methods designed for very different ends are – in any one instance – put together coherently and what makes them successful. Practically speaking, it may well be true that English schools have for a long time been biased towards pragmatism (Reid 1997). And eclecticism is certainly popular with many teachers (Gipps *et al.* 1999; Stahl 1999), possibly because they compromise on the wide range of local and nationally set goals with which teachers have to deal (see Chapter 2). However, to say that teachers are frequently impelled to be pragmatic and (in principle) do not wish to exclude any sort of method as potentially useful (to be eclectic) is one thing. To say that this statement is definitive of teaching as a set of professional decisions to be made about classrooms and curricula is quite another.

The nature of teaching is such that decisions about purposes always affect decisions about method, even the most routine and insignificant. Neither pragmatism nor eclecticism are helpful in linking strategies to purposes as strategic policies (see also Chapter 2), simply because – where circumstances *are* deciding factors – what may work for one teacher in one setting may not work for another faced by equivalent problems. Suffice it to say that teachers who are clear-sighted about aims, provided these relate to each other (the achievement of one increasing the likelihood of reaching others), have what they mostly need for tackling practical issues. For these teachers will know which problems need resolving, which can be ignored and which kinds of pragmatic solutions will best keep aims in sight.

Although it makes intuitive sense to see teaching and learning as complementary rather than as contributing unequally to outcomes, the real justification for partnership teaching is its promise to realise a value-driven ideal specific to it. In teacher and learner-centred systems, it isn't so much that either adults or pupils dominate the relationship, but that each approach serves *separate* ideals, or categories of values, with methods devised to make the satisfying of these possible. Usually, these values focus on 'knowledge' (traditionally defined) and 'person-centred' learning processes (empowered individuals able to choose their own educational goals), and have been judged incompatible when pursued seriously as goals of the highest priority. For teachers cannot consistently 'transmit' ready worked out texts and techniques while helping learners gain personally approved ends for themselves. But this does not imply all process- and content-oriented teaching is by nature incompatible.

All forms of school-teaching are forms of partnership, in the sense that teachers and learners cannot work together unless each consents to what is happening. What marks out partnership policies *per se* is that teachers balance different sets of aims and objectives against each other as a matter of course. That is, they welcome the potential value-conflicts built into the 'partnership' concept full-heartedly as grounds for their negotiations and (as will be seen) a high-octane fuel for the curricular car. They aren't thrown back on negotiations, somewhat reluctantly, as a means of choosing between subject transmission or learner-facilitation. They negotiate classroom roles so as to exploit the dyadic (individual/social) interchanges which most characterise teaching, developing, by doing so, new rationales for their practices.

It is assumed that if learners and teachers are regarded as (notional) equals, concepts, skills and qualities embedded in partnership curricula will reflect the bipolar manner in which they are acquired. At a premium, whatever teachers and learners tackle together will from the start have both personal and public validity. This implicit rule of negotiation overcomes (for example) that residual difficulty of teachers choosing between 'absolutism' and 'relativism' when deciding aims. Curricular routes of a purely personal sort (relative to context), or publicly mapped ('universally' agreed), are neglected in favour of those which both teachers and learners together admit as appropriate. Put simply, democratic values underpin partnership curricula (see Kelly 1995). And the educational ideal pinned to the mast of partnership teaching is that of freely embraced, responsible, democratic citizenship. It no longer matters whether learners agree to adult expectations, or teachers bank on procedural skills, attitudes and qualities to deliver personally fulfilling aims. Through negotiation, both possibilities are fitted together in ways acceptable to teachers and learners and (by extension) to other community members. Partnership policies are contractual between teachers and pupils. But because each group (of teachers and pupils) refers to wider groups, and because democracy itself needs a benign context in which to flourish, educational policies must involve all those parents, school governors and inspectors, industrialists and other prospective employers, politicians with abiding interests in the school enterprise.

So what defines a partnership system is not any distinctiveness of method as the democratically transformed nature of its values. Learners take dual perspectives upon what is being learned, appreciating its role both in their public and personal lives. In principle, the desirability of such outcomes is obvious, in that it would seem ideal for school-learning to function for the benefit of both individuals and the wider society. In practice, the very desirability of the outcomes will warn us that they might not easily be put in hand. After all, teacher-centred methods are often resorted to because it is thought learners cannot by nature be curricular equals with teachers; only teachers (by virtue of their authority and training) can know what will work in terms of aims and methodology. Learner-centredness often rather perversely clings to the opposite assumption, that teachers are never faithfully able to represent learners' own individual and often idiosyncratic views, yet have somehow to respect these to make in-depth learning possible: learner-perspectives are taken to be truly intransigent factors. But in partnership systems, conflicts of interest and perspective shirked by the other two approaches are taken as routine, because their resolution becomes part of what we mean by educational progress.

The democratic basis of partnership policies give rise to curricular and organisational ploys only fully grasped during theoretical study. For convenience (and to keep continuity with earlier chapters), four dimensions are, again, discerned. First, the way classroom democracies function needs explaining (a). Second, psychological issues engaged when learners co-construct their school knowledge (bringing personal and public viewpoints into line) takes on board the types of two-way transactions which modern school-learning often assumes (b). Third, the idea that we invite conflicts into classrooms gives us a glimpse of why conflict-resolution is often at the heart of this type of teaching (c). Finally, the egalitarian, community-oriented and pluralist extensions of partnership systems go beyond the teacher–learner partnership itself (d). Many have argued for a 'social reconstructivist' education (Brehony 1992; Dewey 1916; Engelund 2000; Jones 1983), not especially because they see reconstructivist teaching as itself virtuous, but because they think it is the route to a more egalitarian society. These four dimensions compose socio-political, cognitive, affective and ethical dimensions of classrooms, and in their integration suggest special criteria for competent, successful, excellent teaching.

(a) Democratic classrooms

A democracy is a place where people rule themselves. But, as Carr (1998) reminds us, this simple idea begs questions of who, exactly, rule (who are the 'people'?), and what 'ruling' involves. In schools and classrooms, to empower pupils *at the expense of teachers* is hardly egalitarian though it might appear so to champions of pupil rights. Similarly, to insist that teachers rightfully represent pupils' interests when speaking for a wider *adult* society is to nod towards democratic inclusion but only honour teacher-centred values. In other words, competing models can be invoked as in their different ways democratic. It is those curricula where all with a stake in education act together in line with their functional relationships

with the two main partners (teachers and learners) which get closest to
the liberal-democratic or civic humanist ideal (Bryant 1997; Pring
1995b; Weale 1995). They reiterate in their contractual basis what
gives rise to the discussion in the first place – how, best, to help adults
and pupils together reach common goals. For what is promised is not
just a way of teaching as the initiation of pupils into interdependent
roles within a democratic state. This particular form of teaching is
tailor-made for the citizenship-education much debated in recent educational literature (e.g. Anderson *et al.* 1997; Bryant 1997; Hall *et al.* 1998;
Osler and Starkey 1998; Roche 1999; Starkey 2000).

Pupils who help devise a rule-governed system learn something about
the public nature of values (that some degree of public acclaim gives
credence to all values), in a way more suited to citizenship teaching
than via processes of transmission or individual study (Anderson *et al.*
1997). Reaching this conclusion clarifies short- and long-term aims, for
if it is agreed that the point of setting up democratic classrooms is to
teach through example a democratic way of life (long term), teachers
will insert opportunities for democratic decision-making into curricula
(short term). In other words, teachers will teach the attitudes and skills
which democracies demand as natural by-products of their daily practices
(as Carr 1998 and Kelly 1995 propose). Schools can be 'deliberative
democracies' (Engelund 2000) within which pupils come to their
rights, roles and responsibilities as members of communities (White
1993). Pupils may not only experience democratic milieus and join in
democratic decision-making, but also find out at first hand how to be
democrats and take full part in communal life.

Distinguishing between the two ways in which school classrooms can
be democratic helps us meet a long-standing objection to pupils making
classrooms and curricular decisions normally left to adults. For what
matters will not be so much the fact that schools are always hierarchically
organised (Wilson 2000a), affecting the democratic quality of decisions
made, as what pupils learn from making it. We will assess classroom
policies according to how far empowering pupils does make it more or
less likely that they learn to become fully fledged citizens, able to enjoy
community occasions, take part in community events and, in the end,
flourish as individuals.

Within a democratically governed classroom, constraints on pupil freedom are precisely those teaching pupils how to regulate self-referenced
views from the perspectives of others. Dewey (1916; see also Carr
1998; Horne 1938) famously believed that life in a democratic state
demands more than the sophisticated know-how of formal skills. It
requires thoroughly imbibed attitudes and personal virtues without

which democracies cannot function and which schools have somehow to teach. For Dewey, as for Carr (1998) and Kelly (1995), democratic teaching is one where all pupils have equal opportunities to 'formulate and achieve their collective ends by confronting shared problems and common concerns' (Carr 1998: 335).

Watchwords of democratic teaching, then, are those which make the unit of educational action and of evaluation a dyadic or team enterprise, rather than an individual effort. A school's success is to be judged not by pointing to prizes won by gifted individuals but by the excellence of teamwork and group ventures. These latter will be springboards for individuals in the sense that group members will take pride in their group's achievements and grow accordingly. Various types of co-operative activity can be deployed to teach key skills and concepts (Covington 1998), replacing tasks where students succeed or fail and are threatened by low self-esteem. Procedural rules for managing curricula as well as social behaviour build the frameworks within which school communities function, and within which various socio-political hierarchies enfranchise all members' views and affect decisions made. Representational democracy is likely to be a model for all but the smallest communities for the obvious reason that one can seldom give all who are to be affected by decisions the right to speak. But nominees can speak for groups, and any member of a school community can be delegated as nominee. At the level of school management, schools' councils contain individuals who speak both for themselves and for the various groups they represent. This is true for school governing bodies.

Of course, schools' councils, whole-school policies and governing bodies exist outside democracies. Hargreaves's 'new' professionalism in teaching (1994, 1999) is collaborative but not democratic in enfranchising pupils. Collaboration (in Hargreaves's thinking) appears to be for adults alone. Here, a democratic pupil–teacher partnership is said to depend on maximising pupil involvement. Relevant policy-making may even include *at some level* those policies most obviously assigned to adults, such as financial management, staff appointment and curricular design. There is no reason in principle why pupils shouldn't have opinions about how moneys are spent, the kind of teachers who should be employed in a school, and what they (the pupils) should learn. Staff appointment is perhaps a prime example of where one wouldn't expect pupils to have informed views, since the context of staff appointments (involving other staff, local education authorities (LEAs), governors, taking account of financial constraints etc.) will in practice be familiar only to adults. Yet it is odd that the group most able to judge the expertise of teachers, pupils themselves, are seldom consulted by school managers taking procedural action to improve a school's staffing resource. Pupils make their views known implicitly of course in how they respond to teachers and the quality of the work they produce, and it is these judgements which matter to managerial decision-making. But for that very reason – that pupils must, to a degree, evaluate what is happening to them – some attempt by teachers to research pupil views on a school's teaching provision would seem part of what we mean by a school democracy.

Still, we must remember that even though the youngest pupils have a far richer sense of what is happening to them than one might expect (Silcock and Wyness 2000; Trigg and Pollard 1998; Woods 1990), the point is not so much whether they join in informed debates about school policies as how they move towards democratic citizenship. The educational gifts which may accrue from doing so justify their having a say (if only limited) in decisions about finances, staffing and so forth. Anyway, people of any age who are expected to act or speak sensibly on issues concerning them often learn how to do so (cf. 'child-carers': Roche 1999; and pupil-advocates: Sherwin 1996). If pupils are elected to represent other views, they may, credibly, research these, take responsibility for correctly putting them, possibly even come to respect a diversity of opinion even minor episodes of school life conceal. Children growing as citizens of their local and wider society are being prepared by their becoming school 'citizens', assimilating values meant to serve them in future. What matters is that this co-ordinated system, where pupils habitually take note of reflections other than their own, lays down cognitive stepping stones towards the broader, academic goals which schools promote.

(b) Co-constructivism

Constructivist theory is of three main sorts. Two have already been studied within teacher-centred (Chapter 3) and learner-centred (Chapter 4) paradigms. First, socio-culturalists tell us that the 'internalising' or 'appropriating' of social knowledge is the critical event in children's lives. Education *is* acculturation (Cole and Wertsch 1996; Gingell and Brandon 2000; Smith and Standish 1997). The job of adults is to get school curricula, management and accountability structures right. Second, there is the belief that concepts of the physical and social world are fashioned by individuals from a unique mental resource. Students tailor their thinking in ways making sense to themselves, and to ignore these ways is to misunderstand what they are, really, learning in school. So teachers must fund individualised learning at (if necessary) the expense of whole-group resource management. Third, there are those who position themselves between these extremes (Adey and Shayer 1994, 1996; Biggs 1992; Broadfoot 2000; Bruner 1995b; Cobb 1994; Silcock 1999). Bruner (1995b), who has flirted with both camps in past writings, looks now to a middle way between personal constructivism and socio-culturalism. He asks: 'can schooling be construed both as the instrument of individual realisation and . . . as a reproductive technique for maintaining or furthering a culture? . . . Finding a way between this antinomic pair does not come easily . . . But if one does not face it, one risks failing both ideals' (Bruner 1995b: 7).

A simple way of separating the three stated positions is to name the first constructivist, the second socio-culturalist (in some versions, social constructivist), and the third co-constructivist (Nelson *et al.* 1998). Regarding partnership models of teaching, the co-constructivist case rides on the notion of complementary tendencies within any curricular task integrating learner with teacher policies. In schools, these twin tendencies mediate a pupil's personal knowledge, ambitions and skills and a teacher's professional knowledge, ambitions and skills. Most rationales rely for this integration, somewhere, on a symbolic interactionism where the restructuring which takes learners from one conceptual level to another combines self-conception with social-perspective taking (classically analysed by Mead 1934). Pupil thinking is normatively a reworking of some personal insight in the light of possibilities suggested by someone else.

So reflectivity, for purposes of concept formation, involves an imagined 'self–other' transaction, or a *dual transformation*, whereby the personal recasting of experience for purposes of adaptation (constructivism) happens in cultural contexts (most human contexts being culturally defined) by a repositioning of oneself *vis-à-vis* significant others. Education as such a culturally specific process of improvement can be defined in terms of this dual transformation (Silcock 1999). In co-constructive teaching, teachers and learners counterpoint their ideas against each other in face of common difficulties. Each 'constructs' the other's view as a standard against which to make judgements. A base assumption, then, is that the *conceptual change* which education demands (Driver 1989; White and Gunstone 1989; see also some review in Georghiades 2000) is an outcome of critical self-review following from critical dialogue.

In partnership teaching each partner scaffolds the thinking of the other so that the outcome is a joint effort, though it will be recorded first and foremost as a pupil triumph. The point is worth repeating. Teaching can be seen as an adult either scaffolding a child's faltering efforts or guiding a pupil from a naive to a more sophisticated viewpoint. The nub of co-constructivism is that pupils scaffold adult thinking in order to assimilate it for purposes of self-transformation (i.e. there is *two-way* scaffolding). This means that, in pupils' eyes they (the pupils) are not so much giving up their naivety or losing ignorance as taking up more defensible positions within public arenas (Georghiades 2000). Teaching is not so much the slow nudging of pupil views from ignorance to knowledge (though it can be that) as a joining of two independently built edifices within a new superstructure. Democratic spin-offs are obvious. In a partnership, education is not thought of as the beating into shape of inferior, uncivilised and untutored beings by older and wiser superiors, but the sharing of a difficult if potentially exciting adventure (Pring 1995b).

Those who knit together Piagetian and Vygotskian theory (see contributers to Demitriou *et al.* 1992) use both traditions to model the learning-teaching task. They typically harmonise otherwise distinct pedagogies: those which respect the personal needs of learners (bottom-up) and those which reach towards what is traditionally known and respected (top-down). Each takes meaning from the other. That is, learners are challenged by new arguments, while standard debates are counter-challenged when learners have properly dug out their own beliefs. It is usual that learners come to know about their own attitudes and experiences, as a first step. Ongoing conceptual development happens in a *publicly* measured sense in its assuming a hierarchically scaled improvement in pupils' internalising of core learning procedures (formal operational rules in Piagetian psychology, higher-order skills in Vygotsky's terms). It is *personally* transforming in that pupils' 'distancing' of themselves from given views in order to analyse, synthesise, appraise or criticise (Georghiades 2000; Kuhn 1999) fosters the sorts of 'metacognitive' control seen by many as a highway to a number of worthwhile destinations. By adapting from situation to situation, school pupils learn to rethink what they already know.

The moot point is that, in terms of pedagogy, where pupils tease out general principles from school learning, these feed diverse imaginings of events in the world, creating a ubiquitous capability which accelerates pupils' thinking (Adey and Shayer 1994). Multiple perspective-taking leads both to a broadening and a deepening of knowledge. Pupils learn to transfer understandings, since effectively what they are learning is that knowledge is fluid and vulnerable to infinite possible transformations, seldom finalised or static.

(c) Conflict-resolution

Co-constructed learning happens when two different views (starting in self and other) become one. These views may or may not at first be incompatible. It is likely enough that pupils will see flaws in their thinking without suffering anxieties or stress. However, in some respect conflict is latent in all conceptual change processes (and therefore in all educational processes), since, as learners shift perspectives they must notice what divides a superior from an inferior view. A degree of cognitive conflict precedes all learning producing conceptual change. We don't have to share Piaget's conviction that conquering *disequilibria* lies behind any conceptual manoeuvrings (Piaget 1971, 1978), to know that, somehow, for a learner to move on he or she must detect the flaw or contradiction in what is already believed. Pupil-thinking is not by its nature unstable. It is only provisional, like all thinking. Indeed, there is always a fair durability to whatever is learned if it is worthwhile (see Georghiades 2000). A well-learned principle never wholly leaves our minds but is either altered or strengthened by what comes later.

Yet there can be ongoing (even perhaps permanent) instability in the mind of someone whose learning strategy is to add ideas together somewhat randomly as, purely, a means to memorisation. This can be thought an unstable learning strategy since it will almost unerringly lead the learner into situations (including exam situations) they cannot cope with. Learning concepts randomly is not learning a subject. For the application and knowledge-transfer which spell out a subject's utility rely on its vulnerability to various (possibly endless) transformations (see also Chapters 6 and 9). A mathematical or scientific principle (to be a principle) must assume a range of practical and theoretical guises in service of its parent studies. It will be built up through the arduous business of testing out and rejecting endless possible solutions to problems before one is settled on as at least provisionally worth entertaining. As is well known, conflicts leading to conceptual change fire academic debates within the distinct disciplines. Academic progress is guaranteed by people championing ideas against each other, testing for rigour, fitness for task, capacity for generating ideas, and so on.

This conclusion makes conflict (rather than collaboration) the pearl in the educational oyster, though conflict is not the inevitable concomitant of group activity. Co-operating groups sometimes seek to ward off disputes, looking for a form of 'groupthink' which short-cuts discussion and facilitates decision-making. Such 'groupthink' was reputedly responsible for President Kennedy's failed Bay of Pigs invasion of Cuba (Philips 2000). Kennedy's successful resolving of the later Cuban missile crisis is believed to be owed to his fostering of disagreement, objection and doubt among his advisers. For related reasons, in schools, writers suppose that grasping the nettle of conflict not only is a prerequisite for academic debate (Driver *et al.* 1994) but also can inspire an invigorating and exciting way to teach. Johnson and Johnson (1994; also Covington 1998; Silcock and Stacey 1997) write about a 'co-operative' teaching which welcomes disagreements between learners as healthy clashes of ideas. Debates and discussions, group game-playing, organised arguments, comments and critiques (in class or school journals), committee discussions and socio-political confrontations provide various sorts of public context within which individuals can convert their thinking from one sort to another.

Learners able rationally to debate with others earn skills of negotiation, tolerance and affective control as well as rising towards novel perspectives on issues debated. Tensions arising within groups are resolved to the satisfaction of all (Osborne 1997), providing teachers are capable of dealing with disputes in a sensitive as well as impersonal fashion (Kaplan 2000). This sort of ethos dignifies a socially and emotionally as well as intellectually healthy classroom. Indeed, there is a sense in which co-operation cannot happen unless individuals quell emotionally charged misgivings, overcoming implicit disequilibria as a presumption of sharing in group discourse. It is common enough for anyone co-operating with others first of all to suspend existing prejudices in order to make a new synthesis possible. So skills of resolving internalised conflicts (reconciling conflicting views conceptually) have to underpin staff collaborations which, for example, mark a modern-day teacher professionalism. Certainly, the possibility of reconciling conflicts within groups is important for truly democratic co-operation since co-operation alone, as Lester (1992) points out, may not involve democratic negotiations. People can co-operate in all kinds of undemocratic ways: only when group members are able freely to debate their views do co-operation and collaboration become democratic.

It also goes without saying that skills of conflict-resolution help anyone (teacher or learner) mediate between entrenched positions, so preventing dangerous or harmful conflicts. Dangerous conflicts are not deliberately sought. Conflicts based on prejudice and discrimination are self-evidently harmful. Where such harmful conflicts (e.g. racist) occur, it is nonetheless of the utmost importance that those who experience them know how to deal with them. So skills of conflict resolution will often help foster attitudes needed for social reform, such as attitudes of 'critical realism' and 'critical policy-making' (Corson 1998). Social and political conflicts are, sometimes, to be faced head on, and resolved by reference to egalitarian principles, rather than in a wholly neutral fashion.

(d) Egalitarianism

A weakness of partnership teaching is that there are no built-in criteria for resolving likely conflicts between competing values. Teachers and pupils may share values from the outset. But in modern pluralist societies, value-consensus can never be taken for granted. Teacher-oriented approaches avoid such hindrances by not questioning the legitimacy of dominant values. Teachers favouring pupil-oriented systems legitimate pupils' own goals and value-commitments. Partnership, or democratic systems, rely on democratic values as ways of resolving both natural and potentially disruptive conflicts.

However, democratic values are, by and large, procedural values: that is, they promote rule-governed ways of life, such that community members have a hand in organisational and curricular decision-making. Only when they are married to other types of value, related to forms of knowledge and ethics, can they be taken as fully fledged models of good educational practice (since good teaching is more than the realising of procedural aims). Embedding partnership systems within co-constructive, conceptual change theory has been introduced. Binding partnership teaching to egalitarian principles follows because members of democratically governed communities must think of themselves as equals in some fundamental ways. Cued by egalitarian principles, not only do teachers find themselves impelled to treat pupils (and other members of a school community) as co-equals in the school enterprise, but also they become enmeshed in strategies meant to enfranchise all individuals and social groups. This is always likely to happen because educational opportunities are not part of any community's natural inheritance, they may have to be won, defended, clawed-back, according to circumstance. Some prizes are on offer to some social classes and genders more than others. Age and disability may handicap because resources suit some people (young, able-bodied) more than others. Linguistic and cultural diversity are facts of modern life we may find problematic just as much as we may celebrate.

Nevertheless, partnership teaching, tied to egalitarianism, is securely tied to policies of *social reconstruction*. Such policies have, in the past, been thought out and followed by reformers who found traditionalist modes of teaching oppressive in their ethnocentricity, and progressive models too individualistic to help groups whose difficulties lie in their cultural identities (Lawton 1989). Some (such as Freire: see O'Cadiz *et al.*

1998) have sensitised students and others to the causes for their own oppression. Social-reconstructionist teachers may opt for what Tamir (1995) calls a 'thick' multiculturalism, outfacing social conflicts that are barriers to progress (as opposed to 'thin' multiculturalism which is, less assertively, more accepting of circumstance). Dewey's (1916) social-reconstructivist form of 'progressivist' teaching (Jones 1983) not only helped individuals realise personal ambitions but also made these intrinsic to democratic systems (Blatchford and Blatchford 1995; Silcock 1999).

Teaching which works to topple barriers between social groups while (through its democratic virtues) helping group members realise their own talents and ambitions in their own fashion is working bi-directionally. Teachers are doing two things at the same time. They are ridding classrooms of unwanted differences (or at least neutralising the harmful effects of these) while helping learners preserve essential values. This bipolarity of aim asks for teaching which goes beyond facilitating a learner's personal aspirations. Teachers may well find themselves acquainting pupils with a wider knowledge of cultural diversity than that naturally met, alongside ethical standards and egalitarian attitudes without which mature democracies founder. Because partnership teaching establishes equal opportunities by legitimising cultural difference, the global, international, European dimensions of education, presupposing diverse interests and values, logically entail partnership systems.

Crowning partnership teaching with egalitarian attitudes allows these to pervade all curricular activities and bring coherent perspectives to core studies in the humanities, arts and sciences. It is the very fact of classrooms being democracies which stops teachers indoctrinating beliefs sometimes associated with the over-enthusiastic pursuit of culturally biased ends. Respecting the points of view of others does not oblige us to adopt them. There is nothing within an ethnocentric topic itself (such as the study of English history) which makes it in some sense 'undemocratic'. How it is studied is the factor which saves it from cultural indoctrination, not its content (it is co-constructed, not delivered).

Competence, success, excellence in partnership approaches

Primarily, democratic and egalitarian ideals are at the heart of partnership methods, composing ways of life to which people can become committed. Methods are thus more than optional ways of reaching agreed goals. Hamilton (1999) contrasts rather narrow, bureaucratic ways of interpreting the role of schools which obsess current political thinking with teaching wedded to ways of knowing the world and of being in the world. Hamilton's point, as here, is that to adopt one model of good practice rather than another is to adopt one ideal of human development rather than another, a principle which must jog our thinking when we look for quality indicators in a 'partnership' system. Teachers who pursue democratic ideals are hardly likely to do so unless they are sincerely committed to those ideals. A tokenistic attitude may work superficially, but will never deliver the educational goods. The starting point for any study of quality partnership work is a recognition of those attitudes on which partnership teaching depends.

It would be palpably absurd to expect someone who embraces an ideal of cultural transmission to take a critical or multicultural stance on curricular content; basic stances on curricula (as on human ideals) contradict each other. This does not mean that a sincere democrat will painlessly learn to teach democratically, it merely says that fruitful soil for the growth of skills exists. As a viable hypothesis, then, a minimal requirement for competent partnership teaching weds democratic, egalitarian attitudes to co-constructive, conflict resolution skills. These split down into skills of negotiation, tolerant attitudes, and those recursive insights which will benefit any leader. They comprise a desire to co-operate yet welcome conflict, adapt yet debate and stand firm where necessary, to follow as well as to lead, to listen closely and explain oneself in ways which others can understand, to analyse in order to synthesise, fashion and refashion, to be critical of oneself as well as of views which appear undemocratic, intolerant, unyielding, and so on (see also Chapter 6). Competence becomes excellence through the refinement of such emotionally and cognitively complex abilities.

On any level of performance, inserting into democratic teaching a critical attitude is crucial because conceptual change in schools does not usually involve sudden or radical change. It is as often the ironing out of flaws, the glimpsing of a somewhat better task-solution than the one started with. We always have to evaluate our own as well as another's thinking to pan gold from dross in both areas. Co-construction is not a pupil's habitual acceptance of a teacher's opinion (or vice versa) or a habitual championing of a personal conviction at any costs: it demands critical analysis of *all* incoming information – including that from one's own past judgements. What is most signalled is that in order to teach skilfully in a partnership manner, it is seldom enough to follow an uncritical line. For instance, it might be thought enough, when teaching a multicultural curriculum, to familiarise pupils with other cultural mores, stressing the need for tolerance and understanding. But this risks teaching moralities, religious precepts and so on in essentially undemocratic and discriminatory ways: pupils are better both submitting their own attitudes to critical scrutiny and questioning the culturally grounded attitudes of others (Tamir 1995). Political correctness and the hallowing of sacred cows have no place in a democratic classroom. Following through this obligation might of course be difficult, where others' cultural sensitivities (not to mention one's own) might well stand in the way.

An excellent democratic teacher will be one who is not only competent at interactive teaching but also able to deal with the disputes, quarrels, hurt feelings, and so on which follow. These problems are likely to arise outside classrooms as well as inside them; and in a society which is especially xenophobic, homophobic or ethnocentric, teachers might well find themselves to a degree alienated within their own community. Parents in such a society who resent their children learning to be tolerant of views they themselves find strange might well believe a school's policies are actually out of line with modern thinking. This possibility leads again to the rather paradoxical conclusion (rehearsed in earlier chapters) that a competent and possibly even an excellent teacher (within this model) will, in a given circumstance, fail to reach goals at which he or she aims (see also Chapter 6). That is, prevailing circumstances can shackle someone whose professional values bring them head-on into dispute with managers who decide what counts as successful within any one school.

A truly democratic education, which models society as a humane, egalitarian community, is one where the dominating context is the human one, with universal moral values as criterial for cross-cultural judgements. What democratic values create are contexts where individuals pursue self-chosen life-styles without fear of oppression (providing they don't oppress others). A post-modern culture without value-priorities may survive only within a democratic state (as Kelly 1995 argues; see also Chapter 2), for it will be quite in order for post-modernists to establish their views as having parity with others. But it is hard to see how 'partnership' teaching can succeed where external pressures are non-democratic. A teacher impelled to deliver a curricula without the consent of main stakeholders may well survive by deploying co-constructive, conflict-resolution skills; but no one should underestimate the difficulties and hardships involved.

Up to a point, democratic values promoted currently via citizenship teaching in UK schools represent compromises, since children do not have rights of negotiation and teachers' powers of altering curricula are severely restricted. This does not mean teachers cannot use a 'partnership' approach. It is actually hard to see how any other approach can deliver citizenship curricula currently devised (Osler and Starkey 1998; Starkey 2000). But imposing these curricula in the first place and maintaining them through legislation does close large areas of decision-making to practitioners and pupils alike. Only where there is flexibility at all levels of curricular organisation can anyone work in a thoroughgoing and uncompromising co-constructive manner. Accepting the status quo, however, may also mean that school communities find out where political battle-lines are drawn and confront them suitably. After all, within socio-political democracies (within the UK), it is perfectly in order to criticise educational legislation, even if to disobey such legislation would usually be thought subversive.

The other option, of discarding partnership policies for ones which assure teaching success when, for example, Ofsted criteria apply and standard tests are used to measure pupil performance, is tempting. And one suspects that many British teachers take it as self-evident that teacher-centred pedagogies are asked for by a centralist system. Alternatively, teachers might abandon 'models of good practice' *per se* and simply follow given schemes as faithfully as they can. Possibly, the hardest stumbling block to anyone who believes there are effective ways of chasing different values (i.e. models of 'good practice) is the widespread view that such models are themselves restrictive and that teachers should just try to 'teach well', whatever that might mean. Eclecticism and pragmatism are resilient ideologies of the late twentieth and early twenty-first centuries: whether they survive long in the new millennium, depends on how soon we realise they represent models of *bad* practice.

Summarising first principles

The educational ideal

Any teacher guided by partnership principles will expect learners (just as teachers) to commit themselves to democratic decision-making, critical thinking, negotiation and responsible citizenship. This model of learning subsists as a model of education and of an educated person working to further democratic ends within a democratic state.

Associated principles

Practices and procedures are best affirmed through discussions attached to modal activities. There are three main ones, corresponding to the concepts of learners and teachers differentiated from the democratic ideal itself, associated types of curricula and the main thrust of methods used.

First, teachers and learners 'in partnership' are not equal, except that their roles are seen to contribute equally to learning outcomes. It is in the maintaining of parity while acting differentially that the challenge of successful partnership teaching lies (see Chapter 6 for clarification).

Second, classroom decision-making entails teachers and learners taking each others' (potentially conflicting) viewpoints on academic issues. Argument, debate and conflict-resolution are seen as the stuff of democracy, with the egalitarian basis of democratic rule maintained throughout. Curricula are designed so as to provoke discussion, disagreement and the gradual teasing out of principles of critical thinking, the transfer and interpretations of knowledge.

Third, teaching methods are not prescribed but follow the to-and-fro of democratic debate and decision-making. It is irrelevant whether teachers take a 'formal' or 'informal' stance to topics, provided that the class (or school) group concedes the rationale for the stance taken. Given that pupil views often reflect their backgrounds, partnership teaching will commonly involve other educational stakeholders in the formulating of policies and practices.

Notable strengths and weaknesses

Strengths

Democratic, partnership approaches are currently popular, fitting much current thinking on how to reach educational ends. Strong doubts about alternatives (top-down and bottom-up: see earlier chapters and Chapter 6) sanction a way of uniting apparently opposing strengths without suffering the consequences of teachers behaving in self-contradictory ways. The widespread belief in pupils becoming responsible citizens reaches apotheosis in this paradigm. Also, new theories of conceptual change (while still recounted in Piagetian and Vygotskian lore) accept conflict between individual and social pressures as the meat and drink of mental improvement. Partnership policies wholeheartedly accord with this formula for educational success.

Weaknesses

Partnership teaching's weaknesses are exposed by comparing it with competing paradigms – for the very reason that it risks losing what they promise. It cannot reliably deliver traditional tried-and-tested knowledge: it cannot reliably deliver the classical ideal (though it might). Nor can one be sure that students through negotiation will win for themselves unique lines of enquiry (self-actualisation). They need not find their self-esteem intact after repeated debates where (especially with the intellectually weak) they might repeatedly perform poorly. Pupils regularly defeated in argument might become confirmed victims rather than confident adults.

However, the partnership stance is specially vulnerable to the charge that its 'social' orientation makes it prey to dominant ideologies. Its reliance on critical perspective-taking might save it from being a rather subtle way for adults to socialise a new generation into an already stable (yet possibly corrupt) society. But if the point of discussions is to establish democratic rule, consensus *is* the stick which will be used to beat anyone with a deviant cause or who wishes to buck popular trends and return to more traditional forms of study. As can be seen from many so-called democratically governed societies, calling a process democratic does not always make it tolerant or egalitarian, since the rule of a majority can easily become the rule of the strongest at the expense of the weakest. What needs discussion are the curricular and organisational strategies belonging to partnership ways of teaching, to reassure teachers that there are ways to counter difficulties of this sort (Chapter 6).

6 Co-constructive teaching
A practical guide

Introduction

Working out, in more detail, how teachers can teach co-constructively clarifies a model tailor-made for modern classrooms at primary, secondary and advanced levels. Given that no teaching approach is without weaknesses, in-depth analysis might also turn up ways of dealing with these. So this chapter contains a reasonably full guide to that form of teaching underwriting partnership approaches. Its eleven sections discuss: reasons why co-constructive teaching is given special treatment; the sorts of value-commitments teachers will make; the nature of conceptual content co-constructive strategies teach; methods and techniques used; professional skills deployed; how to keep social order within co-constructed curricula; modes of assessment and evaluation; age-phase differences; the variable roles of pupils and teachers; dealing practically with endemic problems and, finally, a summary of guidelines determining quality practice (competence, success, excellence), preparing for later chapters.

Why choose co-constructive teaching?

As introduced, co-constructive teaching is the operational arm of any partnership approach. Its likely classroom effectiveness is promoted for four main reasons, gleaned from earlier chapters.

First, the English/Welsh National Curriculum is 'heavy' with content (suited to many vested interests). It can become fatally unmanageable, unless teachers route themselves through it. Mapping out curricular programmes via democratic negotiations would appear a valid way of responding to legislated demands.

Second, 'partnership' approaches are popular in today's schools – usually involving whole-school policies, parents, higher education tutors and other stakeholders (a recent government green paper on future educational policy makes much of its own 'partnership' with teachers: DfEE 2001). Making (or confirming) pupils as partners in curricular decision-making is both logical and far-sighted, given that pressures towards the fulfilling of children's rights will increase over coming years. It is also believed that teachers will find extending the 'partnership' concept to include children welcome and workable.

Third, seeing teaching as a form of 'performance management' does not, really, suit the essentially collaborative cultures found in a modern teaching profession. Subjecting the profession to strict control dilutes that very professionalism meant to deliver quality practice (see Chapter 3). Yet uncompromising learner-centred alternatives, too, are virtually impossible to reconcile with standard curricula. Even in their own terms, it is hard to see what realistic safeguards can be used to prevent pupils from pursuing self-chosen ends which turn out to be academic culs-de-sac (see Chapter 4).

Fourth, the trend in developmental studies (underpinning educational paradigms) is to find a middle way between putting learners in charge of their own progress and making cultural influences prime movers in intellectual change. This middle way is the co-construction of knowledge, qualities and skills (Chapter 5).

How teachers commit themselves to relevant values

First principles of good teaching are that teachers decide what typifies the thinking, behaviour, achievements of learners relative to some overall concept of education. Professional skills are deployed accordingly. No matter how sharply they fix more particular aims (e.g. to teach 'scientific method'), unless they see where these lead, teachers will miss out on key practices. Essentially, co-constructive teaching helps learners place their own perspectives in relationship to what others believe and do. Such a formulation (of the 'ideal learner') guards against the twin dangers of pupils assimilating attitudes and beliefs of little relevance to their lives and of rejecting traditional views purely to indulge personal ambition or an overweening self-preferment.

If teachers' ideals govern their practices, teachers who teach in a collaborative manner for no other reason than they have to (via 'contrived' collegiality: see Chapter 7) are missing out on just those discussions which best deliver their main purposes. Indeed, the purposes prescribed for the teachers may not be their purposes – except by default (they have not chosen others). Their success as teachers will depend solely on their conformity to conventional wisdom, which will be of little value to them when ideological climates change (as they do, often enough). Nor should we underestimate the difficulties of asking anyone to commit to values with which they have little natural sympathy. Value-commitments *per se* are problematic (as theorists tell us: Silcock and Duncan 2001; Smith and Standish 1997; Standish 1997). Acquiring a new 'vision' implies considerable thought, including – possibly – a thoroughgoing reappraisal of earlier convictions. At least, democratic values shoring up a co-constructivist ideal are borne these days upon strong tides of opinion, world-wide, and not just within western democracies. There is a fair chance that British schoolteachers will prefer them to the hard-edged, traditional fare they have had to swallow of late.

Closing in on how teachers come to make a relevant commitment: what we can guess is that a person's professional ideals crystallise throughout their training and career, via reflections on notions of learning and education, and during their professional lives. As said, these reflections link to preferred pedagogies and explain why the integration of dimensions of a teaching model equates with competent teaching. It is never an intelligent dealing with classroom situations alone which decides teaching quality. It is sensitivity to circumstance in the light of known commitments which give rise to those actions and judgements we prize. On this argument, we must reject some popular beliefs that it is largely the job of a headteacher (or institutional 'manager') to shine up a school's guiding mission (see Weindling 1997: 226). Unless all staff share in formulating it, the whole-school enterprise will be fragmented and unsatisfactory (Senge 1990).

Evidently, headteachers are those who present the public face of their school and must explain its special features to others (parents, inspectors and so on). But if they are thought wholly responsible for a school's ideals, why should classroom teachers make sense of what is not thought their duty? Fullan (1991) attests how that educational mecca, 'school improvement', passes out of reach unless a school's vision 'permeates the organisation with values, purpose and integrity for both – the what and the how of improvement' (Fullan 1991: 83). He has to be right. The relationship between ends and means in education is such that to grasp one properly we have to grasp the other. For teachers to know how to teach, they must have some notions of the ends to which they strive (essentially, what a 'model' learner is, relative to some longer-term ideal). Such knowledge is not a 'bolted on' extra: it is fundamental to the job.

Curricular content

Many basic questions in education cluster round disputes about what an 'ideal learner' is really like. How do teachers know that they are succeeding? An element of the answer has to lie with the knowledge and skills that successful learners are thought to have. Co-constructed curricula have a special sort of content, which should show itself in pupils' work, exam answers, classroom discussions and so forth. Such content may not be the only sure-fire indicator of good educational practice but it is probably the most obvious and easiest to see. This is important. Knowing how the mind of a learner works during a teaching process is to guide that process (by way of feedback affecting teachers' thinking).

Pupils who learn through multiple perspective-taking are learning the complexity of the academic concepts they study. This factor influences most school learning, though within some sessions more than others because concepts differ in how much they extend into distinct areas of study and are reciprocally defined. Put another way, the 'content' of what school students learn is not determined purely by a syllabus (i.e. what is taught), it is determined by how it is learned. For example: at the simplest level whether some dimensions of topics are faced at all will depend how a teacher approaches a subject. Fairly inevitably, learning history within an autocratic society via top-down instruction reinforces dominant values and the legitimacy of the autocracy. By contrast, learners who determine their own curricula need not confront autocratic principles at all (they may have little interest in political history): so different ways of teaching can present different means for avoiding disputatious topics or dealing with them fairly superficially. Only when overtly critical stances are taken can socio-historical evils such as racism be directly confronted. Partnership curricula develop capabilities learners need to join in discipline-related activities (research and so on) which thrive on argument, ambiguity and multilayered problem-solving.

They also develop a multidimensional way of grasping what is taught. Again, to illustrate: a moral concept such as honesty stipulates truth-telling as superior to falsehood. But the concept has diverse meanings according to how it is learned. It can appear to matter just because one is told that it does: one accepts the concept's meaning and its supposed role in our lives but (possibly) no more than that. For it to be learned in terms of one's personal experiences is for it to serve self-willed ends within the limitations of those experiences – it could become a central plank of one's character marked out by one's rigorous conformity to truth-telling. But honesty can, also, mark a special relationship between self and others transforming both its straight definition and its personal significance. People can be naively or cruelly honest to others; they can subscribe to honesty as a moral principle without integrating the principle into their lives or integrating it to the extent that it overrides more humane principles. Or they can seek to preserve their own and others' integrity even when this entails distorting known truths.

What one is *not* saying is that modes of teaching always convey particular truths or particular ways of thinking (for we learn in many settings). But the models of teaching discussed lean towards stipulative (socio-culturally given), idiosyncratically formed (individual constructed) and co-constructed ways of knowing. All concepts are altered in usage (this is the essence of theories of 'grounded' or 'situated' knowledge: see e.g. Bereiter 2000). And teaching situations, by nature, govern usage by learners. Even a taught fact will be memorised differently depending on how it is acquired. One can learn that the battle of Hastings happened in 1066 as a factually occurring event. One can learn it as part of a broader personal interest in, say, battles, warfare or the geography of southern England. Or one's hold on the event can be governed by its historical status for present-day historians. Such associations will be part of its meaning (implicit in my memorising of the date will be the significance accorded it).

So the relationship of a concept to others is part of the way we learn and memorise it. Although there may be one concept to be learned, which can be taught in different ways, there will also be variant products extending into other areas of study. 'Holist' thinking, whereby meanings arise from their interconnections within a wider network, implies that both the personal and publicly ordered nature of learning interrelates within distinct epistemologies. As ideal types, a straight transmission of knowledge is based on a knowledge where meanings are sanctioned by academic subjects, teachers, and schools backing them. A learner-oriented system systematically links what is learned to a personally organised store of knowledge (concepts are built up experientially). In a partnership system, the two types of meaning contextualise and in some sense capture each other. Someone learning history, geography or whatever will take public perspectives on personally significant ideas, and personal slants on what is publicly valued.

What is at once noticed is that this way of looking at concept-building and concept-mapping clarifies why we should not automatically think that valued skills (such as literacy and numeracy skills), because they are valued, can be taught in that way we find most expedient. The maxim of doing 'whatever works' is the black hole into which many educational policies have fallen, just because how one learns decides the significance and meaning of what is learned ('best' ways to teach must match to given ends which can be managed skilfully or not). Curricular content is tied as much to values and ideals as are aims, methods and so forth, in that distinct types and classes of concepts are outputs from different teaching models. If we value conceptual correctness, we have to adopt a transmission approach to teaching. When we shift towards personally valued knowledge and application, we will see the virtues of allowing pupils to follow concept-trails laid by their own talents and interests. If we are concerned about contextually applicable knowledge (implying learning transfer), we will look to the cross-perspective taking of co-constructive teaching, knowing there will be some trade-off in terms of correctness and personal significance and application. This trade-off between models needn't imply that curricular content has to be stated or written differently (it could still constitute elements of a National Curriculum, providing that curriculum isn't regarded as knowledge to be 'transmitted' or 'delivered'). Only, the meaning of written content will alter from learner to learner according to the way the content is treated pedagogically and acquired.

Curricular management and teaching strategies

Socio-political skills of democratic teaching mastermind curricular management to ensure that subjects are learned, tasks accomplished, lessons completed successfully. As introduced in Chapter 5, programmes devised by those who take recent cognitive developmental theory seriously (in Demitriou *et al.* 1992; see also Adey and Shayer 1994; Resnick 1985; Resnick *et al.* 1992) are dedicated to co-constructivist techniques (Chapter 5; see also 'integrated learning theory' in Broadfoot 2000). Twin perspectives (top-down *and* bottom-up: Biggs 1992) spring both from pupils' experientially based attitudes and capabilities and the special features of subjects being taught (perhaps clarified as challenges to pupils' stated positions). Dual transformations (framing curricular content within one's preconceptions in order to change one's preconceptions) align with the simple formulae devised by Adey and Shayer (1994) teaching science to young adolescents and Resnick *et al.* (1992) teaching mathematics to infants. Their bare bones are as follows.

1 Pupils' existing viewpoints are elicited, clarified, sanctioned as legitimate on topics to be discussed. Pupils realise what they already know.
2 New knowledge challenges viewpoints already established. Pupils sense what they don't yet know and begin to probe for new meanings.

3   Pupils seek to adapt the one set of viewpoints to the other through hypothetical and critical thinking, discussion, debate, argument, game-playing, trialling and so forth.
4   Final syntheses are reached (if only provisionally), tasks accomplished and new tasks sighted.
5   Pupils' viewpoints are elicited, clarified and so on, regarding the new tasks.

Notably, the starting point for co-constructive teaching is for pupils to clarify what they already know. One can hardly adapt to other views if one is unclear about what one's own position is (it isn't just that teachers need to understand pupils' experiences; pupils need to understand their own experiences). Then it is the clarifying, challenging and restructuring which matter: i.e. curricular goals are in the main procedurally defined (process values) rather than reached through the teaching of a set content. Adey and Shayer (1994) think that pupils must hypothesise and defend positions in face of peer challenges and teacher questioning, not in a way so as to reveal some 'correct' view, but to lift learners to a hypothetico-deductive thinking typical of scientific debate. Resnick *et al.*'s (1992) intent is to overlap pupils conceiving of problems in their own intuitive language with those in a more formal mathematical language, not to show the first as wrong and the second as correct, but to force each to supervene on the other.

What teachers in this approach model is the reaching for an ever more challenging scepticism and questioning attitude. Because such a strategy is complex, it is worth elaborating on earlier discussion. The high-road climbing to a 'metacognitive' control over subjects (Adey and Shayer 1994) comes through our subjecting ideas to challenges which, themselves, are evaluated as part of cross-perspective taking. Learners discover what challenges work, and which not, integrating these in the end within reliable, flexible, rule-governed operations. Metacognition (self-monitoring) is not just a form of hierarchical reflection or propensity for mental detachment. Piaget's ideal of formal-operations has meta-perspectives built into areas of knowledge, tools of any academic's trade. Recognising that academic judgements are never more than staging points towards an ever subtler view is to keep a distance from known solutions, forever having the option of reconceiving what is already known. The general process of cross-perspective taking implies seeing the way a single idea 'works' in diverse contexts: i.e. it must (as claimed earlier) prepare ground for knowledge transfer.

Crucial to this sort of teaching is peer interaction whereby pupils habitually challenge, support, comment, evaluate, debate each others' and standard views. A co-constructivist classroom is one where such talk is staple. Adey and Shayer's (1994, 1996) and Resnick *et al.*'s (1992) evidence (see also Kuhn 1999) is that such talk works not only with science teaching but in developing critical states of mind (Piagetian formal operations; Vygotskian higher-order skills) and integrated forms of thinking (Broadfoot 2000). Such ways of applying and testing out knowledge imply a 'no-holds barred' attitude tolerating extensive disagreement. This attitude must be modelled by teachers themselves, who may well take a critical stance on public life, but by doing so acknowledge fashionable attitudes and contemporary idioms rather than ignore these. Pupils talking about 'green' issues, drug abuse, sex education, religious and political tolerance, or whatever are not being taught the wrongness of 'traditional' attitudes or the rightness of alternative life-styles. Via debate (rather than through repeating what they have been taught or rediscovering individually within topics), they use collaborative problem-solving as a means of fashioning the resulting judgements into a personal stance, which was Dewey's (1916; see Horne 1938) criterion for gauging the appropriateness of a teaching process.

Teachers will bring the widest possible range of people into classrooms to put informed views – artists, scientists, politicians and academics. Formal techniques associated with discussion and debate, committee work, the recording of views, a constructing of dialectical cases, philosophising and so on, would fall within the purview of democratic teaching. Models of political and philosophical debate and parliamentary decision, boardroom discussion, law-court procedures, workplace and trades union operation, are among curricular possibilities. 'Game playing', whereby (e.g.) international companies bid for control of each other and seek to dominate a marketplace, will also promote the sort of critical thinking and contemporary know-how which should well prepare pupils for later life.

Professional skills

All teachers co-operate, negotiate, reconcile views sympathetically, resolve differences, mediate between options, contest issues generously, present dialectical cases in ways making them vulnerable to argument, and generally act in a socially skilled manner. Those teaching through partnership will make most of such capabilities if only because someone who typically instructs others (teacher-centred) or empowers others to work independently (learner-centred) will spend less time negotiating, debating, collaborating etc. than someone whose teaching is at heart negotiative and collaborative. It follows that teachers in partnership with pupils will – instinctively – appreciate alternatives, experiment with radical positions, show a tolerance usually untested within monocultural settings, and use mediation and conflict-resolution as markers for their professional territory. These latter skills live side by side with capabilities for arguing a case critically, since there is little use conceding an argument if the other disputant is in error, although the art of critical debate is more often to compromise with contrariness than try to dismiss or eliminate it. What is recalled is that skills etched out by discussion are not professional skills which, somehow, are regularised through training prior to their deployment (though lessons inducted in training will need to acknowledge them). They become part of a teacher's professional armoury as a consequence of their primary commitments.

Partnership skills not only assume social knowledge, but also imply a pro-social capability. Educated adults often restrain their own intellectual powers in order to nurture those which are immature. Skilled teachers may suppress their assertiveness in order to give courage to the reticent or, indeed, calm the nerve of those who are over-assertive and should be circumspect. Although partnership teaching often means working with a single class group, it may just as often mean adjusting views from pupil to pupil and group to group. This sort of teaching is unusual in the imaginative leaps required to blend radically opposing perspectives born from ability, gender, class, cultural background, personality and experience. It demands enough self-knowledge and knowledge of one's pupils to make the congruent integration of both a platform for conceptual change. This is after all what 'partnership' means: teaching and learning are cross-determined – notwithstanding the chance that learners, themselves, may not always consent to contractual duties imposed. Over a period, and assuming any chance at all that learners become converted to educational values, this approach does have the merit of accepting the problem itself (the need to negotiate endemic conflicts) as real.

Self-restraint ought to be a by-product of any sincere effort to work in a partnership manner – as should a flexible attitude towards curricular innovation. In pluralist settings, large groups will bring to task novel ambitions, insights, prejudices and so forth. To adapt to differences, synthesise arguments, defend in order to refine immature views, persist with a case until it can be overruled, incite both dogged reasoning and flexibility of opinion is to be ubiquitous in a way not normally asked for within the intimate confines of classrooms. Democratic teaching may be shunned by some, because it faces up to social dilemmas we will otherwise avoid (Moore 2000). It asks for the expression of disagreement and criticism, a probing for weaknesses, a search for person–group discord in order to reach a higher-order person–group accord.

Often, teachers will not find themselves teaching in the conventional sense, but mediating between options (Mason 2000). They will put hypothetical alternatives to what is conventional in order to persuade learners to give up personal biases and standard beliefs for more promising ideas. So democratic teaching is not made easy by being cradled on a raft of social skills. One can imagine that the various capabilities listed will integrate differently according to that degree of conflict endemic in a school or classroom community: some inner-city schools demand a resoluteness of will not demanded in less stressful environments (see Chapter 5). Where pupils have an appetite for debate and criticism, a sound subject knowledge combined with a creative approach to problem-solving may well be a teacher's mainstays.

Preserving social order (discipline and social control)

Partnership teaching has pupils ready to defend and challenge, recon-struct, 'play' imaginatively with old and new options, and so forth. Their co-equal actions (whatever their respective ages, backgrounds and so on) topple barriers to democratic citizenship. However, the very fact that disagreement and arguing is expected rather than, simply, tolerated is always likely to spark 'class management' situations. Bitter arguments are not always healed. Disputants may have to lick their wounds and stand on their disagreements for longer than either can reasonably tolerate. As already admitted, managing such classrooms is not always straightforward. But the principles of classroom management implied are intrinsic to the process. That is, the rule is that one listens, argues, disagrees and tolerates the disagreement provided no person or basic procedural rule is harmed by it. Learners who wish to make head-way within such situations have little choice but to self-manage them-selves, emotionally and intellectually.

Ultimately, it is the educational ideal itself which rules how deviant behaviour is to be judged and dealt with. With a partnership ideal, social control ceases to be purely a teacher's prerogative but becomes an instrument of group decision-making. Pupils are enfranchised, but only so as to be on par with others (including teachers as 'first among equals'), and only on the back of suitable preparation. For example: peer-mediation training of pupils in conflict-resolution skills (Johnson *et al.* 1998; Osler and Starkey 1998; Silcock and Stacey 1997) precedes their intercession in peer disputes. Peer teaching and peer counselling, pupil conferencing (Eskeland 1996), children's 'courts', child philosophy

(Lipman *et al.* 1980) hint at what is possible once we abandon prejudices about what we believe are childhood's limitations. Notions of classroom management become in the end inseparable from notions of school management where all groups rightfully persuade individual members to swing into line behind rules to which they have, themselves, agreed.

Generally speaking, this is not to be formulaic. There is no 'right' way to organise democratically. But an advantage that this social organisation has over its rivals (such as Rogerian student-centredness) is that it does not erect moral barricades against the wider social context – i.e. trying to be morally superior to the world at large. Just as there will always be adults who wish to live and work 'outside' the system, so in a democratically run school there will be students who will refuse (perhaps on principle) to conform to any group decisions on rules. How one 'manages' such students has to be decided by the group itself, in the light of circumstances inside and outside the school. Quite likely, those unable to live within a democratic community might be better working in some other environment, chosen by themselves.

Assessment and evaluation

Assessing (as part of *evaluating*) the effectiveness of a democratic classroom has to be somewhat different from assessing pupil progress within teacher and learner-centred systems, since group processes are centrally engaged, and classrooms (and schools) will therefore have to be judged prior to the assessment of individual pupils and teachers. Only when one is clear as to the contribution one individual is making within a group will it be possible to assess that contribution in its own right. To judge a pupil's moral status, say, outside of a study of the moral context within which he or she operates daily is to invite a wrong assessment. Standard measures of intellectual capability (tests of all kinds) do have a place in any educational system, but anyone who devises them should know that social contexts may have fostered subtler ways of thinking which standard measures do not touch. In effect, democratic classrooms have to be judged within their own terms, notwithstanding any judgements about the democratic and egalitarian nature of classroom processes themselves which, for obvious reasons, are non-negotiable.

To meet the likeliest question regarding assessment, whether standard testing works or not has to depend on whether it is standard within the community being tested. The problem with 'nationally' standardised tests and comparisons of test results is that they give nothing to local or individual circumstances. Some children will always be treated unfairly by tests that cannot properly discern what such children actually can do. And all children will have some capabilities untouched by measures geared to a 'standard' which applies to enormously varying situations. Pretty certainly, such tests *always* mislead (see Davis 1998; Fielding 1999) and their outputs (as records, result portfolios or whatever) will work to divert pupils from building up the cognitive apparatus which is their most valuable, developmental heritage, towards refining examination skills. Yet it is not beyond the wit of educationists to devise tests which have local validity and standard utility. These tests would have to be equivalent in difficulty to national tests while distinctive in content. That is, we need not suppose there is no way of checking teaching success and making cross-school comparisons just because existing ways are flawed.

Age-phase differences

The need for tripartite transactions in teachers' preparation for their work (between general teaching models, specific ideals and local circumstances) is never more blatant than when one considers how teaching changes through age phases. As a rule, children's capacity for coping with the demands that teachers make on pupils alters over time. For example, two main characteristics of the very youngest are their instinctive independence – in areas where they already have control (largely sense-motor control) – and their lack of control in those other areas where teachers expect conformity (i.e. obedience to adults, consideration of others and so on). Correspondingly, it is probable that 'child-centredness' will always dominate early childhood teaching, and that early-childhood practitioners will develop techniques applicable to all children who are developmentally young (i.e. whatever their chronological age).

Passing into the primary age phase proper (5–11), a current tendency in English schools is for teachers to socialise children into a format suited to formal testing, competitive league-tables and so on. What has been supposed is that a co-constructive model is actually more suited to the culture of professional teaching and the demands of modern societies (and can be employed with situations vulnerable to inspection, testing and so forth). Collaborative primary schoolwork gives more to pupil choice than at secondary level (referring to the developmental principle introduced above). One might suggest as a paradigm strategy the group topic, where subgroups negotiate sub-topics, roles, ways of learning and so on (to compare with the child-centred 'integrated day', where children negotiate as individuals pursuing personal interests and ambitions: see Fisher 1996).

Co-constructive teaching is eminently suited to secondary age work, in that its features reflect the academic traditions by which most subjects progress (peer-referenced problem-solving, debate, argument, testing through rational discourse). Only when a need for pupils to be tested competitively arrives might one think that a top-down, teacher-centred way of teaching becomes obligatory. However, Adey and Shayer (1996) contend that a way of teaching whereby teachers doggedly work with – rather than against – developmental processes, fostering metacognition and learning transfer is, actually, a good way to prepare youngsters for formal tests. The difficulty lies mainly in the fact that where teachers need to prepare pupils quickly for exams, top-down 'cramming' becomes, often, irresistible. Where such circumstances exist, it is often pupils themselves who turn to cramming as a solution, rather than teachers prescribing it. To pre-empt obvious complaints: a system where memorising information for testing purposes is the modal way of teaching and learning is hardly an educational system.

At advanced and higher levels of teaching, adults should have the flexibility to cope within any teaching model. But co-constructive teaching might well be used, in that it is usual for older adolescents and adults to wish to be agents for their own learning while accepting that they have, to a degree, to acccomodate to curricula embracing other interests than their own.

Teacher and pupil roles

When teaching co-constructively, teachers sometimes initiate activities, sometimes follow pupil suggestions. Rather than 'recruit' to task (student-centred) or expect routine obedience (teacher-centred), they will propose possible ways forward, argue cases, suggest likely solutions to problems and so forth. One might query such a position. After all, teachers have knowledge pupils do not have and must regularly, simply, tell it to pupils. What point is there in 'proposing' that the battle of Hastings occurred in 1066 when there is no doubt that it did? Yet, for that very reason (that there is no point in proposing as a possibility what all know is factually correct), both teachers and pupils will state facts in a factual manner – this would be true for any human being. There is not a teaching issue involved. However, little in teaching is so straight-forward. And even in factual areas, topics we believed wrapped up and closed off to further debate tend to get revisited as scholars mull over long-established theory (see also under 'curricular content' above). According to Smolin (1997: 29), a basic reason why physics is unpopular in universities is that much of the curriculum, taught as factual, is actually untrue (i.e. out-dated). Students sense that it is.

So co-constructive teaching treats knowledge as by its nature provisional. It is worth illustrating with a possible scenario. Rather than a humanities or science topic being a vehicle for information-gathering (book and computer research), questions pupils are asked to answer are, themselves, tested out. Why are these questions important? Why not others (pupils themselves may come up with)? Once such background questions are known, pupils are invited to research how people have attempted to answer questions (again, why are these approaches the 'right' ones, and why aren't others used?) or to suggest other ways forward. They might wish to carry out some first-hand research themselves. Information thrown up by this tactic becomes provisional by the very fact that different groups of learners will discover both different routes to solutions and (thereby) different solutions, or different slants on standard theories. Temporary closure will be reached fairly arbitrarily, following exploration of available texts, project work, visits and so forth.

Learners, in co-constructive systems, are in some respects on par with teachers, except that teachers ('first among equals') are those knowledgeable group members able to keep other group members 'on the right track', arbitrate where necessary, link to outside circumstances (parents etc.) and known expertise, manage resources, model skills. Still, learners should recognise themselves as provisional authorities on the subjects and topics they study. A good test of the success of a co-constructive system, then, is for teachers to leave their classrooms from time to time, asking a pupil (or a pair of pupils) to take on a teaching role. This should be perfectly possible for pupils given that their roles already have parity with those of teachers (in a way such a strategy could only be partially possible with other approaches).

Dealing with endemic problems

Because two agencies are always involved in co-constructive work, mutual trust is assumed. Where pupils and/or teachers are unable to work with each other (because personalities 'clash', or whatever), outcomes are likely to be more serious than in teacher or pupil-oriented systems. This is because with the former, curricula are largely prescribed by agencies outside the school; and in the latter circumstance pupils can assert their own personalities in a way they cannot when they are constrained by group decision-making. One has to suppose that democratically organised schools will benefit from being part of a democratic

society. This means that where situations internal to a school are unsatisfactory these become vulnerable to modification from outside. This
possibility is already built in to present-day teaching situations (mainly
via an inspection system) and some equivalent system is assumed here.

What needs adding is that democratic teaching is – by its nature – a
way of teaching which subjects itself to critical scrutiny as part of its
way of working. Democratically run schools have to be self-evaluating
schools. And given that the present Ofsted system is likely to be replaced
by a new form of inspection contingent on school self-evaluation, this
fact adds further weight to arguments in favour of democratic or co-
constructive teaching. The point to stress is that co-constructive teaching
depends on ongoing critical self-evaluation: generalising from ongoing
particular circumstances to gain a picture of any one school's achievements should be a fairly straightforward business.

The other difficulty, regularly revisited, with promoting co-
constructive teaching at the moment is that as a form of pedagogy the
implications of its practice are rather 'out of tune' with legislation of
recent years in England and Wales. What has been argued is that it is possible to marry a standard curriculum to partnership work and that, in fact,
it is hard to see how a standard curriculum can ultimately succeed unless it
is embraced within some such system. The gradual easing of top-down
policies by central government (of which a watershed move will be the
shift from hard-line Ofsted inspections to school self-evaluations) must
herald some re-empowering of teachers (i.e. giving back to them some
degree of curricular autonomy). What partnership systems allow (by definition) is a sharing of authority between various 'partners' which can just
as well include politicians and their advisers as children and parents –
provided each group is considered co-equal with other groups in the
way its views are treated.

Teaching co-constructively: a summary of guidelines

First, competent teaching will stem from teachers' commitments to an
ideal in full awareness of other options (models of good practice).
These, too, are part of a professional context within which all teachers
work. Regarding 'partnership', competent teachers are likely to be those
whose commitments to negotiation and democracy (etc.) model suitable
ways of behaving for their pupils.

Second, quality teaching means skills are matched to context. What has
been supposed is that successful and excellent teaching are not prescribed
purely as 'outputs' from well-intentioned skill. They will be products of
the successful integration of skills with regard to known circumstances.

Such circumstances will include age-phase conditions, gender-biased settings, cultural inputs from a diverse community, disabled and disadvantaged pupils and so forth. In some cases it will be the social demands of the job which loom largest; in other cases, it will be the academic. Sometimes, good teaching will rely on critical debate, sometimes what is required is a sensitive easing forward of immature opinion towards a more principled understanding. Pragmatics do not determine quality teaching; but a teacher's dealing with circumstance in a studied manner has to help propel a teacher beyond mere competence.

Third, if there is one principle which most signals the value of co-constructive teaching it is that which tells us of the fluid nature of knowledge itself. Because a concept's meaning alters through its relationship with others, the same idea will be understood differently according to whether it is learned as provisional or an element of some unassailable theory. And the issue is not one, simply, of 'explaining' to pupils that knowledge is provisional, for what could that mean for someone not used to disputing propositions? Children can learn as a stipulative idea something which takes real meaning only from experiencing the idea in application (someone can learn as a 'fact' something which does not, then, impinge at all on what they do, think or understand). How a topic is learned gives meaning to what is learned.

Fourth, the above principles affect all others – forms of assessment, social control and so on. 'Pupil management', for example, assumes unassailable criteria by which personnel issues can be judged. Sometimes there are such criteria (to protect physical safety for example). Often there are not; and social organisation depends not on human management (a strange notion – the idea of 'managing' autonomous people who can by definition manage only themselves) but on negotiation, mediation, compromise around given rules of procedure. Which is not to claim that all pupils feel at home within a democratic rule-governed setting. This is another reason why a knowledge of alternative models benefits teachers: sometimes parents and pupils can be counselled that a particular form of teaching is not suited to their needs. In such circumstances, and given that other schools using a different type of approach exist, migration to one of those schools should prove a solution to the difficulty identified (rather than operating a policy of exclusion, for example: see Chapter 8).

Fifth, as it happens, the possibilities for teachers working effectively in a partnership manner is currently expanding exponentially. This is because, in many societies, human rights and democratic movements are now powerfully able to channel minority views in such a way as to ensure their proper discussion. Mass communications, an information technology revolution, a globalisation of trade and associated socio-economic aspects of life, increasingly confront groups in ways both demanding and facilitating negotiating and debating skills. The world shrinks daily. Opportunities for teachers to learn the 'democratic' skills being championed proliferate. To repeat a sterling point: teachers may well find that models of good practice attractive to them in a cosmopolitan world approximate to a partnership model. Governments, too, may in future find themselves constrained to allow some democratic decision-making (i.e. involving pupils) in schools, if only to bow towards human rights' principles which underpin modern, international law (though the greater a government's power the longer it can defend undemocratic positions, should it wish to do so).

Even if this does not occur, there is a fairly respectable stance democratic teachers take to a non-democratic educational governance, in order to leave them with some chance of success. They can work within a centralised system, treating it as one within which curricular decisions are made democratically. That is, they can use the system to illustrate dilemmas which often arise in a democratic state, perhaps showing how wider policies have dangers, weaknesses and may even be ethically dubious, despite being democratically decided. As discussed, truly excellent practitioners are those who integrate their various capabilities in such a way as to keep faith with ideals while admitting the realities of circumstances they cannot alter. What bears repeating is Kelly's (1995) observation that democratic education is exactly that approach to teaching which prepares a person for compromise, tolerance and a general 'giving' to the other person, except in relinquishing democratic principles themselves.

7 Achieving competence
The role of initial teacher education

Introduction

How do teachers learn to teach in a competent manner?

Earlier argument suggests that teachers are guided by emerging professional concepts (of education, teaching and learning) and by their actual classroom experiences. Over time, the ability to apply principles associated with a favoured ideal of good practice firms up, boosted by novel insights and innovations during periods of training and further professional development. But the varying *situations* in which teachers learn how to teach are complex. They are complex because teachers' professional expertise is – from the start – subject to multiple influences from central government legislation, from classroom and school communities and (initially) from the kind of help and instruction given on teacher-education courses. These latter courses are, themselves, prey to competing political, professional and academic demands. Course leaders must combine a top-down managerial approach (conforming to political legislation) with bottom-up school-based learning, via school–college partnerships, often exhorting student-teachers to integrate these various strands of influence through a form of reflective appraisal or critical thinking.

In other words, when we look at teachers as learners (i.e. as learning to become competent) we find they must integrate a bewildering variety of experiences in order to benefit from them. For this reason, it is likely these days that any coherent system of teacher education and professional development will fall back on various sorts of collaborative (or collegiate) methodologies, just to cope with multiple, diverse pressures. However, they will do so for other reasons than as coping strategies. Modern, democratic states expect young teachers to learn from other practitioners, experts and interested stakeholders while refining their skills. Such expectations, feeding on a seemingly insatiable public appetite for ever higher educational standards, take for granted that teachers (including novices) will get involved in many advisory, academic and mentoring networks. Learning how to teach is neither simple nor straightforward, as will be seen.

Learning to teach: three paradigms

As discussed, young teachers adapt existing social and personal skills to three sorts of context – to particular schools and communities, to the general requirements posed by their own professionalism, and to legislated frameworks. So learning to teach is never just a matter of 'applying theory' or of being trained in generic skills, though theoretical study and skills' learning have supplementary roles – the first to direct the deployment of skills (argued throughout), the second as adjuncts to a more basic theory. We are always returned, when debating the professional development of teachers, to questions of how discrete strands of influence (theory/practice/ideology; workplace/academia/society; school/college/ community) combine to shape professional skills. And the overriding issue will usually be that of how (while combining) to give sensible, functional priorities to these distinct strands.

For simplicity, we can summarise the various solutions to problems of combination, or integration, as being of three kinds – again corresponding to the three paradigms which always appear when we study human improvement and conceptual change. Practical repertoires can grow around a core of learned 'competencies' decided by some central authority. They can evolve within some personal 'construction' managed by individual teachers. Or some form of partnership arrangements can operate whereby learners integrate, more collaboratively and democratically, different contributors' overlapping and varying demands. Although the education of professionals for vocational purposes is rather different from the general education of pupils in schools, this does not mean we reach different conclusions about good practice. The aims of Initial Teacher Education (ITE) are to initiate professionals into the teaching profession with a base level of skill or competence. Trying to divine how such initiation is fruitfully managed will be revealing if analysis confirms exactly those conclusions earlier reached when looking at the more general nature of competent, successful and excellent teaching.

Paradigm 1: the competence model

That model of training and development known as the 'competence model' implies not only that a generic approach to teaching capability is academically and professionally respectable but also that it can be realised for professional training and development purposes. Now, it has been conceded that common standards for professional education and development can be set, providing one accepts the contrasting ways very general statements are interpreted, and providing one accepts that what works in one setting may not work in another. When assessing good teaching, we can never dispense with interpretation: those making assessments must be professionally equipped to see whether skills are, properly, deployed to fit both aim and circumstance.

But, issues of interpretation apart, the tough question for anyone relying on generics, is whether these can *sufficiently* bind together what we call competent or good teaching without anyone having to add on more basic capabilities – of a procedural or conceptual sort. The assumption that they can was made during the 1990s in the UK. Successive governments stipulated (via a Teacher Training Agency: see TTA 1996, 1997a) that skilled teaching is circumscribed by discrete 'competences' or 'competencies' strung together within a taxonomy meant to stand as any professional teacher's repertoire. Implicitly, higher quality or 'excellent' teaching was (and still is) thought measurable, by examining the special character or application of such competencies regarding important tasks or within important categories of teacher-action (see e.g. Sutton *et al.* 2000).

Competences, then, function both as 'standards' for Initial Teacher Education and for various levels of school leadership including preparation for headship from the National Professional Qualification for Headship (NPQH) and induction into headship through the Headteachers Leadership and Management Programme (HEADLAMP). They constitute a national curricular structure for ITE (TTA 1996, 1997a) and for the *National Standards for Headteachers* (TTA 1997c, 1998) which offer a mixture of functional and personal competencies. Moreover, research commissioned by the DfEE from the international management consultancy firm Hay McBer of a series of 'professional characteristics' has, now, mapped out teacher effectiveness throughout different stages of professional development (Hay McBer 2000). The tantalising possibility is held out of a competence system structuring the whole of a teacher's career.

This extraordinarily successful system seems to have had its origins in the 1920s when the drive for technical and rational management systems first gained momentum, though it became influential in the late 1960s and early 1970s (Adams 1996: 44). A prime mover in promoting it was David McClelland, a Harvard psychology professor who founded the consultancy firm 'McBer' – later to evolve into 'Hay McBer'. McClelland believed that traditional academic examinations did not predict job performance or success in life, and were often biased against minorities, women and others (Adams 1996: 44). He proposed such 'traditional' forms of assessment be abandoned and advised researchers to look for other variables that could predict success in an unbiased manner. It was onto a background of egalitarian ideals that McLelland projected his concept of the centrality of 'competencies' (Adams 1996: 45).

In the 1970s, consultants at McBer began to seek ways of defining competencies and refined the technique of 'behavioural event interviewing', based on the earlier 'critical incident method' (Adams 1996: 44). During the 1980s, a number of studies of these emerging techniques were carried out leading a McBer consultant, Richard Boyatzis, to come up with a definition of a competency as part of his attempt to put together a 'generic model' of managerial skill. He defined a competency as: 'An underlying characteristic of an individual which is crucially related to effective or superior performance' (Boyatzis 1982: 64). So Boyatzis placed the concept of competency firmly in the context of *effective* performance from the outset, enhancing the conceptual worth of higher levels of performance by refining his definition as: 'Those characteristics that differentiate superior performance from average and poor performance' (Boyatzis 1982: 66).

McClelland's work, elaborated by Boyatzis, continues to be influential in the United States though it separates from the competence movement in the UK in two crucial ways. First, whereas McClelland and Boyatzis believed that people are those who 'possess' competencies, most UK approaches suggest they are intrinsic to 'the job' not the person. Second, McClelland and Boyatzis are concerned with what counts in professional behaviour as *superior performance*. By contrast, occupational standards in the UK have tended to be made up of elements of competence with performance criteria indicating *minimum competence* levels. Even the terminology has been used differently. While United States writers refer to 'competency' (plural: 'competencies'), much UK literature talks about 'competence' (plural: 'competences').

Reservations about the competence model collect around the two convictions that, first, the competence model contains within it an inappropriate and reductivist model of learning which is educationally and philosophically inadequate; second, it is morally repugnant since it denies notions of professional autonomy. The central idea, here, uniting both elements, returns us to the notion that the competency paradigm fairly desperately underestimates the complex nature of any teaching and learning as processes involving human agency, as discussed in earlier chapters. In its attempt to 'atomise' its topics, it may actually destroy what is being studied.

Everard (1990: 15), for example, declares the competence approach 'is like using a quantity surveyor rather than an artist to capture the grandeur of St. Paul's'. Cullen (1992) finds competencies period-specific; they may date very quickly. Using them, he suggests, is like 'driving using a rear-view mirror'. Chown (1994: 161) believes profiles of competence lead to 'static and partial models of teaching' and are an inadequate base for the development and accreditation of professional practice. Bridges (1996), an erstwhile supporter of competence-based systems, has given in to attacks on the philosophical inadequacy of the competence movement, agreeing that the concept is defensible only if a 'more generic and cognitively laden concept of personal and professional competence' is found (Bridges 1996: 361).

A dramatic example of a 'lack of conceptual clarity' (Leat 1993a: 499) in the competency system can be found in the oft-quoted *Florida Catalogue of Teacher Competencies* which lists no fewer than 1,276 competencies for teacher education. The ludicrous complexity and sheer range of such lists provides a striking example of the potential futility of anyone seeking to excavate to some unchanging basis of teaching skill (Leat 1993a: 500). Drawing on Ryle's (1949) distinction between 'the knower and the known', and Pearson's (1984) more recent separating of 'habitual skill knowledge' from 'intelligent skill knowledge', Leat (1993a: 509) concludes: 'The development of competence needs a curriculum for the affective and explicit attention to cognitive processes within an experiential framework'.

Competence, according to Hyland (1993a: 127), is tied to a 'narrow and mechanistic' behaviourist theory of learning. Competence systems fail to take account of a human capacity for adapting skills to what is known of particular circumstances and particular ends. Hyland (1993b: 59) sees 'a reluctance on the part of certain enthusiasts for competence strategies to make any concessions to knowledge and understanding'. A rather primitive attitude to human development creates an epistemological profile of competence-based education involving 'a bewildering range of conceptions of knowledge' (1993b: 63) naively dividing the mental and physical components of performance.

It is strange that a reductionist model of teaching and learning should come to the fore when many other areas of intellectual endeavour accept the increasing complexity of any human ontological position. Whereas most of the humanities, social sciences and even science itself grapples with and concedes multiple possibilities inherent in all aspects of our lives, competence systems of education ignore 'postmodern uncertainties and reasserts the modern certainty that the situation can be managed to produce a better tomorrow' (Edwards 1993: 125). Of course, it isn't wholly out of the way to reduce teaching and learning processes to a finite number of basics, providing paradigms admit within their rationales the complexities introduced into any 'ideal type' by our perceptions of human autonomy and variability. These perceptions have been marshalled within separate options for teaching depending how teachers themselves view limitations set by open-ended assumptions about the varying aspirations, social backgrounds and values of pupils. It is the over-simplistic and over-ambitious nature of competency theory (that we can ever achieve closure when seeking to define good teaching practice) which are questionable.

Beyond competence

Three models of competence dominate research in the field. These are a 'broadly behaviourist' approach, a 'process model which attempts to map out the process of competent action in terms of flexibility' and a third approach which 'may be described as a cognitive model, since it attributes such importance to knowledge and understanding' (Reynolds and Salters 1995: 350). As one moves from the first to the third model, one is moving from a belief that secure professional skills have bedrock position in teaching to one which sees that professionals themselves must decide how to react to difficulties and tasks. It is how they decide to deploy skills (rather than the skills themselves) which is significant.

> The three models reflect different interpretations of knowledge and understanding. Within the first model knowledge is subsumed into behaviour and competence is task completion. The second model makes some reference to the role of understanding in contributing to the ability to use knowledge in changing situations. On the other hand, the third model extends the ideas of a personal dimension to knowledge, identifiable in the human ability to recognise and act in situations which are similar, yet not identical.
>
> (Reynolds and Salters 1995: 352)

The above tripartite analysis inspires Hager (1995: 142–143) to find weakness in both task-based, behaviourist theory and in the alternative reliance on general personal attributes, dismissing the former as 'reductionist' and the latter as having little capacity for predicting future occupational performance. Hager remarks that most professions have chosen a third 'integrated' conception as their adopted model and accepts that this model can have beneficial effects in that it can offer 'valuable guidance for course development' (Hager 1995: 146–147). It is this last model that offers some integration of the more raw-edged elements of competence systems with traditional 'academic' forms of learning and give us our best hope of integrating the more helpful aspects of competence into such areas as teacher education.

Such qualified concession to the continuing centrality but deficiency of competence-based systems is echoed by Boyatzis, who has decided that 'competency can be developed' (Boyatzis *et al.* 1996: 26). Defending the role of competence in management theory, he admits 'certain ingredients' need adding to make the process effective (Boyatzis *et al.* 1996: 35). These include 'individualised assessment and development program or activity in which people can develop'; an 'atmosphere of interpersonal support for the exploration to develop the image of their desired future'; and 'opportunities to experiment and explore the use of these competencies and knowledge in "work" settings' (Boyatzis *et al.* 1996: 35). Boyatzis's more holistic model of education and training incorporates and extends competence ideals, addressing concerns about them as expressed in recent debates in the wider sphere of training and development.

Cheetham and Chivers (1996), too, stay confident about the future of professional competence, offering their own 'holistic model'. They harmonise the 'outcomes approach' which they see as characterising much of the National Vocational Qualification (NVQ) system with the 'reflective practitioner' approach worked out by Schon (1983). Within this new synthesis, the notion of 'meta-competencies' developed by Nordhaug (1990), which carries the idea that competencies may assist in the development of other competencies such as 'communication, problem-solving and analytical capacities' (Nordhaug 1990: 23), becomes central. Cheetham and Chivers (1996) attempt to integrate these competence hierarchies within a framework exploiting Eraut's (1994) proposals on overlapping sets of values underwriting ethical issues encountered in the workplace.

Despite all this revisionism and continuing optimism expressed by supporters, the worm eating away the core of the competence approach is that it unashamedly offers *training* rather than *education*. Whereas training endeavours to impart knowledge, skills and attitudes necessary to perform job-related tasks and to improve job performance in a direct way, education is a process whose prime purposes are to impart knowledge and develop cognitive abilities applicable to all important life-situations. In this sense, education is not primarily concerned with job performance (Truelove 1992: 273), it is concerned with the deployment of more subtle and flexible human capabilities for dealing with fleeting problems, seldom vulnerable to trained skills.

Specifically, teachers need broad intellectual abilities to solve the most severe problems currently facing schools. For this reason, Duignan and Macpherson (1992: 48) define the 'educative leader' as 'a practically effective theorist'. Similarly, Leithwood and Stager (1989) list various types of problem-solving capability as crucial. They distinguish between 'expert' and 'novice' problem-solvers (1989: 129), while, in later work Leithwood *et al.* (1992: 49) add that new school leaders are often 'hostages to their existing knowledge'. In the broader area of teacher education, Tomlinson (1995a, 1995b) who has shifted somewhat from accepting a strict competency paradigm for teaching, admits a leaning towards more recent work on 'skilled expertise' (Tomlinson 1995b: 299). Hyland (1993c: 119) has drafted a five stage skills acquisition sequence consisting of 'novice, advanced beginner, competent, proficient and expert'. 'Experts', Hyland writes, have been found to have high levels of knowledge in their own domains, to make faster and more economical professional judgements, perceive large and meaningful patterns in professional activity, excel in their own spheres and have strong self-monitoring skills (Hyland 1993c: 120). Leat's (1993b) model of competence-based experiential learning, introduced earlier, has the three core components: 'cognition, what teachers know; the affective, what they feel; and behaviour, what they do' (Leat 1993b: 35).

'Capability' purports to offer one way of integrating the strengths of the competency model into a wider notion of educational development. Stephenson (1994, 1996), one of the movement's pioneers, agrees that 'narrowly defined competences are only part of human capability' (Stephenson 1994: 4). Cave and Wilkinson (1992: 39) have adapted the language of 'capability' to educational management to sort out three constituents of such 'education management capabilities' which they define as knowledge relating to the school's 'context, functions and processes'. They further decide that 'higher order capacities and generic cognitive abilities determine appropriate action'. Four of the latter are identified as crucial: 'reading the situation', 'balanced judgement', 'intuition' and 'political acumen'.

To begin to finalise where we are with this topic, the competence movement is one of the most influential paradigms in the history of educational training and development. The challenge to move beyond its declared limitations towards the kind of 'life-world becoming' programmes envisaged by Barnett (1994: 178) which reach towards reflective knowledge and critical understanding has to be addressed. Certainly, one way forward is to see that the bare (albeit courageous) attempt to list a *unitary* set of prescriptions of effective professional capability (whether for school leaders, managers or, just, teachers) is what defeats the competence movement, even when writers move to more holistic ground to set up new positions. It is not hard to find chinks in the armour of those who believe they have captured expert practice comprehensively within a single formula or framework, however sophisticated or process-driven its structure.

This realisation has to make us stop dwelling too single-mindedly on seemingly endless attempts to retrieve a position in face of a barrage of criticism. For the point of critiques is usually not to destroy accounts altogether when they are found faulty (and almost all will have faults given that the nature of the task is to prescribe for an enormous diversity of purpose and situation). Following negative policies of that sort makes general progress near impossible. Rather, we must see whether or not some virtue or quality can be salvaged from the competency model, once criticisms are properly assimilated. And, indeed, when we look hard at the principles behind the model (notwithstanding its actual recommendations), we find that its simplicity and directness have much to offer. The challenge, perhaps, is to retain some degree of clarity of pre-scription when going beyond it towards more intellectually convincing and relevant paradigms.

Paradigm 2: learning to teach in classrooms

There are those who see such revisions of teacher education as a conspi-racy to remove teacher education from higher education institutions in order to place it in the hands of schools. These people warn that teacher education policy during the 1990s has been taken over by the 'new right' (Maclure 1993). It is undoubtedly true that the Education Act 1993 gave great powers to the Secretary of State for Education and the Teacher Training Agency to shift training to school-centred schemes. Schools can now (at least in principle) decide on the funding and location of student numbers. They can accredit courses, and can – up to a point – control educational research (Mahony and Whitty 1994). There are even those who argue that the actions of the TTA in its development of the standards for teacher education raises questions about the state of democratic government (Hextall and Mahony 2000).

Higher education (HE) has, nonetheless, shown remarkable resilience in retaining its dominant position in teacher education: successive attempts to replace HE courses with school-based schemes have met with only minor success. Some reasons why the flight to school-based work has halted confirm, as argued, an acceptance that teaching is complex, and relies on many very different cognitive and behavioural insights and capabilities. It cannot be reduced to simply stated competencies learned or trained *in situ,* though it does, of course, have a core of 'reflective' capabilities which are not products of theoretical teaching or debate, but must, somehow, be learned in face of real pupils in real classrooms. Teaching skills are, in fair measure, 'constructed' by individuals in response to unique school circumstances (see Chapters 4–5).

But the essential difficulty for supposing that teachers can acquire competent teaching skills wholly in schools is that people expect more from professional teachers than the skills they acquire there. This 'something more' has to be won outside of the workplace (though not necessarily in other socio-physical locations: it is just that general theory is learned differently from concrete, perceptual or pragmatic skills). For many teachers, key professional understandings – discussed in earlier chapters – can be gained only by spending time (during initial training and later) in academic study, whether in higher education institutions or on distance learning courses.

Now the only point of returning to the topic is to remind ourselves of something quite important. A theory–practice dualism (like pupil–teacher dualism, public–personal dualism and so on) is endemic in teaching. It is unavoidable. It is unavoidable because of the way we normally see professional teaching not because practical skills are learned theoretically (lay teachers who have never studied theory can be very skilled). Much time and effort has been wasted while policy-makers surge from beliefs in one sort of training (theoretically based) to another (school-based), i.e. in trying to divine the problematic nature of the practice–theory or theory–practice link rather than accept that its built-in dualism makes it problematic to deal with.

To repeat: this is not to deny that practical forms of teaching competence arise and are beaten into shape in the fire of classroom dilemmas, hardships and intermittent failures. Knowledge of teaching *is* a 'subject to be created', and, in large part not to be learned from others (see Freudenthal's 1978 view of mathematics, cited by Korthagen and Kessels 1999: 7). Each teacher's understandings reflect unique encounters with pupils and situations which cannot be 'schooled' by college and university tutors. Korthagen and Kessels (1999) cite this fact to explain why college educators have, for so long, been unable to resolve difficulties of 'transfer'. They are adamant (as are others: see their literature review) that student-teachers simply do not acquire practical knowledge in seminar rooms which they, then, somehow transfer to classrooms. Learning teaching skills is not like that. It is much more a 'situated' or 'grounded' form of learning whereby practice decides its own theory (rather than theories breeding good practice). And this remains true no matter how well general theories are 'linked' to practical circumstances. Korthagen and Kessels (1999), like Schon (1983, 1987) and others, denounce 'technical rationality' because of its assumption that techniques and skills learned 'rationally' (i.e. through study and discussion) can, somehow, be applied to the myriad settings teachers face during their careers.

Yet, to some degree, good teaching *has* to involve transference of capability. Teaching, itself, by nature, lifts knowledge from one circumstance (geographical, historical, scientific research etc.) to another (classrooms, seminar rooms, lecture halls). Education is crucially reliant on knowledge transfer to be regarded as successful in any sense (detailed further in Chapter 9). Writers such as Korthagen and Kessels (1999) take it for granted that what they call *episteme* (formalised, academic knowledge) does not feed directly into teaching, but that professional practice relies on *phronesis* – a sort of refined sensibility or awareness of what needs doing in any given situation, which only benefits from theorising tailor-made for it (Labercane *et al.* 1998 exemplifies such moment-to-moment theorising).

Unfortunately, this argument infers from the real difficulty anyone has transferring knowledge (not just teachers), the dubious conclusion that it is near impossible, *in principle*, to manage such transfers in any efficient manner. It assumes we have to rethink the whole business. As Biggs (1992) puts it, the point of conceptual development (and presumably professional development) is to overcome the situatedness of knowledge, not give in to it. Bereiter (2001) makes a similar case. Writers like Korthagen and Kessels (1999) unambiguously admit the role of theory ('the bigger picture' as they put it). But it is hard to see from their discussion of 'theorising about practice' where the sorts of theorising considered, here, to underwrite teaching models fits. And if it is true (as argued) that teachers inevitably encounter circumstances demanding judgements about these models, this problem is a dire one for those teacher educators who press for 'practical' thinking *at the expense* of academic theorising.

Let's not procrastinate on this matter. Only by a degree of hard study and academic debate, is it possible for teacher educators to safeguard the nurturing of truly professional teachers. Schools cannot be sole custodians of this task – indeed schools can be intellectually and professionally impoverished situations (providing poor teaching models). Largely, this is why HE providers maintain links with school 'mentors' through partnership arrangements. If they did not do so, we could expect teachers learning in a 'constructive' manner to become proficient in terms of their school-based settings. They would not necessarily develop as professional educators.

Paradigm 3: acquiring competence through partnership

Two positions have been reached. It was argued that competence theories do not deal well with the ambiguities and uncertainties of school life. It was also been shown (directly above and in earlier chapters) that a purely 'constructivist' or school-based approach to professional development risks teachers learning poor practice as much as good practice. There has to be more to professional skill than skill itself – i.e. there have to be some guidelines of some sort directing practitioners, however we formulate these. Earlier chapters have found the only secure guidelines in concepts or theories of education which, in turn, give birth to principles of practice realising constituent values. However, what is especially noteworthy about collaborative ideals, such as those engaged by partnership forms (Chapters 5 and 6), is that they satisfy both stated requirements. And, taking account of above discussions, they seem to be the only kind of practice which does.

First, they assume uncertainties built into all educational circumstances and seek to reconcile or resolve these. Although we can never detail exactly how a teacher should behave, we can put forward practically fruitful procedures to deal with conflicts of interest and judgement. These have been called 'co-constructive' in that they hinge on reconciling conflicts between independent agencies in ways which teach learners not to be stymied by the uncertainties they encounter in schools and in the lives outside school. Second, the important (yet often overlooked) outcome of school–college partnerships in initial training is that the system itself enforces a degree of knowledge-transfer. There would be little point to such partnerships if tutors and mentors did not collaborate to make sure that school-based learning and college-based learning enriched each other. Admittedly, just to state that co-constructions are transferable does not make them so. Earlier discussions (Chapter 6) supposed that transferability must, to an extent, hinge on the way knowledge and skills are learned. Partnership systems by nature foster multiple-perspective taking. And there is a sense in which the ability to take perspectives on learning from differently located perspectives (environmentally or in terms of knowledge bases) has to be termed transferable knowledge (further elaborated in Chapter 9).

In its generating of a democratic, egalitarian ethos, the co-constructive option is usually named 'collegial' or 'collegiate'. At this level – i.e. as a 'whole school' collaborative enterprise – it not only survives in colleges, universities and schools, but also flourishes through groups of people having to respond coherently to top-down legislation, and as an offshoot of modern tendencies towards democratic, egalitarian policies. Some think it already the 'official model of good practice' in British educational institutions (Wallace 1988 notices a remarkably consistent view underlying national surveys conducted by Her Majesty's Inspectorate and occasional papers by HMI and other publications based on HMI reports). Much of the recent work on school improvement and effectiveness in Britain such as that of Hargreaves (1994), Hargreaves and Hopkins (1991), Hopkins *et al.* (1994) and Gray *et al.* (1996) makes either open or tacit acceptance of collegial management styles as passports to school improvement.

Technically speaking, collegial models work in organisations such as schools and colleges which contain significant numbers of professional staff, especially teachers, possessing authority arising directly from their knowledge and skill. Teachers thus have an 'authority of expertise' offsetting their positional authority, associated with formal models of management and providing that 'professional authority' needed for decisions made individually rather than according to some standardised rules. Education demands a professional autonomy from teachers because pupils and students need personal attention; and autonomous teachers (at least in principle) have little choice but to collaborate to guarantee coherent systems of teaching and learning. Collegial models assume that professionals also have a right to share in the wider, decision-making process (Bush 1995: 53).

Collegiality, then, implies a sharing of expertise according to role and capability, without recourse to artificial hierarchies or to 'contrived' collegiality where professionals co-operate only to deliver what someone else asks of them. Student-teachers, expected to teach in a democratic manner, will learn (as pupils do: Chapters 5 and 6), through their participation in democratic decision-making. This form of professional learning does not make vital studies optional but it does assume what is and is not important for teacher novices is uncertain and ripe for negotiation. Accepting students into partnership with tutors and mentors (a system practised in HE institutions though with varying degrees of success) is integral to a coherent system of professional education preparing them for life in modern classrooms.

Conclusion

Although competence-based professional education is still policy-makers' bottom line for teacher assessment, problems found with it mean that teachers should, sooner or later, enter 'true' partnerships with government (as well as with pupils, parents, teacher-educators). If, or when, this happens, one suspects they will opt for more flexible criteria for deciding professional standards than any single set, no matter how sophisticated and detailed their lists might turn out to be. They will, almost certainly, admit the problematic nature of trying to decide what is or is not acceptable teaching, given the unpredictable nature of modern life and post-modern conditions. Ideally, their new General Teaching Council will support them in their quest to set professional standards for themselves and administer those standards in ways safeguarding quality teaching. As yet this is very much an unrealised ideal.

Least of all will teachers deny that there are other factors entering the educational equation to determine their own professional success than those arising from pedagogic skills alone. Safeguarding professional standards safeguards the best hope we have of building a successful education service. It cannot guarantee that it will. However, by entering into partnership with those most likely to influence learners (such as parents, and learners themselves), teachers at least bias matters in their own favour, as will be shown in Chapter 8.

8   Achieving success
Dealing with 'out of school' factors

Teachers are not the only people deciding how state education proceeds or whether it is working well or badly. But the extent to which teachers can or cannot deal with 'out of school factors' mediating their success (especially with 'social' issues of disadvantage and poverty) is a judgement anyone trying to prescribe good practice has to make. This chapter looks at where we are with questions about how far schools and teachers can make a difference to pupils, regardless of the background or social attitudes of pupils themselves. It returns finally to considering how far a modern, partnership approach to education might, in practical terms, improve on those odds which seem forever stacked against the most 'disadvantaged' or 'difficult' schools.

Introduction: historical background

Research on school effectiveness and on school improvement has expanded enormously over past years, becoming, in the words of one commentator, a 'major international industry' (Willmott 1999). School effectiveness research has had a major effect on policies at national, local and school levels (Barber and White 1997: 1), suiting policy-makers' ambitions to justify curricular innovations across schools. Such ambitions are understandable. Early in the twentieth century, educational thinking and policy became acutely deterministic, with early and middle decades turning towards policies of selection under influence from 'weak' theories of equality. Pupils seemed well served by an education suited to their supposedly fixed abilities. They were routed along educational pathways (and sometimes along career pathways) via selection tests meant to plumb their fixed intellectual potential as well as their developing talents.

At the same time, the 1960s and 1970s saw some partial justification for such policies in pessimistic theories that schools could not 'compensate' for the effects of social class. Educators and policy-makers alike became captivated by the idea that school outcomes were decided either by inexorable laws of genetic or by social predisposition. What makes one human being more likely than another to succeed in school was thought decided either by biology or by socio-cultural inheritance, or by some unfathomable mixture of both. By contrast, the emerging educational 'effectiveness' movement supposed that schools could make a difference. It was lent power by a 'positivist' or scientific superstructure of statistically based research techniques, freeing researchers to assess the relative performance of different schools even after features of intake had been factored out. The very concept of 'effectiveness', and its sometimes quarrelsome sibling 'improvement', prescribed refreshing antidotes to the pessimism and fatalism of the 1970s (Chitty 1997: 50).

Quickly, however, the new optimism acquired worrying overtones. The effectiveness movement assumed a 'hegemonic' status when explaining how schools function (Proudfoot and Baker 1995) which soured the enthusiasm of some early advocates. It became strongly associated in the UK with central government policy, inviting accusations that its newly won role in educational discourse was ideologically partisan and antagonistic to sections of the educational community. It seemed to favour ways of teaching linked exclusively to paradigms of a fairly traditional or ultra-pragmatic nature. One could claim that research findings had become harnessed to an instrumental view of the educational system as a whole, better called 'schooling' than education. Yet, for those with 'technicist' aspirations it was, as Smyth and Dow (1998: 291) have it, 'the only game in town'.

The rise of effectiveness studies

Coleman's (1966) large-scale survey of equality of educational opportunity in United States' schools found no apparent relationship between resources available to schools and pupil outcomes measured in terms of the academic achievements of the students who attended them. For Coleman, different types of academic achievement were by-products of the social background and personal characteristics of the students themselves. In Britain, an equivalent view was propounded using theories of linguistic difference put forward by Basil Bernstein. Working-class children appeared to lack a capacity for conceptual thinking that was a feature of the cognitive resources of middle-class children. An 'elaborated code' of linguistic representation was superior to a 'restricted' code in its potential for advanced reasoning and abstract thought (Bernstein 1970a; Bernstein and Henderson 1969). In a phrase that was to prove ominous for subsequent generations of researchers, Bernstein declared that 'schools cannot compensate for society' (Bernstein 1970b: 344). The limits of school achievement were set at an early age by linguistic mechanisms children acquire within families (Chitty 1997: 49). Subsequent work by Jencks *et al.* (1972) in the United States revealed that 'if all high schools were equally effective, differences in attainment would be reduced by less than one per cent' (Ouston *et al.* 1979: 67). Similar conclusions were reached by those who carried out the initial evaluation of Head Start programmes (Ouston *et al.* 1979).

Bernstein subsequently protested that his work had been misinterpreted (see e.g. Bernstein 1970c). As Mortimore (1998a: 476) points out, re-evaluations of Coleman and Jencks' work and the Head Start programmes (studying long-term effects: Lazar *et al.* 1977) give a better insight into the circumstances and educational circumstances they were studying. These early researchers worked at a time when they were only able to check out or control macro-level variables, such as the size of a school site and main facilities and resources available to staff and students. This, Mortimore argues, restricted questions which could be asked by researchers and severely limited the quality of research outcomes. Being confined to broad-brush predictions, such large-scale sociological studies were almost bound to overlook 'micro' effects (such as the way particular schools might effect attitude change over a long term or teach very specific vocational skills). They contributed to a mood of 'fatalism' that seemed to dominate educational thinking in the 1960s and 1970s (Chitty 1997: 50). Such a mood was unlikely to last. When, eventually, a new breed of empirical researchers set out to overturn it, they did so with high expectations and much public support.

The development of newer, powerful research tools shifted focus from macro-variables to micro-variables, facilitating research programmes trying to fathom the role of individual schools in learning outcomes. A subsequent outflow of research produced an enormous and still expanding literature. Over a period of no more than a single generation, leading researchers joined forces in attempts to discover the factors that can enhance school effectiveness (Brundrett 2000a). The work of Rutter *et al.* (1979) and Mortimore *et al.* (1988) attained seminal status in finally (possibly conclusively) demonstrating that some schools are more effective than others, even when the social background of students is taken into account. Even more important was the simple affirmation that schools *do* matter and can affect pupils beneficially. This positive effect happens despite severe social disadvantage among individuals in school catchment areas. In other words, school effects are owed to schools and teachers, and not to covert factors such as parental attitudes, degree of affluence or dominant type of linguistic code.

Contributory factors to differences between schools had also begun to emerge. Rutter *et al.*'s (1979) findings revealed which school variables are associated with good behaviour and attainment and which are not. Taken as a whole, main features of schools linked to their success make a formidable list. They include teachers starting lessons on time, praising and rewarding pupils consistently, making explicit the academic content of lessons, setting homework systematically to consolidate learning, arranging good learning and leisure conditions for pupils. What also matters are the extent to which pupils are able to take responsibility for their own learning and the life of the school as a whole (Rutter *et al.* 1979). Mortimore *et al.* (1988), in their turn, were able to isolate factors responsible for effective schooling just as compelling for teachers as those of Rutter. These include the purposeful leadership of staff by the headteacher, the involvement of the deputy head and other teachers, and (significantly) a number of very specific teaching factors. Plaudits are earned by teachers who use a consistency of teaching methods, structure teaching sessions, are intellectually challenging, organise a work-centred environment, keep a limited curricular focus within sessions and communicate well with their pupils, keep high quality records, believe in parental involvement and ensure a positive school climate (Mortimore *et al.* 1988: 250).

Such findings were replicated and extended in North America, the UK, the Netherlands and Australia. The 'effectiveness movement' had arrived, world-wide, though its base remained in the west. In the UK, a new mood of public optimism about schools and their general social roles was bolstered by the researchers themselves, their supporters and the politicians who hoped to capitalise on the early, positive research findings. Teddlie and Reynolds (2000: 4) wonder whether the bewildering number of summaries of school effectiveness findings which ultimately resulted, published in a very short space of time, hint that its development became a modern obsession, a *zeitgeist* of present-day educational enquiry. North America seemed to be a particular favourable location for studies in educational effectiveness. The briefest reviews of the literature would have to respect the work of Anderson (1982), Averch *et al.* (1971), Purkey and Smith (1983), Rosenholtz (1985), Stringfield and Herman (1995, 1996) and Teddlie and Stringfield (1993). Notably, however, many of these summaries concentrate on the first twenty years of effectiveness research – during the period from 1966 to 1985. Bosker and Witziers (1996) hypothesise that, since the mid-1980s, school effectiveness researchers have been much less active in North America than in the UK and Netherlands.

This recent falling away of American enthusiasm may well be more than a straw in the wind to be blown away by the first return of research interest. It can be traced to a number of factors, including scathing criticisms of the whole tradition (see, for instance, Cuban 1993), a growing preference for applied research and a decline in educational research funding during the late 1980s and early 1990s (Teddlie and Reynolds 2000: 13). In other parts of the world, effectiveness research has continued to flourish. Eminent reviews of the UK literature are available in the work of Gray and Wilcox (1995), Mortimore (1998a) and Sammons (1999). In the Netherlands the work of Knuver and Brandsma (1993), Scheerens (1992), Scheerens and Creemers (1995) and Scheerens and Bosker (1997) stands out. In Australia, the influence of Caldwell and Spinks (1988) gave impetus to studies of interrelationship between school effectiveness and learning skills of self-management (see Caldwell and Spinks 1998; Townsend 1997). In the UK, the movement took out a new lease of life by metamorphosing into 'school improvement' programmes.

The rise of school 'improvement'

To keep the tide flowing in its favour, a plethora of international research projects implemented during the 1990s used increasingly sophisticated techniques, hoping to refine its findings at school level. Yet factors first observed by Rutter and Mortimore and their researchers continued to emerge with tantalising consistency. For instance, more recent UK research produced startlingly similar lists of conditions upon which high quality teaching and learning appear contingent (Alexander 1992; Barber *et al.* 1995; Sammons *et al.* 1995). Indeed, the most compelling fact about school effectiveness research is the remarkable consistency of its findings over time and across different cultural contexts. Such consistency is on the face of it a virtue. Replicated findings across environments suggest that underlying truths about schooling have been glimpsed. But it is also a weakness. The problem with almost all these research findings – especially those which list desirable elements of school management and organisation – is that they are both too descriptive and too normative (Ouston 1999). As stressed earlier (Chapter 3), they almost always tell us something about the nature of institutions and organisation by reminding us of why we organise them in the ways we do. It is of little surprise that good schools have good leaders and that the staff of successful schools work together. This is not really what we need to know. What should occupy us is devising the means by which institutions can develop such desirable features.

It is partly as a response to this sort of criticism that many researchers have chosen to pursue the related but divergent path of school improvement. That is, the two types of research are not antithetical, for (as often stated) whereas school effectiveness seeks to tell us the *what* of change, school improvement tells us the *how* of change (Stoll and Fink 1996). However, there are differences between researchers trying to define 'improvement', in their varying stances towards change itself in terms of its role regarding educational outcomes (Duncan 1999). For example: in the formulation set out by Hopkins *et al.* (1994), what most marks out school improvements are their effects on pupils. Hopkins *et al.*'s aim is to bring about closer links between changes within school organisations and classrooms. This postulating of a complex relationship between institutional constructs and learning processes recurs in much recent well-reviewed work in the UK (MacGilchrist *et al.* 1997; Stoll and Fink 1996). Gray *et al.* (1996) remark that the gap between the two traditions of effectiveness and improvement is beginning to close. Increasingly, researchers are drawing on both traditions to find out how to help schools make desirable changes (Mortimore 1998b; Teddlie and Reynolds 2000).

To summarise so far: school effectiveness research has sought to identify what makes schools more likely to reach academic goals regardless of social class or intake and other variables. School improvement studies have sought to help schools develop those positive virtues and qualities with which effectiveness researchers have made us familiar, so that schools can aim at specified goals (White 1997: 30). It would be a fair defence of each tradition to say that anyone wishing to improve the quality of teaching in schools needs to examine both together, and regard them as complementary in what they tell us. But, as it happens, neither a clear differentiation between the two movements, nor their complementarity, saves them from ever-growing and ever sharper critiques.

Critiques of the school effectiveness movement: calculating the role of social factors in teaching success

Despite, or perhaps because of its foundations in positivist inquiry, the school effectiveness movement has been subject to accusations of methodological inadequacy. Looking at Rutter *et al.*'s (1979) work, which has attained almost mythical status among many educators, Heath and Clifford say that its findings suggest little more than 'all things being equal, bright, clean, well-ordered schools promote the production of well-behaved pupils with high academic attainment' (Heath and Clifford 1980: 3). Nevertheless (and perhaps ironically), it is a resurgent sociological campaign which may in the end reverse the ascendancy of school effectiveness and improvement programmes (Mac an Ghaill 1996: 163). This campaign is dedicated to attempts to 're-connect that which has become disconnected – the relation between sociology of education, social class, state schooling and inequalities' (Mac an Ghaill 1996: 164). From the viewpoint of this reworking of staple sociological themes, the effectiveness improvement texts are seen as 'innocent of class relations' (1996: 165). Such an indictment returns educational debate with a vengeance to the disputatious controversies of the 1970s.

For some, the eradicating of social class as a dominant paradigm in representing school achievements is part of the wider erasure of social class from sociology as a whole (Wood 1986). Contemporary analyses of society in terms of social class have largely been abandoned in favour of descriptive measures of social status (Ainley 1993: 1). As Mac an Ghaill (1996: 169) reminds us, earlier critical sociologists of education named schooling itself as a social, cultural and political process, a fact ignored by the currently dominant perspective on school effectiveness (Angus 1993: 334). Schools may at one and the same time 'reproduce' wider social relations that rationalise working-class failure while acting in the best known publicly sponsored way to enhance social mobility (Ozga 1988).

The grandiose claims of effectiveness and improvement research are coming under searching and largely hostile sociological scrutiny. As Chitty (1997: 58) tells us, calculations suggest that school effectiveness factors can account for only between 8 and 15 per cent (Reynolds 1992) or 10 to 15 per cent (Brown *et al.* 1995: 10) of differences between pupils' attainment. Indeed Brown *et al.* (1995) insist on 'the fundamental importance of social class'. They name 'the population served by the school [as] the central source of the concerns that have to be taken into account in making decisions for improvement' (1995: 13). This claim is supported by Benn and Chitty's (1996) large-scale survey of schools and colleges which also found socio-economic background to be a primary determinant of school achievement (see also Marshall 2001; Mortimore and Whitty 1997).

Critics, therefore, base their attacks on much hard evidence as well as on a revival of 'old-style' sociology. This is not to forget that in high-lighting that schools can assist social mobility and social outcome for individuals, if only to a limited extent, the effectiveness movement at least begins to counter the pernicious 'deficiency' thesis which condemns working-class students to failure, just because of their socio-economic origins. But in so doing, it swings us too far to another extreme. It fails to acknowledge necessary social preconditions for teaching success, inside and outside school (Mac an Ghaill 1996: 169). Worse, 'reductionist' notions of schooling like those which rely on generics encourage a similar reliance on 'technicist' approaches to school-management which reject or exclude more sophisticated notions. This is not to suggest that effectiveness and improvement readings deny altogether the profound effects of social class on outcome. But despite the fact that measures of social class correlate strongly with school achievement and measures of achievement underpin most school effectiveness studies (Brown *et al.* 1995: 12), much effectiveness literature views social class as an index of disadvantage (Angus 1993).

One cannot, wholly, reject positive spin-offs from effectiveness and improvement studies. They have, as said, been successfully used to challenge orthodoxies with fatalistic notions about the influence of social background on learning outcomes. Only, there is a fairly urgent need, now, to return to the fairly common-sense principle that family background and social origin do have profound effects on how learners achieve in schools. And this principle need not stand in the way of any political ambition to make sure schools provide the best opportunities possible for all pupils, regardless of background. There is nothing wrong with the aspiration to 'add value' to student experiences. But teachers, just as importantly as governments, need to be aware that there is only so much that an education system alone can do.

Political inadequacies

A second attack on the effectiveness and improvement movement concentrates on its failure to locate research in a broader critical policy framework. Its cosy positioning to policy has been described as 'by turns naive and opportunistic, and at worst complicit in a divisive model of schooling' (Fielding 1997: 9). One of the reasons why the movement has assumed a dominant status in recent years is that politicians and other policy-makers have 'made use' of its findings (White 1997: 29). It has become politically bound up with a market-led model, developing a myopic obsession with test scores and external examination results linked to a preoccupation with league-tables which serves to marginalise large numbers of pupils (Fielding 1997: 11). Despite the apparent cross-party investment in the movement (politically speaking), those who align themselves with this critique suggest that such research is being used to lend spurious support to right-wing aspirations.

More precisely, the effectiveness movement 'advocates an approach in which it is assumed that "educational problems" can be fixed by technical means and that inequality is an intra-school affair' (Willmott 1999: 254). These problems are easily remedied as long as teachers and pupils alike

adhere to 'common sense truisms' (Willmott 1999: 254). It is also argued
that the *oeuvre* has caused a substantial rise in school exclusions as schools
seek to slough off those students who do not fit the template of desirable
market characteristics (Fielding 1997; West and Hopkins 1995). Because
of its links with politically engineered reforms, the movement also has a
predisposition to overstate the impact of change on schooling (see, for
instance, Fullan 1993, 1999). But much exploration bears fairly singularly
upon methods of coping with such change rather than on analysing its
origins or effects (Mac an Ghaill 1996: 171).

There is a drift, too, from notions of effectiveness to efficiency (Beare
et al. 1989). The Ofsted school-inspection regime conflates the two concepts without unpacking the complex interrelationships usually existing
between them (Fielding 1997: 11). The point is that schools can be
effective but profoundly inefficient if (in the terminology so frequently
employed) they 'add value' to student experience at unacceptable cost.
Equally, schools can be efficient but ineffective if they arrange schooling
at minimal cost but fail to educate students. One must question the nature
of a school's efficiency if it leads to burgeoning workloads and surveil-
lance for and of teachers (Ball 1990). As Fielding (1997: 12) points out,
any recognition of the 'non-neutral' status of efficiency begs the question
as to whose interests shape the nature and process of work. Market-led
visions of schooling exclude any exploration of the potentially problematic nature of the curriculum. Schoolwork is usually seen as dealing
with a fixed, immutable body of knowledge, with any alterations justified
according to the dominant paradigm of increased effectiveness.

Without too much distortion, the school effectiveness research findings
can be seen as setting the 'ideological legitimations of socially coercive
schooling' (Elliott 1996: 200). Elliott (1997: 63) places the effectiveness
and improvement movements within what he considers one of the dominant educational discourses of advanced modern societies – namely that of
quality assurance. Drawing on the work of Lyotard (1979), he suggests
that to see reflection on education as a form of 'meta-discourse' based
on rationalist foundations and those who take part in it to be 'aloof
arbitrators' is misconceived. Rather, 'we should view the philosophy of
education as the reflexive deconstruction of the dominant mode of educational discourse we are all more or less caught up in' (Elliott 1997: 64).
Any pretence at a rational or scientific objectivity which (for example)
school effectiveness researchers adopt is exactly that. It is a pretence.
They have striven to establish the superiority of their paradigm by

> the dual strategy of excluding dissenting voices in the educational
> community and trying to subordinate qualitative methodologies . . .

> [These have been] co-opted into the service of a school improve-
> ment process defined in terms of performance indicators established
> through school effectiveness research.
>
> (Elliott 1997: 65)

In other words, once administrators have decided what are quality indicators in schools, the only function for researchers is to discover how to
achieve them. Any other ambitions are to be dismissed as subsidiary or
misguided. Elliott's own efforts to improve schools are very different
from those he criticises. Rather like Schon, he mounts action-research
projects framed within 'imaginative constructions' of 'innovative experiments' (Elliott 1997: 81), counteracting the 'victory narrative' dominant
in language of quality assurance which attempts to reach 'consensus by
exclusion' (1997: 82). However, to an extent, Elliott's protests are not
so much aimed at quality assurance as at the new 'idolatry of measure-
ment' which supports it (Fielding 1999: 277), since this invariably
seems to result in the voice of the student being ignored. Duffield *et al.*
(2000) take the same view. They write that although pupil performance
is seen universally as an indicator of school success, pupils' own perceptions find little place in the discourse on standards. Their study found
that relationships between teachers were characterised by the absence
of discussions on learning.

Apart from these matters, the sidelining of long-term educational goals
by researchers has had the effect of marginalising what was once central to
any wider discussions of educational practices (White 1997). In place of
such discussions have arisen policy initiatives, such as 'fresh start' schools,
receiving media approval and financial backing. Unsupported and often
rather facile propositions are taken as likely remedies for school ills –
such as the view that individuals can reconstruct or reinvent schools by
dramatic intervention on the heroic scale. The idea that one individual,
or even group of individuals can, in the common parlance, 'turn a
school around' is superficially attractive but somewhat lacking in plaus-
ability (Chitty 1997: 55). Even the leadership qualities of the headteacher
may be less important than the practical consequences flowing from a
market philosophy leading inevitably to regional disadvantages, 'failing'
schools and educationally disenfranchised groups. Adopting all the practices deemed 'effective' can only take schools so far if they are locked into
a local or national system where a polarisation between social groups is
taking place (Chitty 1997: 56). 'Below certain levels of intake quality . . .
it may be very difficult to be an effective educational institution'
(Reynolds and Reid 1985: 194).

Ball is one of the most trenchant critics of the effectiveness movement, though the language he uses is not always easy to grasp. He argues that 'effectiveness is a technology of normalization. Effectiveness research both constructs a normative model of the effective school and abnormalizes the "ineffective" or "sick" school' (Ball 1995: 260–261).

> Effectiveness studies and school difference studies [re-centre] the school as the focus of causation . . . of student performance and variations in levels of achievement; displacing or rendering silent other explanations related to the embeddedness of education in social and economic contexts.
>
> (Ball 1995: 260)

Thus the school, the process of schooling, the culture of the pupils, and the nature of the community, the society, the economy, are rarely seen in relation to one another.

Or, as Chitty (1997: 56) puts it, effectiveness researchers 'mostly inhabit an homogenized, sanitized world which ignores social and cultural differences and awkward political antagonisms'. By refusing to engage either with wider social or political constructs or to analyse many of the most salient features of classroom life or policy-making, they have contributed to a new and very dubious educational philosophy. This, the philosophy of blanket prescription, not only does injustice to teachers who find themselves unable to follow it, but also it risks harming the very pupils it is most meant to help.

From quality assurance to partnership

The influential model of effectiveness developed by Creemers (1994) has it operating on a number of levels including social context, school, classroom and student. All too often (as discussed on pp. 123–124) it is focused on a quality-assurance driven agenda emphasising external accountability and structural alterations to school management, neglecting the welfare of the classroom and the student. Arguably, we need a manifesto for *educational* rather than school effectiveness (a broader remit which looks outside schools for deeper sorts of change than the purely institutional). The key issues that such a manifesto would address would include:

- an acceptance of the effects of social background on pupil outcomes
- a commitment to a unified approach to social deprivation at the local, regional and national level

- a sharper focus upon pedagogic practice with associated research programmes led by practitioners and theoreticians working in partnership
- true rapprochements between higher education, local authorities, teachers and other caring professionals, and policy-makers.

We lack a national discourse and research effort on teacher effectiveness as vigorous as that on school effectiveness (Muij's and Reynolds 2001). The development of the teacher-focused research strategy by the TTA and the DfEE-sponsored 'Teaching and Learning Research Programme' are welcome signs that such a discourse is on its way. There is some chance, now – given the overwhelming evidence for the failure of 'structural' and managerially focused policies to deal with the really intransigent factors – for achieving lasting school success. We could do worse than heed the advice of researchers such as Mortimore and Whitty (1999: 11) who want politicians to 'bring together partners from across society rather than seeing problems as being solely in the realm of the educational service'.

Mortimore and Whitty (1999) stress the point offered repeatedly in this book that teaching skill, alone, does not guarantee effectiveness. Teachers cannot win tough educational battles unless client groups have the material, cultural, emotional and intellectual resources to fight hard alongside them. The inevitable outcome from such judgements has to be that purely top-down policies whereby 'structural' interventions alter school management policies, or bottom-up (within school) improvement strategies will seldom work. Teachers must reach beyond their own school walls towards the 'local authorities and other caring professions' (Mortimore and Whitty 1999: 12), not just to co-operate with these, but also to learn from them.

Partnership systems are systems where people both work together (e.g. consulting and communicating reciprocally) and compose groupings where they can, when necessary, act as a single agency. To do this, they have to know how to act. Which means being clear-sighted about the hardships that disadvantaged learners actually face. Half the difficulty with teachers persuading pupils whose minds are not on learning tasks (because they are emotionally hijacked by the more pressing matters of physical, social or cultural insecurity) that education might solve their problems is that teachers insufficiently detect such viewpoints. This is hardly surprising, given that they are not superhuman social workers nor do they have mind-reading capabilities. But the realisation that – somehow – teachers have to work harder at understanding views of schools which are, for whatever reason, deviant from that normally expected, fuels partnership methods of teaching.

For example, to make debating controversial issues routine in classrooms might persuade members to open up about their own (perhaps unusual) circumstances. Certainly, it is unrealistic to believe that teaching (however skilled) can in itself transform learners from impoverished backgrounds. The aim must be for teachers to bring whatever ambitions learners already have into increasingly fruitful relationships with others, so that learners transform themselves. That is, teachers who can empathise with learners from backgrounds very different from their own have some chance of introducing new ways of looking at the world, some of which are likely to reap personal rewards for learners. This returns us to the co-constructive paradigm. It doesn't return us to sure-fire success. But it opens the way for what may well be the only route forward with any chance of getting beyond the very limited triumphs of recent political endeavour.

Conclusion: teaching success via partnership

The work of the school effectiveness and improvement movements grew in reaction to overly determinist and pessimistic accounts of schooling that emerged in the 1970s. These accounts revealed that schools never ameliorate the negative effects of social background (Barber 1995). What we, also, learn from both traditions is that effective teaching *can* be developed within any schools and that such developments gain from supportive relationships among staff, pupils, parents and other stakeholders within school communities. What appears to matter is the fostering of a positive, learning-centred culture, where relationships between participants combine, ultimately, within a single, coherent view. It cannot be one where one group 'remedies' or 'turns around' the legitimate aspirations of another, in order to improve a school's position in league-tables say, or prevent a school's failing in standard, Ofsted terms (Marshall 2001).

'Inclusion' policies which work, on this book's argument, will be those where criteria for inclusion (what different groups are included in) are negotiable. We have to get past believing that by getting managerial or curricular structures right, we will bring lost sheep into the educational fold. What we have learned by accepting the limitations of the effectiveness movement, historically speaking, is that factors outside school are frequently, perhaps inevitably, determinants of school outcomes and teaching success. Evidence from relevant studies almost invariably finds the correlation between social class and student outcomes high (see e.g.

Marshall 2001; Nash and Harker 1998). Economic class structure gener-
ates social classes within which families are located and, as a result, families
have access to differential levels of resources, financial, education and
social (Nash 1999: 124).

What is claimed is that other forms of relationship between pupils,
parents, politicians, teachers and others are possible which do not
combat social class cultures but admit their potency. Such partnership
arrangements involve members in a grouping with educational purposes
that encompass those they at present hold (rather than denying them).
These have been discussed as difficult to manage (Chapter 6). But, they
do offer some chance of our putting right a situation where disadvantage
equates with educational failure. This situation (according to commentators such as Marshall 2001), and despite the best efforts of recent
governments, is getting, depressingly, worse rather than better.

9 Achieving excellence

On the face of it, there is fair agreement about what – in general – we mean by excellent teaching. HMI (DfEE 1997), former Chief Inspector Chris Woodhead (Ofsted 1996) and academics writing about pedagogy (Alexander 1998; Sutton *et al.* 2000; Turner-Bisset 2000) decide that the best classroom practice does two things. Unfailingly, teachers make as sure as possible that pupils hit important learning targets (pass exams and so forth). At the same time, they strive to arouse committed interests and enthusiasms in learners over the longer term. Teachers, these days, must 'prepare for lifelong learning and the world of work' (Alexander 1998: 65), rather than settle for lesser ambitions. Our best schools will be those which lay foundations for pupils' professional and vocational futures as well as taking them to thresholds of personal fulfilment.

At first, such a picture appears slightly at odds with standard teaching models, as these have been described. Such models are usually oriented towards knowledge-delivery and formal exams (Chapter 3), to persona-lised knowledge construction (Chapter 4) or to forms of collaborative learning (Chapters 5 and 6). Yet these models counsel bias ('orientation') not exclusive preoccupations. And they do so for good reason. To believe 'high culture' is a mainstay for schools (Gingell and Brandon 2000; O'Hear 1987; Winch and Gingell 1996) is to believe it enriches pupils minds while it prepares them for formal exams. It isn't inapplicable to per-sonal life-styles and pastimes, it is timeless in what it has to offer (Rossbach 2000). And although learner-centred thinkers and those committed to democracy in schools (e.g. Kelly 1995) denounce curricular prescription in favour of 'processes', they are unlikely to deny that exams and tests have their place in teaching. On the contrary, enskilling pupils as inde-pendent or collaborative learners should widen their scope for taking tests as for self-improvement. So commentators differ in *how* they think teachers can realise everyone's dream of a learning society, occupationally skilled and economically profitable as well as culturally rich. They don't part company much on the equivalent (though not always equal) desirability of reaching instrumental and expressive goals.

Yet questions about what makes for an 'excellent' or efficient learner do occupy writers who trade in teaching models, earmarking competing concepts of education discussed in earlier chapters. Being crucial educational questions, they, naturally, bring controversies with them – of a practical as well as theoretical nature. 'What is it that gives pupils control over "narrow" exam skills while also embedding worthwhile, satisfying interests to sustain them throughout their lives?' is a practical, classroom question par excellence. And despite the fact that theoretical battles constantly rage over it, we may well find that quality teaching cannot be designed at all without our having some answers we can rely on without too much ambiguity or qualification.

What is 'excellent learning'? The problem of balance

Teachers' brief to guarantee pupils' personal, social and cultural development as well as to hit curricular and exam targets represents a tall order for them. And recent legislation binding schools to exam targets rather than to enthusing pupils about the 'broad and balanced' curriculum can be regarded as a somewhat unhelpful streamlining exercise, given that teaching does have expressive as well as instrumental aims. Indeed, it is exactly such policy-contradictions which have earned the most scathing criticisms from commentators (e.g. Alexander 1998; Broadfoot 2000; Davis 1999; Silcock 1999; Silcock and Duncan 2001; Silcock and Wyness 2000; Turner-Bisset 2000). Broadfoot (2000: 103), for example, rams home her point that a preoccupation with target-hitting and summative testing means that 'questions which focus on how . . . [learner] performance can most effectively be encouraged go not only unheard but even *unthought*' (her italics). She wants to replace an obsession with measuring capacity to exploring the diverse ways in which pupils learn effectively in classrooms.

One suspects that policy-makers won't be diverted from test-driven curricula by such complaints. Probably, they believe that students' short-term losses in enthusiasm are usually recouped over time. If learners, alone, judge what is or is not personally satisfying, whether test-driven curricula herald longer-term fulfilment may have nothing to do with the curricula themselves, but may chiefly reflect students' own attitudes to their studies. Certainly, student purposes and attitudes are critical variables in the educational equation as will be seen. However, we already have good grounds for believing that modern-day learners find scaling both summits of educational excellence – formal (public) performance and individual (personal) fulfilment – difficult. To consider, again, whether anything can be done, on both counts, it is worth, briefly, isolating some main points of argument.

As Davis (1995, 1998, 1999) puts it, pupils working towards standard targets in set ways (e.g. as laid down by UK national literacy and numeracy strategies) cannot assimilate learning to that more personal knowledge allowing wider application. Prescriptive teaching leads pupils towards narrow procedural goals rather than towards knowledge and understanding. This is true because teachers following set procedures cannot, at the same time, adapt their actions to individual learners. Targeted work by its nature is not geared to comprehension, it is geared to technical knowhow needed for success in exams. Davis (1995) believes that making criterion assessments reliable (skills being fairly tested across schools and localities) has to diminish their validity (in terms of what pupils actually know and understand). Pupils will not understand work being tested exactly in so far as they cannot reconcile and integrate it with their more personal, 'richly textured' conceptual systems (see also White 1999).

Davis's (1995) argument is part of the broader case (put earlier) showing why school-learners tend either to be enthused by personally relevant projects or strive towards criterion-based, standard assessments. It isn't that pupils can't learn in different ways at different times. But educational policies *persistently* striving for skills' training and exam success are different, by nature, from those enriching and extending pupils' familiar experiences. Policy-makers, it seems, like teachers and academics, fall prey to the paradigm-clash which bars our way to the upper reaches of educational excellence.

Still, the point of returning, yet again, to this impasse is to rediscover (and better understand) how to avoid its worst effects. Without recanting on agreed contradictions met by anyone teaching exam skills while helping learners follow their own agendas, there is a let-out clause in the experience-based case, as outlined. Experience, itself, is not some immovable rock on which all learning must be founded. To figure in conceptual growth, both concrete and social experiences have to be symbolically interpreted and reinterpreted by individuals in diverse ways. How learners interpret experience is up to them – it will depend to an extent on their purposes. Moreover, the symbolic framing of experience (largely linguistic) will be derived from 'standard' sources. In other words, although personal experience is the fertile soil for all intellectual change, the plants of knowledge which grow from it do not grow naturally – they have to be cultivated by learners, aided by others. Bereiter and Scardamalia (1993) point out how, with advanced forms of writing, pupils do not merely report their thinking but rework it, restructuring their minds. The process engaged is aided by students learning a formal language (i.e. of science, maths etc.) which can, then, be tested, provided we do attend at some time to both things – uniquely gained experiences and a formally learned language. Whether there is interchange between the two is not so much dependent on the texturing of pupils' minds at any one time, but on whether or how experiences can, over a period, be adapted to agreed purposes.

This qualifying argument does not dodge the thrust of Davis's (1995) case. For there always remains the need for teachers to respect learners' responses to task while they proceed (which they cannot do, as he says, while they teach in strictly defined ways: Davis 1999). Only, sometimes, 'respecting' is not so much a concession to individual 'need' as one of gradually bridging between what is individually known and what is publicly valued. Although there is a 'gap' between standard and unique attainments it is not one in principle unbridgeable. It is possible for students' experiences of (say) the natural world, or a favourite literature to be rethought in dual (i.e. personal and formal) ways, allowing transfer from broadly personal to narrower public settings such as scientific or literacy studies and vice versa.

This conclusion reinvigorates our trying to reach what are otherwise seen as mutually exclusive goals. It does so by recasting the issue as one not of trying to reconcile contradictory types of teaching and learning but of seeking to teach learners so that they can, themselves, flexibly 'transfer' whatever they learn from situation to situation.

Excellent learning is transferable learning: escaping classrooms

Sticking to terms introduced, excellent learners are those who 'transfer' their knowledge and skills from home to school, school to home, personal to public domains, and so on. Those who write about learning application and transfer agree (Bereiter 2000; Desforges and Lings 1998; Georghiades 2000; Lings and Desforges 1999; Perkins and Salomon 1989; Resnick 1987; Resnick and Neches 1984). Knowledge-application (involving transfer) has been called the 'holy grail' of education (Desforges and Lings 1998, citing Resnick 1987) because these outcomes are exactly those confirming how teachers prepare pupils for life outside the school gates. School-learning must be transferable for education to happen at all (by definition). It must extend into life-skills – which implies students will, also, import personal enthusiasms into their schoolwork.

As it happens, evidence suggests that transfer, though possible, is not easily managed (Georghiades 2000; Perkins and Salomon 1989). Problems already met when wishing pupils to enlighten their own lives through school-lessons are more than confirmed by cognitive theorists working in this area. Dishearteningly, these problems often rearise as more complex when stated as problems of transfer, for, apparently, it isn't, just, arid exam-oriented work which doesn't easily fit out-of-school contexts, most schoolwork (however much pupils enjoy it) tends to be school-bound. What is slightly more encouraging is that there is fair agreement among writers as to the reasons why school-learning is situation-specific; though there is less agreement about how teachers can deal with such specificity in the light of what is known about it.

Looking at one or two theories in some depth helps us recognise these problems while glimpsing possible ways in which learners can bridge between personal and public circumstances. Bereiter (2000), for example, believes that 'knowledge-building' is the way pupils free themselves from institutions to win wider attainments. Knowledge-building, as he describes it, follows a developmental continuum from 'unconscious learning in early childhood . . . to . . . inquiry that is focused on World 3 objects' (Bereiter 2000: 80). 'World 3' objects are abstract ideas which exist only in human thinking – i.e. in linguistic or scholarship form. Knowledge-building takes students from personal (grounded) experience to those ideas schools embed in advanced curricula which can be applied more universally. Bereiter separates learners whose flexible attitudes let them flourish in distinct environments from those who cannot, making this separation the core of his theory.

He cites two maths students whose work he studied. Both knew their mathematics. But whereas one could transfer symbolically framed ideas between contexts, the other could only apply skills she had gleaned from teaching and could not transfer what she certainly knew, even between arithmetic and algebra. Bereiter connects his observations to Resnick and Neches's (1984) research into maths teaching which finds that pupils typically learn computational skills they cannot combine to solve 'real-life' problems. His diagnosis is not that the two students he studied differ in innate capacity though they differ in their conceptual and symbolic skills. What separates them most are the conscious purposes they have acquired relative to the settings where they work.

One student simply cannot see beyond classrooms, where she has learned to deal with tasks in set ways. She is imprisoned by her own limited awareness. She isn't so much building knowledge conceptually as fashioning procedural skills (she can't see beyond simply getting her maths 'right'). The second glimpses a different sort of end. She has acquired a 'personal agenda' (as Bereiter 2000: 78 puts it) which takes her imagination beyond school boundaries and entails her developing a mental symbolism applicable to out-of-school settings. She has mastered 'intentional learning' (Bereiter and Scardamalia 1989) which means she deliberates over longer-term, personal goals which, themselves, require abstract types of thinking transcending concrete tasks.

The issue, then, for Bereiter, is one of type of consciousness that learners have of the nature of school learning and what it is for. He proposes that for teachers to get students to move from known to unknown (knowledge-building rather than, simply, knowledge-acquisition), they must first raise students' awareness of where they are being routed. He probably realises (though he doesn't say) that there is something of a 'chicken–egg' difficulty here, as cognitive development is usually thought to give as well as require consciousness of the purposes of such activity. Feasibly, teachers can pass on something about the wider uses of 'knowledge objects' apart from their narrow functions within school-based curricula. Pupils will transfer their learning from situation to situation where they grasp these uses, freeing themselves from school-bound studies. Bereiter is supposing a conscious dimension separate from the organisation of concepts which frames how the concepts will be used, and how they will function to regulate further concepts.

Desforges and Lings (1998) have similar theories (see also Lings and Desforges 1999). Their 'ideal' learner, too, is someone who can apply ideas within diverse settings since they agree this criterion indicates depth and relevance of understanding. They also fix the problem for teachers as one of students having a mind-set whereby what they learn is applicable only in schools (see also Paechter 1998). People can have a sort of tunnel vision about what is being taught. Desforges and Lings think the answer lies in the 'modularisation' of knowledge (how it is framed). With suitable modularisation (a wider framing of what is learned), students will come to see outside the narrow confines of institutions and academic studies.

Relevant to their theorising, Lings and Desforges (1999) interviewed primary age pupils. They found these children uniformly unable to separate ways of applying historical, scientific, literary knowledge (presumably the point of separating a school curriculum into subject areas). Children interviewed thought the main point of school-learning was to deal with classroom or homework routines. The broader roles of science, the humanities and the arts in the outside world, apparently, passed them by. These distinct 'ways of knowing' (as Lings and Desforges call them) didn't figure much, if at all, in pupils' minds. School subjects consisted of fairly undifferentiated tasks to be tackled with varying degrees of skill. Lings and Desforges generalise that curricula will stay school-bound unless they are, somehow, reconnected to wider environments; though their project leaves us a trifle pessimistic about teachers managing this.

Fairly unanimously, it seems, writers agree that learners have to move beyond the confines of institutionalised life to realise that school-learning can be applied elsewhere (see also Georghiades 2000; Strike and Posner 1985). Although few explore in detail how to make such escape from the immediate possible, this is because their focus on application and transfer is sufficiently challenging in itself to occupy them. Their practical recommendations are certainly pertinent. Bereiter and Lings and Desforges make the problem largely one of students' attitudes to context. They place store on raising teacher-awareness so as to raise learner-awareness. Some way of widening students' horizons is required (in Bereiter's case by students' building from the familiar to the unfamiliar intentionally, so as to forge symbolic means for applying ideas and skills).

Another way of putting this is to say that the theories cited propose a fairly top-down solution to giving learners more bottom-up control of their own minds. Obviously, they may be right to do so. A clear stating of a problem can bring in its train one or more solution(s), and there is no contradiction in stating it is adult actions which liberate (or not) children as flexible learners. What is suggested, nonetheless, is that we need to detail better that process freeing learners from institutional contexts found in both the above writers' treatment of issues, related to an individual's purposive awareness. Once we have such detailing under wraps, we just might be able to deliver, in schools, the capacity for learning transfer which is the holy grail of educational achievement.

Excellent learning: learning transfer in schools

What makes learning transferable? Technically, it isn't hard to state criteria. Georghiades (2000) lists four requirements:

> a) recognition of similarity of the two contexts, b) acknowledgment of the potential of a certain skill or conception that has worked in the past to give solutions to a new problematic situation, c) mental testing of the applicability of the potential solution and d) an attempt to apply the skill or conception to a new context.
>
> (Georghiades 2000: 123)

But these criteria are built in to the business of knowledge-transfer itself (anyone must engage with them during transfer). What remains uncertain is why some pupils fulfil these conditions and some do not. Ultimately, Georghiades (2000: 127ff) pins his faith on 'metacognitive' awareness. Once students can monitor the activity of their own minds there is a chance they will, then, think across environments. He advocates 'cognitive conflict' as a means to stimulate learners into self-monitoring through a regular reconciling of conflicting perspectives, noticing that just to advocate knowledge-building alone leaves learners with existing misconceptions (see Chapters 5 and 6). Only through testing new ideas against conflicting views do they have any chance of reaching that principled status which brings mental flexibility.

Georghiades' (2000) affirming of a layer of awareness as critical brings his theories into line with those of Bereiter (2000) and Lings and Desforges (1999), who, as described, also take students' controlling purposes as important. But Georghiades' developmental stance allows him to go a little further than other writers. Along with neo-Piagetians such as Adey and Shayer (1994, 1996), Resnick (1985, 1987) and so on (see Chapters 5 and 6), he sees learning transfer as, actually, part of any learning which produces conceptual change – it isn't an extra ingredient added to more basic capacity. He reminds us that Adey and Shayer's (1994) CASE (Cognitive Acceleration through Science Education) technique of asking students to defend their ideas against criticism from others gives them a controlling 'overview' of science. So it also helps them transfer their knowledge to other circumstances (such as exam situations). He is sure that 'Effective CCL [conceptual change learning] . . . cannot be considered achieved, unless ability to transfer new conceptions has been established' (Georghiades 2000: 123).

Georghiades' work suggests we might understand learning transfer better if we look at what is actually going on during much intellectual progress – seeing, it is hoped, why transfer sometimes happens and sometimes does not. To agree with his point, it is timely, now, to remind ourselves of this book's broader argument. It was earlier claimed that different kinds of learning (including achieving transfer) are products of different situations, including different ways of teaching (Chapter 6). We can state a little more clearly what such situations are. Bereiter (2000), for example, does not think they are basically 'experiential'. He mildly reproves progressivists for 'having learning come about naturally through the social life of the community' when this will not naturally facilitate knowledge 'of an abstract or theoretical nature' (2000: 80). Counter to progressivist thinking, he believes that students succeed at knowledge-building where they are aware of what the enterprise involves – what matters is learners' relationship with their own learning rather than how it occurs.

Yet what was noted was that such criticisms hinge on how we regard 'experience': learner-centred teachers may see experience only as an absolute limitation, conceding that any single experience can be interpreted (i.e. symbolically) in a variety of ways. So agreeing that knowledge gained 'naturally' may never fully equate with school knowledge does not entirely remove the role of 'naturally' gained knowledge. Building on what is known must, somewhere, mean building on what we learn in the normal course of our lives. If we recall Bereiter's point that students learn to transfer understanding in the light of their purposes, it was thought worth speculating whether purpose and understanding (built experientially) might not actually amount to the same thing. It may not be so much that the former produces the latter, since to see the way knowledge transfer works beneficially for us is by the same token to have mental flexibility. Wider purposes (than just solving specified problems) and flexibility of thinking are different destinations, but they do presume each other. We may find that we arrive at both destinations on the same bus, so to speak. What we need to know is where to catch the bus! We must know the sort of experiences likely to bring both the 'mindful', purposive awareness and the capability for knowledge-transfer (i.e. a type of cognitive development generated by a particular way of teaching).

To get to the point: these experiences are – it is suggested – more than those of school-learning as this is normally arranged. Earlier chapters pointed out how 'knowledge-building' means more than moving from known to unknown. Bereiter's pervading image of 'building' can mislead in its suggesting a one-way upward progression, a placing of one 'brick' (one 'knowledge object') onto another. These metaphors don't at all capture the *two-way* transformations which happen with radical manoeuvres we find in knowledge-transfer. That is: although to gain new concepts we must interpret them in terms of what we already know, once we do so, we will grasp what we already know differently.

Fundamental conceptual change which builds distinct levels of understanding is always a two-way transfer (an applying what one knows to familiar as well as new contexts by means of flexible thinking). It isn't only that we apply what we know to what we don't know. There is a reverse-transfer, whereby we grasp, better, what we previously knew. This contention is visible enough in ideas such as 'conceptual change' which say that mental improvements happen not by building new ideas on old but by giving up present ideas to accord with new circumstances. Its full implications are seldom realised because writers tend to fix on (for them) more salient issues – such as the effect of context on transfer or the role of intentionality in conceptual change.

In fact, the concepts 'knowledge transfer' and 'knowledge application', too, can mislead. For they imply that we take what we already know to a new setting and 'apply' it, benefiting from what is newly revealed. But knowledge-transfer is never just that. If I 'apply' Shakespearian lessons to modern times and realise better, say, something about the tragedy of human relationships, I am not only improving my knowledge of relationships, but also tightening my mental grasp on Shakespearian drama. The oft-repeated example (e.g. in Desforges and Lings 1998) of mathematically wise, child street traders being poor at school mathematics is usually presented as one of their not shifting wisdom from one place to another. But if such children were to become mathematically competent in school, they would also become different sorts of street traders (perhaps, initially, less sure of their skills).

Much depends on this fairly obvious point. For it helps us see that to transfer ideas, in practice, demands two things. Students must grasp relevant features of the two contexts concerned, and they must see a way of conceiving their expertise relative to both (i.e. not just applying it to the novel setting). That is, it isn't enough for students to see – for example – that mathematics can be applied practically (commonly taught in schools). They have to grasp how practical maths also transforms the theoretical (two-way thinking is implied). Anyone who can transfer mathematical knowledge between settings not only sees how to apply maths to concrete problems but also grasps something about the nature of mathematics. This is, partly, why teaching was revolutionised by Piaget's research on children's misconceptions of maths and science, and why his ideas still hold a deal of sway in these areas. Children may talk about the way gravity affects objects they have played with, yet still not see how to generalise the scientific rule, because their underlying conceptual assumptions are unchanged. And until these assumptions are changed, not only will they be unable to transfer their scientific knowledge – simply because they will not understand the principle which is transferable – but also they will make slow progress in their development as scientists.

A little thought confirms that if students really know that a mathematical computation applies in the real world, they also know that objects in the real world are represented by mathematical formulae. But such awareness does not inevitably follow from pupils becoming familiar with out-of-school settings. It really isn't just a question of students or teachers (or both) becoming sensitised to the nature and purposes of knowledge and skill. Pupils given lots of practical experiences of mathematical application may still think inflexibly, not through lack of first-hand experience or lack of purpose. They may simply not grasp the principle bridging contexts (they are working from old, faulty templates). School-learning so easily becomes one-way, or one-dimensional learning where pupils are led from known to unknown without sufficient thought given to how what is being learned is affecting existing assumptions. And the point is that it may not *be* affecting existing assumptions at all (because pupils' preoccupations are elsewhere and the knowledge acquired makes little impact on their real concerns).

Bereiter's, Desforges and Ling's, Georghiades' and Paechter's convergent point on the power of context to constrain transfer is well taken in what has been said. Schools easily become places for one-way learning (moving from one state of ignorance to another, without pupils ever fully understanding anything). This happens because there would appear to be two critical moments of knowledge-transfer which conquer situation (or 'situatedness' as Bereiter sees it). And this is not at bottom an issue of what sort of situation we choose or how clearly what is taught is shown to apply widely – i.e. it is not only or even, perhaps, basically a modularisation matter.

What makes the difference is likely to be this. The altering of an existing view is not the same as applying learned knowledge differently. The former asks us for a self-engagement in a way the latter does not. We can judge that what boosts the quality of school-learning is not merely how students initially frame knowledge as how they relate to it personally (experientially) and how confident they feel in their own judgements. Put this way, we see that there is an emotional dimension to knowledge-transfer (in fact to qualitative conceptual change generally) which is easily missed (see Georghiades 2000: 121). Giving up an existing idea is often hard, for this implies a self-reflection marked by our treating what we already know as always provisional and vulnerable to the new. Recalling that experience is never a permanent halter on learning, the optimistic point is that pupils *can* move to a different view, provided they are convinced that it really does place them in a surer position than before.

Cognitive development engages our most personal attitudes to ourselves and to our existing knowledge: the intellectual and the emotional are married in key instances of learning. Students differ in how comfortable they are with themselves. So they will differ in how far they can rehearse conflicting scenarios regarding what is learned, rather than just accept whatever they are taught. But it is perfectly possible to teach using an approach which helps learners treat themselves and their existing learning as staging-posts to other things, rather than fixed positions which they must defend at all costs. In short, knowledge-transfer is reinterpreted as a dual transformation. It is never just a one-way transformation (as often mistakenly seen because that's what the term implies) where what is already known illuminates a novel circumstance. On the contrary, learners forging ahead in school deploy cross-perspective taking – they take sightings of what is familiar from the perspective of what is unfamiliar, and vice versa. They move easily between positions, exercising both critical (of others) and self-critical (taking the viewpoint of others) thinking. It is rarely just one or the other. And knowledge-transfer is, on this analysis, a particular form of qualitative structural change involved in significant intellectual improvements (as Georghiades says it is). But it need not occur. And usually – in schools anyhow – it does not.

The axiomatic role of this principle is such that education itself can be thought at bottom an instance of it – i.e. a dual transformation whereby learners interpret new meanings in terms of old, in order that the new should transform the old (Silcock 1999). Education is a gradual modifying of a culture by learners in personal ways, to allow the resulting awareness to transform (i.e. educate) them. Effectively, as argued throughout prior chapters, such a dual transformation is effected (and can only be effected) by the cross-perspective taking of co-constructive learning. It can also, we now see, usefully be restyled a form of 'contextual co-ordination'. That is, it is paramountly a bringing together of what were formerly different situations (such as homes and schools, personal and public) such that relevant features are co-extensive.

To summarise, via a last example of cross-perspective taking (resulting in contextual co-ordination or knowledge-transfer): once I have come to see the historical background of – say – the growth of London as a city, my experiences of London (as someone living or simply visiting there) should change. In so far as they do, history becomes a living subject and the two otherwise disparate 'places' (a physically enduring city and an abstractly conceived subject) are bridged. Chapter 6 earlier introduced this topic by suggesting that different models of teaching had different knowledge outputs. What has been added is that the reason co-constructive teaching outputs a distinct epistemology is that it engages, by nature, contextual co-ordination which brings with it conceptual change. It gives a flexibility to our thinking contrasting forcibly with the inflexibility of ideas gained stipulatively or as integral to a purely personal (possibly idiosyncratic) interest. In each of these latter two circumstances, what we learn is grasped within one setting (the public or the personal). Transferable learning has to be grasped from dual perspectives, locked into whatever disparate circumstances need to be allied.

Basics of excellent teaching: confirming the co-constructive option

If we take excellent teaching as that which gives us cross-perspective taking (from examined public or standardised knowledge to those personal insights we find satisfying in our lives and vice versa), we will see co-constructive teaching as the best bet we have to deliver it. Teachers who bridge from personal to public and back again take stances which essentially ask them to take two factors into account as they teach. They will ensure learners make full sense of their private experiences (from a school point of view) and, conversely, that they make full sense of school knowledge from a perspective of personal interest. That is, they will co-ordinate (support or 'scaffold') not only pupils' thinking and problem-solving but also pupils' attitudes and purposes.

The main practical claim is that the two-way transactions of learning transfer are not just cognitive, they involve emotional transactions. Learners anticipating new ideas while revising old ones must trust the teaching/learning situation. They must think outcomes will be a successful one for them – relative to their own ambitions, the way they feel about themselves, and so forth. At exam time, this trust will often be tested to breaking point. And although the principle of reciprocal-transfer works just as well with exam circumstances as any other, we must be cautious when dealing with such matters about expecting too much from teaching. What teachers must do, essentially, is hardly controversial. They have to focus pupils' minds on the relevance of test-driven curricula for pupils' personal ambitions and so foster positive attitudes. By coming to view exams in personal terms and thereby getting a better idea of how tests can help them achieve their aspirations, students are led, unerringly, into the type of mind-set they almost certainly need when preparing for tests (and the one which policy-makers expect). But they may also be led into seeing that their chances of success are poor or even non-existent. Two-way thinking may be essential for cognitive change and learning transfer. It may also be emotionally destructive for those who, then, see the real depth of failure revealed by what is brought into view.

One of the reasons why one-way learning happens so often in life (and is endemic in schools) is probably that it makes learning possible for us which does not threaten personal change. Potential repercussions from taking on-board burdens we cannot easily tolerate are minimised. So, we will deploy such strategies to safeguard identities we cherish. After a while, it may happen that we become incapable of applying what we learn reflectively simply because our emotional investments have become lodged elsewhere. To repeat this in common-sense terms:

learners can reject school just because they realise that what it mainly has to offer (the possibility of exam success) is largely or wholly beyond their reach. Such an outcome should not stop teachers from using a co-constructive approach (which gives them the only chance they have of succeeding). All it means is that whether or not they are successful will not be decided only by their teaching (a possibility rehearsed in Chapter 8).

One extra point is worth making. The need for learners to review experiences in terms of new learning has been aired. But in the light of this chapter's study, it is evident that the concept we tend to have of schooling whereby learners 'move forward' relentlessly towards ever more desirable goals needs burnishing into a very different ideal. Quality school-learning is never be a relentless moving forward to ever 'truer' positions, but is invariably the tentative creation of a possible future in terms of a newly interpreted past, and the past in terms of a potentially brighter future. Naturally, one is not suggesting that new learning must always involve the turgid revisiting of old learning, but that the inter-action between known and unknown should be commonplace – as it is in democratic classrooms. Where pupils are hypothesising, testing, discussing and debating from an established position, they are – neces-sarily – encountering what is new from stances that will change as they move forward. Such encounters should become routine, making intellec-tual development happen as cross-transformations (allowing knowledge-transfer) and not just as school-'situated', one-way knowledge-building.

Excellent teaching: are there hidden features?

We might, yet, expect more of excellent teachers than that they work co-constructively as this has already been discussed. We might expect them to integrate and deploy their skills and techniques in ways especially suited to the localities in which schools are set (Chapter 5). But, as it turns out, this is no more than to reshape contextual co-ordination as co-constructive teaching. Good co-constructive teachers cannot do otherwise than bring together homes and schools in partnership. We might expect a real commitment to democratic, egalitarian principles over and above that expected of any professional teachers (Chapter 5). Yet this, too, is a presumption of teaching in a partnership manner. We might hanker after exceptional charisma, a charming interpersonal style, a warm personality, a flair for story-telling, an engaging humour, unusual flexibility or a highly refined reflective capability (and so on and so on). But although such capabilities are 'extras' to partnership teaching, they are extras to teaching of any sort. They will be found or not found in people who work in other jobs besides teaching, to be imported into teaching by those who enter the profession, to greater or lesser degrees. They will affect what happens in classrooms, certainly, but there is little point legislating for features of personality developing throughout our lives.

So how do we separate the 'good' teacher using a partnership approach from the excellent? All we can say is that there will be degrees of fidelity to the co-constructive model and personal dimensions (related to personality characteristics) which it would be fruitless to waste space discussing. This is not to cop out of a central question at the eleventh hour. It is to take the positive option that anyone who teaches democratically in a co-constructive manner, transforming his or her own knowledge contextually while helping others do likewise, should, eventually, graduate as an excellent practitioner. The teaching stereotype drawn in Chapters 5 and 6 is by no means easy to realise. Yet it does not involve especially complex thinking or technical expertise. It assumes that teachers take a principled stance and grasp a few hard-and-fast fundamentals. Once they do, the sky should be the limit, in terms of their professional development.

As a postscript, it is interesting to recall other candidates standing for election to excellence these days. And although these have received fairly full treatment, it is worth casting a backward glance at them from the perspective of present conclusions. These are the many recommendations that teachers work 'effectively' by – for example – collaborating, keeping records, being purposeful, getting involved in school decision-making, creating a positive atmosphere, setting homework and so forth (candidates for 'effectiveness': see Chapter 3). But what matters to excellent practice is not so much that teachers collaborate, keep records, set homework (and whatever). All teachers must (at some time, according to circumstance) do these things. What, in present terms, we need to know is how particular ways of keeping records (or whatever) fulfil that central criterion of cross-transformation which has been decided to underpin (this model of) excellent teaching.

To illustrate, one might take two examples. First, it is vital that teachers collaborate in the way that many commentators discuss (especially Hargreaves 1994, 1999), forming partnerships with parents, etc. But collaboration between adults may not work at all. It isn't just that all the merits gained through democratic interactions between adults credit adult–child transactions also. Without the latter, the former may not only boil down to time-wasting committee fodder but also work against pupils' interests (it is not at all an outside possibility that adults agree through collaboration to impose an autocratic regime on pupils). This is to underline the flaws in otherwise competent studies (such as that by Hargreaves 1996) which by the very fact that they convincingly show how adult interactions generate school policy show how skilled practice may nonetheless fail in some settings and even work against pupils' long-term interests.

The second example is that of setting homework (in primary and secondary schools). If cross-perspective taking between home and school is integral to good practice, one might say that setting homework is a spin-off from such a practice (i.e. is, truly, an 'effectiveness' criterion, as Barber *et al.* 1997 say it is). But ideas set out above do not validate any homework as worthwhile. They tell us that schoolwork carried out at home should reflect home (and connected out-of-school) cultures such that pupils comfortably regard schools from a home perspective and vice versa. Some forms of homework might help on that score, some – i.e. which are 'one-way' applications of what is learned (school-to-home) – would hinder it. Homework negotiated between home and school, seen by both institutions as relevant to a child's development, should stand a fair chance of fulfilling the criteria laid down. Yet one would have to look at the homework via a child's perceptions. We would have to know how far the homework is school-relevant and out-of-school relevant to be sure.

All that we need add is that teachers who, themselves, learn in a co-constructive manner (see Chapter 7) not only should be expert teachers but also should manage their jobs flexibly, through their bringing into line the personal and the professional. Teachers able to 'co-ordinate' their home and school lives (via cross-perspective taking) should be expert teachers in a way that teachers who insulate one from the other cannot be. This follows from first principles. It also brings full circle theorising about teaching and learning. For, what we can understand, is that those who are excellent teachers are those who share with learners that capacity for intellectual improvement which makes them excellent learners also.

10 The myths, mysteries and magic of good teaching

This book's argument is that schoolteachers, of all subjects and at all levels, use professionally devised theories of good practice in their work, if with varying degrees of conscious intent. Formed, refined and tested over many years, by multidisciplinary debate as well as by usage, these theories, ideals or models serve well-known social and educational values. They are not vulnerable to wayward fashions and trends in the way we sometimes think. Nor are they moved, much, by fine-line compromises within government advisory groups, large-scale consensus and research studies, surveys of professional opinion, or legislation derived from or drawing on these. Teachers are public servants who obey governmental *diktat* without demur. But to stay in charge of their own jobs, they dare not abandon the grounds of their own professionalism.

The argument, itself, can be summarised as a number of general statements, so that anyone doubting any part of it can see what points need overturning. These statements are grouped below in a way meant to show what is essential about them. First, attempts are made to explode the most potent myths about teaching which continue to hypnotise policy-makers. Second, they resolve – or at least throw a little light on – a few long-standing mysteries. Third, they are used to explain something of the magic of competent, successful and excellent teaching.

Myths

The myth of the formula

Myths of all kinds pervade educational decision-making. Many cluster around widely held beliefs especially difficult to banish because they appear to accord with common-sense prejudices about human learning and behaviour. O'Hagan (1999) lists many of these in a book charting the future of comprehensive education, which contributors to his book find partly responsible for continuing hostility to English comprehensive secondary schools. In fact, many myths work their mischief just as much at primary and nursery level (such as the idea of a 'fixed' potential human ability or that good management necessarily makes good schools).

Here, the most damaging and expensive myth for those interested in quality teaching is thought to be that supposing good practice can be reduced to a single formula (albeit very general), such that all worthwhile classroom strategies and techniques cross-relate and mutually reinforce each other. This myth is at first sight plausible as well as pervasive. Governments of modern times have become so convinced by it they have standardised school curricula and organisation across nations and held teachers accountable for obeying its precepts. Presumably, they have believed that all teachers will assent to 'new ways' once these ways are shown to work and are thoroughly adapted to schools through public monitoring (via the 'modernising' of appraisal, inspection and performance management systems). Since alternative views held by the professionals, themselves, are supposed to be no more than optional ways of reaching the same ends, these views can safely be discarded in favour of those chosen. Little thought needs be given to them.

This position has been condemned as false. Different pedagogic means take us to different educational ends – not exclusively (or the fact would be obvious and there would be no need to debate it), but in subtle, often indirect ways not easy to see. The means–end linkages called teaching models have been presented so that one can discern where they merge and overlap (at levels of pragmatics, say) and where they most divide from each other (in main thrusts towards distinct values). Not only do they operate with their own priorities of method and mode of assessment, but also they rule different epistemological outputs.

It was claimed that to ignore the distinctiveness of these models (i.e. to suppose educational curricula are no more than different means for realising the same ends) is to damage teaching as a profession. For it sets the same standards for all teachers and pupils which (in the light of this book's case) all are not able to achieve, or may not wish to achieve where they can. It is also an expensive myth for any government to believe. Imposing blanket expectations on professional groups (rather than admitting a diversity of aim) leads to forms of accountability, professional development, assessment and appraisal which are costly in terms of human resources and effort. Yet the expectations themselves are likely to be impossible to satisfy.

There are three main sub-strands of argument showing why a single formula for good practice is a non-starter, theoretically speaking. These refer to teacher–learner independence working against a backcloth of competing demands from social contexts, value-conflicts and the way teachers' routine experiences pull them in diverse professional directions.

Teacher–learner independence and competing demands from context

School students may fail to learn regardless of how skilful teachers are simply because learning is contingent not only on the behaviour of others but also on a full range of learner-resources. In other words, learning is conditioned by not only factual (cognitive and social) but also personal (i.e. voluntary) conditions to occur. Teachers can modify techniques to suit the former, but may be able to do little about the latter. Learner-commitment is a particularly vexatious idea to get into perspective being always relative both to learners' grasp of the importance of schooling (in turn influenced by their social context), their capabilities and their own personal values. And variable commitment affects all that learners do in school. Naturally, we will always think that there are things professionals can do to inspire committed learning, and we certainly wouldn't admire teachers who sit back and admit failure. The point is that what we can seldom do is diagnose sure remedies for poor student commitment, just because we are not dealing with an unbroken cause–effect chain. We are dealing with a mix of factual matters and voluntary decision-making related to a learner's social circumstances.

So the reasons why some pupils lack commitment may connect only very loosely and misleadingly with teaching skill (there will always be some connections). In turn, the reasons that pupils persist with tasks and are ultimately successful (where they are) may only vaguely correlate with teaching, but may palpably reflect pupils' own ambitions and emotional resources. In sum, there are pupil-specific variables determining teaching success just as there are teacher-specific. And how far teachers think each has a role to play in schools (or should be allowed to play, for we might think that pupils should always have most say on ethical grounds) will decide their professional ideologies.

This factor interrelates with contextual factors such as socio-cultural status and parental attitude which, themselves, intervene in the fates of school-learners apart from teaching skill. For many teachers there is no issue to worry about here: families see eye-to-eye with school staff and support their efforts. Not all do. It is tempting to think that teaching is, somehow, effective or not, instancing 'good practice' or not. Yet humans interpret the same actions (a skill, technique, strategy or whatever) according to their expectations. Children from different socio-economic backgrounds see their school lives differently (Chapter 8). They may respond to standard forms of teaching in different ways.

What is appropriate practice for one group may be unsuited to another. Good teaching in the eyes of a child from one end of a street may not seem quite so good to a child from the other end.

This does not make it impossible to prescribe teaching methodologies. It does deny outright the possibility that a *unitary* set of skills, techniques, strategies linked to a standard curriculum can be recommended likely to resolve all teaching dilemmas.

Value-conflicts

Normatively, to hit one set of learning targets squarely makes it more likely that others will be hit. If education nourishes capability (intelligence or whatever) this must be sound qualification for almost any further improvement. So people mastering one subject discipline should find themselves that much more likely to gain entry to others. A few hard won attainments (e.g. literacy and numeracy skills) are by rule dedicated to other attainments. On the other hand, a few are framed in opposition to others. That is why they exist. People disillusioned by schools' failure to combat, say, inner-city deprivation might be persuaded to apply special sorts of standards to what such schools are doing. Theorists have always disagreed about the function of education in people's lives and whether schools can or should intrude on what people do in the same way for everyone. Models of human development are prey to the same disagreements, since our views about how people grow and change (empirical theories) are always affected by views about how we believe people should grown and change (our values).

This is why Hamilton's (1999) complaint that modern school curricula no longer refer to our ideals of what human beings can become but are devised as technical solutions to technical problems, is apposite. With educational ends pre-decided, professional debates rage about means. Yet decisions about means always entail decisions about ends. Particular types of learning (structuring minds in distinct ways, via different epistemologies, different organisations of personal knowledge) are outputs from particular sorts of curricular management and organisation. Deciding what is to be taught commits us to particular ways of teaching along with special features of assessment, learning use and application. Three approaches to practice preach not only of teacher–learner behaviour but of learned knowledge and skills. They idealise, as said, types of human being. No one *can* be considered superior to the others, except in so far as we commit ourselves in advance to one type of educational value or another. But if we wish to realise any one we must strive earnestly for it; not believe we can win everything with a single curricular throw.

The tacit dimension

The work of Schon (1983, 1987) following Polanyi (1967) has been discussed critically and for its merits. Professional people are agreed to refine effective skills in settings likely to be infinitely variable, socially and physically. Teaching is a highly structured resource differing between individuals as, *inter alia*, intuitively and idiosyncratically wielded styles. Attempts to train these as 'competences' not only may fail but also can mar efficiency of deployment by standardising what must, in the end, work flexibly and adaptively (Chapter 7). Because teaching works flexibly and adaptively, we can only list constituent skills at levels of generality where they are impossible to challenge. By the same token, even teachers will be no more able than anyone to grasp exactly what they do to teach well (because practices are always subject to circumstance), calling into question attempts to set up taxonomies of excellence by recording the opinions of professionals (cf. Hay McBer 2000). Where we can take heart is in our optimism that model approaches *have* flourished around what typifies teaching situations – the variable roles of teachers and learners.

Myths of infinite variability

Just as questionable as the myth that we can define excellent teaching formulaically is the myth that we cannot define it at all – that good teaching is infinitely variable. Some 'reflective practitioner' writing (notwithstanding the above) can lead us into that theoretical wilderness (see Chapter 2). Although teaching situations are infinitely variable, they do have features bending teacher behaviours towards some forms of action (good practice) and not others (bad teaching: see Chapter 2). The two forms of constructive act which refer directly to each other (teaching and learning) generate the three models discussed.

Similarly, knowing that pluralist societies enshrine values we have no sure way of choosing between, does not mean that educators are stopped at all turns from seeking out viable aims. Schools can and do teach many kinds of values. The issue is not one of how to regard multiple values sensibly as how to deal with any that compete for priority. To repeat a crucial principle: professionally approved aims often do compete (how far we can at the same time prepare pupils for the world of work and as life-long learners hangs on a complex set of issues which are not

easily resolved: see Chapter 9). So the moot question for anyone entering teaching, or wishing to assess teachers via standards of accountability
is: to which model should anyone give allegiance? Training systems are
quickly infected by the hidden ideologies of those who condemn this
as a question not worth answering. So are appraisal and accountability
systems. It isn't a matter of whether we can legitimately educate at all
in a post-modern age, but how to deal with post-modernity itself, in
schools, in an acceptable manner.

Empiricist myths

The most deeply rooted empirical myth is that which supposes we reach
final judgements on good teaching through observation and interview,
curricular experiments, questionnaire surveys and self-reports (i.e. by
researching it empirically). This myth arises for the same reasons as the
first, discussed above, and is worth reworking because of the added
thought that what we most need to know is not always discoverable
through empirical research. If excellent teaching is by its nature context-specific (i.e. it depends essentially on successful adaptations to one-
off occurrences), the only effectiveness rabbit that we can draw out of
the empirical hat will be highly visible to attack on grounds of irrelevance
or being featureless (see Chapter 3). At levels of generality where we
mostly agree about practice, empirical confirmation for such agreements
are worth reporting. But research will be very limited in what it can tell
us. Educational researchers regularise what they research to give themselves a realistic framework within which to work and commit resources.
This framework accords with their own standards and expectations.
So people who look to capture 'effectiveness' in some sure-fire way
often enough do no more than take a circular route to clarifying their
own prejudiced beliefs.

Anyone who points to the successes of 'scientific' research in other
areas to deny this sort of claim must remember Carr's (1995) strictures
(see also Pring 2000) that to take value-judgements out of educational
research is to destroy the value of the research itself. Unlike, say, research
in the physical sciences, or even in the social sciences where one is often
not concerned directly with the deliberations of one's 'subjects', the stuff
of educational research is the value-related perspectives and judgements
of pupils, teachers, parents and politicians. To take these out of the
research equation (i.e. to make the research value-free) is to lose those
contrasting judgements and expectations which give us problems in the
first place. For example, anyone who discovers, through research, the
worth of one teaching method (say whole-class teaching) must, to be

helpful, still say what it can and cannot achieve. The fact they will have great difficulty doing this in any precise fashion (because any single form of teaching can be used within complex repertoires of methods) doesn't detract from the point that value-issues in education have priority over empirical discoveries.

This is not to say that empirical research has no part to play in classroom study. Only it cannot, by itself, answer questions which are defined valuatively (like what makes for competence, success, excellence, effectiveness and so forth). For the criteria by which we will assess outcomes are themselves contentious. This is the problem with so much research launched on the premise that it is possible to set up criteria for success or excellence by which to assess competing methods. For those methodologies will be linked to disputed ends (especially when measured through reliable, standard tests) in a variety of logical as well as empirical ways, as Davis (1995, 1998) takes pains to point out. The choices that researchers make in what to test and how to check findings will, in the end, pre-decide what is discovered.

There have always been a number of empirical myths which plague researchers, and influential beliefs which may well turn out to be myths. One which has had a fairly lasting effect on educational policy, and which partly explains an English love-affair with traditional forms of teaching, has attached itself to the seminal writings of Richard Peters (1966) and Paul Hirst (Peters and Hirst 1970; see also Jonathan 1997; Reid 1998). The Peters and Hirst or 'liberal rational' hypothesis (which Kelly (1995) makes culpable for much that is wrong with modern-day teaching) has it that learners have to be 'initiated' into traditionally conceived disciplines before they can take charge of their own lives. Such a belief is empirical in its hanging on the idea that rational autonomy arrives during human development as an acquired capacity (corresponding, perhaps, to Piagetian formal operations, or Vygotskian higher-order skills).

In the light of research with infants (see Chapter 4), we are quickly discovering that this view can be taken seriously only in a severely qualified form. Obviously enough, in any environment, human autonomy has in practice to be bought through learning. Rational autonomy is inconceivable outside some sort of knowledge. Hirst's case that rational thinking always reduces to a knowledge-*related* capability remains important, provided we affirm an underlying process component (which some would call 'agency') giving power to the knowledge it wields (and not just the traditional: see Kelly 1995). We need not perhaps look for an absolute bottom-line for rational autonomy for that is gifted to us. We have to sort out the kind of society we wish to have and what (therefore) will count as rational and autonomous behaviour within it. If it is true that humans are born means-end problem-solvers (underlying rationality), and of initiating this for themselves (underlying autonomy), such truths have profound implications for education. Given that they hardly, yet, constitute received wisdom, they have so far had little impact on theorising (though see Silcock and Duncan 2001). Sooner or later, they must affect a whole range of teaching programmes – especially those parasitic on beliefs about 'independent learning' as a set of definable skills, rather than as the core of everyone's humanness.

Myths of eclecticism and pragmatism

Pragmatism (choosing according to circumstance) was once the Labour administration's bright idea for education, its 'third way' (Hodge 1998). Along with eclecticism, it seemed to give teachers alternatives to ideologically tainted solutions to classroom problems. As pointed out (Chapter 2), the difficulty here is that teachers can be endlessly pragmatic and eclectic in the way they deal with practicalities. This almost goes without saying. But pragmatism and eclecticism are, themselves, subject to decisions about ends. That is, distinct educational aims compel distinct sorts of pragmatic and eclectic policies. Nothing perhaps confuses issues more in teaching than realising how even pragmatic strategies can figure differently in different curricula. Only by seeing how bundles of strategies are integrated within larger groupings (teaching models) can we uncover the grander picture showing us the likely effectiveness of these. To an extent, this is why one useful way of assessing teaching quality is to look at the way skills and techniques are integrated together as professional repertoires in pursuit of aims (Chapters 2–6).

The special variant of the pragmatic myth enormously influential in academic education circles is that suggesting 'reflective practice' is, by nature, good practice (see Chapter 2). It is inconceivable that a teacher (any teacher, good or bad) would not to some extent reflect *in* action since he or she could not teach otherwise. Intelligent action (as Schon 1983 conceives) marries pragmatism to reasoned thinking which is an extremely insightful way to look at professional skill. Yet, as pointed out, any model we might care to set up will involve some reflection *on* or *about* practice. At a minimum, a model of good practice must separate from other models and divide strictly from forms of bad teaching. Reflection (in, on and about teaching) is found in almost any sort of professional work, even that which delivers ends we believe unworthy. That is, it is a modelling of professionalism *per se*. But we should not see it as delivering quality teaching on its own, unless we supplement it with features which, then, turn it into something else.

Mysteries

Public fads and fashions about schools come and go. They do so not so much because teachers lose track of what is and is not good practice but because of changing public attitudes towards some central mysteries. The most persistently pored over of these mysteries are the following.

- What is worth our trying to achieve in schools (questions of value?)
- How do pupils develop psychologically and socially (questions deciding methods, including assessment)?
- How should we decide what to teach (questions of content)?

What was claimed is that all three of these questions (even the second) hinge on the way we deal with the first, and that sorting out the first question makes it fairly straightforward to sort out the second and third. Reasons why this is so help, again, to summarise some key points of argument.

Intellectual change

The 'many faces of constructivism' (Phillips 1995) attract us according to whether as primarily unique individuals, social beings, or as both individuals and social beings engaged forever in some public–private interchange. Certainly, there remain many mysteries about human minds and conceptual progress. But evidence-based constructivist theories tell us that people make progress in a number of different ways, and to stress one way rather than another is to take us into one set of theories rather than another. It isn't that one set is true and another set false. But one set brings with it distinct perspectives relative to the others. And whether we go for one set rather than another will depend on our purposes for doing so (linked, again, to our values). So different sorts of teaching link to distinct ends because different sorts of learning do. Dashing hell-bent for correctness of outcome (checked by written examination) threatens to stop in its tracks a march towards personal-knowledge and skills application and/or transfer (see Chapter 9). Embracing one set of aims usually means freeing ourselves – if only partially – from another.

Choosing between aims

To return to the abiding issue, we cannot choose between competing educational aims on objective grounds. We can only suit ourselves, according to cherished values. For we have to use values to choose, and the only relevant values apart from those recommending the aims themselves, are our own. We can turn to contingent values such as appropriateness or fitness for circumstance. But this still begs the question of how we judge relevant circumstances: there is little point responding to a circumstance (community pressures, say) which is, itself, of dubious provenance. No amount of theorising about teaching is helpful without some judgement about the society for which pupils are being prepared.

Once we know the society we want, then we can decide on how to educate people for it. It is obvious folly to take the question the other way round: to believe that by clinging to whatever we believe is good educational practice (traditional methods, perhaps because we can control these and measure outputs) we can, then, ensure we will create a good society. This latter would be true only if there were one kind of good teaching. And there could be only one kind of good teaching were there one kind of good society. There are a number of versions of the good society, so there are a number of versions of excellent teaching. That is the point.

Magic

But there *is* competent, successful and excellent teaching. The magic of good teaching is that it transforms: it changes people for the better. Whether it does so through direct (teacher-centred) or indirect (learner-centred) interventions, or via negotiated settlement, it helps students set their own standards in life and aspirations for the future. Although there are always difficulties in teaching well, the worst of these are, often, not so much owed to lack of teaching expertise as to teachers trying to satisfy conflicting demands from different client groups. Once teaching goals are clear, there is no shortage of guidance on how to reach them, evidenced and discussed through early chapters. Once we accept such evidence, we are left with conflicts of priorities as the main culprit for uncertain school policies and practice rather than a general ignorance of what counts as pedagogic skill.

This conclusion does not deny that teaching is a complex business. But, at levels of competence for example (Chapter 7), there is little doubt that normal human talents for communication, making relationships and so forth can be refined as professional capabilities, sufficient for successful teaching, providing we don't expect too much from schools. As argued (Chapter 8), educational success will arise from competent performance in situations where teachers' and learners' goals are congruent with wider public values. In circumstances where public expectations outstrip or lag behind teachers' own expectations, or where they do match up to social realities, it will be more problematic agreeing criteria for success than deciding on suitably effective categories of skill.

Proposals reaching towards classroom excellence hang on the same requirement (Chapter 9). There has to be public and professional convergence in deciding on the kind of learners we want (i.e. ultimately the kind of society we want), to give teachers any chance of showing how they can transform immature people into educated citizens. Again, this argument doesn't imply that nothing can be said about excellent teaching apart from that it follows from resolving value-conflicts, since there's more to teacher performance than that. Earlier proposals listed general principles and procedural requirements (somewhat different from competences, effectiveness criteria, taxonomic lists of qualities, and so forth). These are worth summarising.

- Teachers should be *committed* to a value-driven, professional ideal, linked especially to notions of what it means to be good or 'excellent' learners.
- They should have a professional knowledge of the main options for 'good practice' possible for them. They should be familiar with the *theoretical* back-up for these options.
- From this commitment and knowledge – all things being equal – will develop the *skills*, *techniques* and *strategies* which they will deploy pragmatically (in line with the next point).
- Teachers will have a *sensitivity* to local factors, the socio-cultural needs of pupils and the expectations of parents. These factors will transform the way teaching skills etc. are deployed.

The partnership (or co-constructive) model (Chapters 5 and 6) promoted illustrates how one can be specific about these in useful ways for all responsible for teachers' professional development, as well as for teachers themselves; though any specification is meant to exemplify not define good and excellent teaching.

Teaching models are the obvious ways professionals avoid both the single formula myth and the myth of infinite variability. What was pointed out is that teaching capability does not merely reduce to a rather loose grouping of model-related skills but that these will be integrated in ways related to teachers' unique personal and professional experiences. So in the 'partnership' example (Chapters 5 and 6) teachers vary in whether or not their democratic and egalitarian leanings dominate the more practical co-constructive/conflict-resolution skills. Using this sort of conceptual tool one might explain, for example, differences between hard-line and soft-centred ideologies, while the integration of skill components adaptively to context is a way of theorising about how to deal with uniqueness and diversity. A standard professional expertise would vary in the structural arrangement of its components according to circumstance but not in the content of the components themselves. No doubt, it is over-ambitious to try to freeze such possibilities within a full-scale predictive theory. But it ought to be possible to study classroom events via theoretical spectacles taken from such fairly modest hypotheses.

What may be more promising is the potential of co-constructive teaching to save us from some value-ridden dilemmas currently preoccupying politicians, academics and professionals themselves who (for obvious reasons) want to say something solid about high quality or excellent teaching. This model deals directly with the obligation – practically everyone appears to accept – that schools should prepare students for the 'world of work' without neglecting their personal, social and cultural futures (Chapter 9). It does so not by denying that there are inherent conflicts between distinct types of aim, but by making the resolving of such conflicts vital to achieving 'learning transfer' pivotal to the model. It also brings with it insights into academic ways of learning and achieving conceptual change. According to some (e.g. Alexander 2000), human academic development is poorly charted in the educational literature, being usually fragmented into different social, cultural and intellectual strands. Since this development involves the reciprocal transforming by academic studies of our personal and social lives, the way co-constructive insights account for such two-way transformations (forms of learning transfer: Chapters 6, 7 and 9) could be just what we are looking for. They should be of interest to those responsible for any enterprise where intellectual application and practical skill are meant, reciprocally, to inform each other.

On the other hand, the potential co-constructive teaching has for moving us in more than one direction at once shouldn't delude us into believing that it rids us of value-conflicts altogether, if at all. What it does is remind us exactly what is happening when, for example, pupils with exam weaknesses recognise that exams do, still, have legitimate roles to play in school and in life generally. Indeed, partnership systems largely come into existence in such circumstances, where there may be hard options to face. They do so by telling us that it has to be important participants who must resolve (in democratic ways) how the teaching–learning process should turn. At least, while being taught within democratic classrooms, learners do have some access to the decisions most affecting them, even when these remain problematic and sometimes impossible to sort out.

For, in the end, even co-constructed solutions have limited application. To edge towards goals which have personal relevance for pupils usually means to edge away from those which are narrowly aligned to common goals. This does not make everyone's mental development wholly dependent on choice of school or type of education. Pupils may experience culturally broad and enriching events at home, while being trained in academically and vocationally useful skills at school. This is fine for pupils whose home cultures complement schools. It is less promising for those who rely on schools to prepare them for a full life and not, just, for arduous exams or menial jobs. What is not wholly out of reach is for teachers and learners, working together, to decide what are and are not suitable learning goals at any one point in time, taking sight of all the pressures upon them. The proviso has to be that they are allowed to make such decisions freely and without prejudice.

References

Adams, K. (1996) 'Competency's American origins and the conflicting approaches in use today', *Competency* 3(2): 44–48.

Adey, P. and Shayer, M. (1994) *Really Raising Standards*, London: Routledge.

Adey, P. and Shayer, M. (1996) 'An exploration of long-term transfer effects following an extended intervention program in the high school science curriculum', in L. Smith (ed.) *Critical Readings in Piaget*, London: Routledge.

Ainley, P. (1993) *Class and Skill: Changing Divisions and Knowledge and Labour*, London: Cassell.

Alderson, P. (1999) 'Human rights and democracy in schools, do they mean more than "picking up litter and no killing whales"?', *International Journal of Children's Rights* 7: 185–205.

Alexander, P.A. (2000) 'Towards a model of academic development: schooling and the acquisition of knowledge', *Educational Researcher* 29(2): 28–33 (plus 44).

Alexander, R.J. (1992) *Policy and Practice in Primary Education*, London: Routledge.

Alexander, R.J. (1994) *Innocence and Experience: Reconstructing Primary Education*, Stoke-on-Trent: Association for the Study of Primary Education (ASPE) and Trentham.

Alexander, R.J. (1998) 'Basics, cores and choices: towards a new primary curriculum', *Education 3-13* 26(2): 60–69.

Alexander, R.J., Rose, J. and Woodhead, C. (1992) *Curriculum Organisation and Classroom Practice in Primary Schools: A Discussion Paper*, London: DES.

Anderson, C.S. (1982) 'The search for school climate: a review of the research', *Review of Educational Research* 52: 368–420.

Anderson, C., Avery, P.G., Pederson, P.V., Smith, E.S. and Sullivan, J.L. (1997) 'Divergent perspectives on citizenship education: a Q-method study and survey of social studies teachers', *American Educational Research Journal* 34(2): 333–364.

Angus, J. (1993) 'The sociology of school effectiveness', *British Journal of Sociology of Education* 14: 33–38.

Askew, M., Brown, M., Rhodes, V., Johnson, D. and Wiliam, D. (1997) *Effective Teachers of Numeracy*, London: School of Education, King's College.

Averch, H.A., Carroll, S.J., Donaldson, T.S., Kiesling, H.J. and Pincus, J. (1971) *How Effective is Schooling? A Critical Review and Synthesis of the Research Findings*, Santa Monica, CA: Rand.

Ball, S.J. (1990) 'Management as a moral technology', in S.J. Ball (ed.) *Foucault and Education*, London: Routledge.

Ball, S.J. (1995) 'Intellectuals or technicians? The urgent role of theory in educational studies', *British Journal of Educational Studies* 43(3): 255–271.

Barber, M. (1995) *The Dark Side of the Moon: Imagining an End to Failure in Urban Schooling*, London: Times Educational Supplement and Greenwich Lecture.

Barber, M. and White, J. (1997) 'Introduction', in J. White and M. Barber (eds) *Perspectives on School Effectiveness and School Improvement*, London: Institute of Education, University of London.

Barber, M., Stoll, L., Mortimore, P. and Hillman, J. (1995) *Governing Bodies and Effective Schools*, London: DfEE.

Barber, M., Denning, T., Graham, J. and Johnson, M. (1997) *School Performance and Extra-Curricular Provision*, London: DfEE.

Barnett, R. (1994) *The Limits of Competence*, Buckingham: Society for Research into Higher Education and Open University Press.

Barrett, E., Whitty, G., Furlong, J., Galvin, C. and Barton, L. (1992) *Initial Teacher Education in England and Wales: A Topography*, Interim Report of Economic and Social Research Council Modes of Teacher Education Research Project, London: Goldsmiths College.

Beare, H., Caldwell, B.J. and Millikan, R. (1989) *Creating an Excellent School*, London: Routledge.

Benn, C. and Chitty, C. (1996) *Thirty Years On: Is Comprehensive Education Alive and Well or Struggling to Survive?* London: David Fulton.

Bennett, S.N. (1976) *Teaching Styles and Pupil Progress*, London: Open Books.

Bennett, S.N. (1987) 'The search for the effective primary school teacher', in S. Delamont (ed.) *The Primary School Teacher*, Lewes: Falmer.

Ben-Peretz, M. (1995) 'Curriculum of teacher education programs', in L.W. Anderson (ed.) *International Encyclopedia of Teaching and Teacher Education*, Oxford: Pergamon.

Bereiter, C. (2000) 'Situated cognition and how to overcome it', in J. Collins and D. Cook (eds) *Understanding Learning: Influences and Outcomes*, Milton Keynes: Paul Chapman with the Open University.

Bereiter, C. and Scardamalia, M. (1989) 'Intentional learning as a goal of instruction', in L.B. Resnick (ed.) *Knowing, Learning and Instruction: Essays in Honour of Robert Glaser*, Hillsdale, NJ: Lawrence Erlbaum.

Bereiter, C. and Scardamalia, M. (1993) 'Composing and writing', in R. Beard (ed.) *Teaching Literacy: Balancing Perspectives*, London: Hodder and Stoughton.

Berlak, A. and Berlak, H. (1981) *The Dilemmas of Schooling*, London: Routledge.

Berlin, I. (1969) *Four Essays on Liberty*, Oxford: Oxford University Press.

Bernstein, B. (1970a) 'A sociolinguistic approach to socialisation: with some reference to educability', in J. Gumperz and D. Hymes (eds) *Directions in Sociolinguistics*, New York: Holt, Rinehart and Winston.

Bernstein, B. (1970b) 'Education cannot compensate for society', *New Society* 387: 344–347.

Bernstein, B. (1970c) 'A critique of the concept of "compensatory education"', in D. Rubinstein and C. Stoneman (eds) *Education for Democracy*, Harmondsworth: Penguin.

Bernstein, B. and Henderson, D. (1969) 'Social class differences in the relevance of language to socialisation', *Sociology* 3(1): 144–158.

Biber, B. (1972) 'The "whole child", individuality and values in education', in J.R. Squire (ed.) *A New Look at Progressive Education*, Washington, DC: Association for Supervision and Curriculum Development.

Biggs, J.B. (1992) 'Returning to school: review and discussion', in A. Demitriou, M. Shayer and A.M. Efklides (eds) *Neo-Piagetian Theories of Cognitive Development*, London: Routledge.

Biggs, J.B. (2001) 'The reflective institution: assuring and enhancing the quality of learning and teaching', *Higher Education* 41: 221–238.

Black, P. and Wiliam, D. (1998) *Inside the Black Box: Raising Standards through Classroom Assessment*, London: School of Education, King's College.

Blatchford, I.S. and Blatchford, J. (eds) (1995) *Educating the Whole Child*, Buckingham: Open University Press.

Blenkin, G.M. and Kelly, A.V. (1994) 'The death of infancy', *Education 3–13* 22(3): 3–9.

Bliss, J., Askew, M. and Macrae, S. (1996) 'Effective teaching and learning: scaffolding revisited', *Oxford Review of Education* 22(1): 37–61.

Bloomfield, A. (2000) 'The Swedenborgian roots of English progressive education', address to the History of Education Society Annual Conference, Birmingham, 24 November.

Bolam, R. (1997) 'Management development for headteachers', *Educational Management and Administration* 25(3): 265–283.

Bosker, R.J. and Witziers, B. (1996) 'The magnitude of school effects', paper presented at the annual meeting of American Research Association, New York.

Boyatzis, R.E. (1982) *The Competent Manager: A Model for Effective Performance*, New York: Wiley.

Boyatzis, R.E., Leonard, D.C., Rhee, K.S. and Wheeler, J.V. (1996) 'Competences can be developed?', *Capability* 2(2): 25–41.

Boyer, E.L. (1990) *Scholarship Reconsidered: Priorities for the Professoriate*, Princeton, NJ: Carnegie Foundation for the Advancement of Teaching.

Brehony, K.J. (1992) 'What's left of progressive primary education?', in A. Rattansi and D. Reeder (eds) *Rethinking Radical Education: Essays in Honour of Brian Simon*, London: Lawrence and Wishart.

Bridges, D. (1996) 'Competence-based education and training: progress or villainy?', *Journal of Philosophy of Education* 30(3): 361–376.

Brighouse, T. and Moon, B. (eds) (1990) *Managing the National Curriculum: Some Critical Perspectives*, London: Longman.

Broadfoot, P. (2000) 'Liberating the learner through assessment', in J. Collins and D. Cook (eds) *Understanding Learning: Influences and Outcomes*, London: Paul Chapman with the Open University.

Broadhead, P., Osborn, M., Planel, C. and Sharpe, K. (2000) *Promoting Quality in Learning: Does England have the Answer?*, London: Cassell.

Brockmeier, J. (1996) 'Explaining the interpretive mind', *Human Development* 39: 287–294.

Brown, S., Duffield, J. and Riddell, S. (1995) 'School effectiveness research: the policy makers' toll for school improvement?', *EERA [European Educational Research Association] Bulletin* 1(1): 6–15.

Brundrett, M. (1997) 'Who should teach teachers? Political ideology and teacher education in England and Wales', *Education Today* 47(2): 42–49.

Brundrett, M. (2000a) 'Introduction', in *The Beacon School Experience: Case Studies in Excellence*, King's Lynn: Peter Francis.

Brundrett, M. (2000b) 'The question of competence: the origins, strengths and inadequacies of a leadership training paradigm', *School Leadership and Management* 20(3): 353–370.

Bruner, J.S. (1990) *Acts of Meaning*, Cambridge: Cambridge University Press.

Bruner, J.S. (1995a) 'Commentary', *Human Development* 38: 203–213.

Bruner, J.S. (1995b) 'What we have learned about early learning', *European Early Childhood Education Research Journal* 4(1): 5–16.

Bruner, J.S. and Haste, H. (1987) *Making Sense: The Child's Construction of the World*, London: Methuen.

Bryant, C.G.A. (1997) 'Citizenship, national identity and the accommodation of difference: reflections on the German, French, Dutch and British cases', *New Community* 23(2): 157–172.

Buchanan-Barrow, E. and Barrett, M. (1996) 'Primary school children's understanding of the school', *British Journal of Educational Psychology* 66: 13–36.

Burtonwood, N. (1996) 'Culture, identity and the curriculum', *Educational Review* 49(3): 227–235.

Bush, T. (1995) *Theories of Educational Management*, London: Paul Chapman.

Caldwell, B. and Spinks, J. (1988) *The Self-Managing School*, Lewes: Falmer.

Caldwell, B. and Spinks, J. (1998) *Beyond the Self-Managing School*, London: Falmer.

Campbell, R.J. (1993) 'The broad and balanced curriculum in primary schools: some limitations of reform', *Curriculum Journal* 4(2): 215–229.

Carr, W. (1989) 'Introduction', in W. Carr (ed.) *Quality in Teaching: Arguments for a Reflective Profession*, Lewes: Falmer.

Carr, W. (1995) *For Education: Towards a Critical Educational Enquiry*, Buckingham: Open University Press.

Carr, W. (1998) 'The curriculum in and for a democratic society', *Curriculum Studies* 6(3): 323–340.

Cave, E. and Wilkinson, C. (1992) 'Developing managerial capabilities in education', in M. Bennett, M. Crawford and C. Riches (eds) *Managing Change in Education*, London: Paul Chapman.

Central Advisory Council (1967) *Children and their Primary Schools*, Plowden Report, London: HMSO.

Cheetham, G. and Chivers, G. (1996) 'Towards a holistic model of professional competence', *Journal of European Industrial Training* 20(5): 20–30.

Chitty, C. (1989) *Towards a New Education System: The Victory of the Far Right?*, London: Falmer.

Chitty, C. (1992) *The Education System Transformed*, Manchester: Baseline.

Chitty, C. (1997) 'The school effectiveness movement: origins, shortcomings and future possibilities', *Curriculum Journal* 8(1): 45–62.

Chitty, C. and Mac an Ghaill, M. (1995) *Reconstruction of a Discourse*, Educational Review Publications, Headline Series no. 4, Birmingham: University of Birmingham.

Chomsky, N. (1959) 'Review of "Verbal Behaviour" by B.F. Skinner', *Language* 35: 226.

Chomsky, N. (2000) *New Horizons in the Study of Language and Mind*, Cambridge: Cambridge University Press.

Chown, A. (1994) 'Beyond competence', *British Journal of In-service Education* 20(2): 161–180.

Chung, S. and Walsh, D.J. (2000) 'Unpacking child-centredness: a history of meanings', *Journal of Curriculum Studies* 32(2): 215–234.

Cobb, P. (1994) 'Where is the mind? Constructivist and sociocultural perspectives on mathematical development', *Educational Researcher* 23(7): 13–20.

Coldron, J. and Smith, R. (1999) 'The construction of reflective practice in key policy documents in England', *Pedagogy, Culture and Society* 7(2): 305–320.

Cole, M. and Wertsch, J.V. (1996) 'Beyond the individual and social antinomy in discussions of Piaget and Vygotsky', *Human Development* 39: 250–256.

Coleman, J.S. (1966) *Equality of Educational Opportunity*, Washington, DC: US Government Printing Office.

Corson, D. (1998) *Changing Education for Diversity*, Buckingham: Open University Press.

Cousins, J. (1996) 'Empowerment and autonomy from babyhood: the perspective of "early years" research', in M. John (ed.) *Children in Charge: The Child's Right to a Fair Hearing*, London: Jessica Kingsley.

Covington, M.V. (1998) *The Will to Learn: A Guide for Motivating Young People*, Cambridge: Cambridge University Press.

Creemers, B.P.M. (1994) *The Effective Classroom*, London: Cassell.

Cuban, L. (1993) 'Preface', in C. Teddlie and S. Stringfield (eds) *Schools Make a Difference: Lessons Learned from a 10-year Study of School Effects*, New York: Teachers College Press.

Cullen, E. (1992) 'A vital way to manage change', *Education* 13(November): 3–17.

Darling, J. (1994) *Child-Centred Education and its Critics*, London: Paul Chapman.

David, T. (1998) 'Issues in early childhood education', *European Journal of Early Childhood Education* 6(2): 5–17.

Davie, R., Upton, G. and Varma, V. (eds) (1996) *The Voice of the Child*, London: Falmer.

Davis, A. (1995) 'Criterion-referenced assessment and the development of knowledge and understanding', *Journal of Philosophy of Education* 29(1): 3–21.

Davis, A. (1998) *The Limits of Educational Assessment*, Oxford: Blackwell.

Davis, A. (1999) 'Prescribing teaching methods', *Journal of the Philosophy of Education* 33(3): 387–401.

Demitriou, A., Shayer, M. and Efklides, A.E. (eds) (1992) *Neo-Piagetian Theories of Cognitive Development: Implications and Applications for Education*, London: Routledge.

Denvir, B. (1985) *GRAN: Group Assessment of Number*, Centre for Science and Maths Education, London: King's College.

DES (1972) *Teacher Education and Training*, London: HMSO.

Desforges, C. and Lings, P. (1998) 'Teaching knowledge application: advances in theoretical conceptions and their professional implications', *British Journal of Educational Studies* 46(4): 386–398.

Dewey, J. (1916) *Democracy and Education*, New York: Macmillan.

DfEE (1997) *Excellence in Schools*, Cm 3681, London: Stationery Office.

DfEE (1998) *Consultation Paper: Teachers Meeting the Challenge of Change*, London: Stationery Office.

DfEE (1999) *National College for School Leadership: A Prospectus*, London: DfEE.

DfEE (2000) *The National Curriculum for England and Wales*, London: Stationery Office.

DfEE (2001) *Building on Success*, Government Green Paper, London: DfEE.

Driver, R. (1983) *Pupil as Scientist?*, Milton Keynes: Open University Press.

Driver, R. (1989) 'Changing conceptions', in P. Adey, J. Bliss, J. Head and M. Shayer (eds) *Adolescent Development and School Science*, London: Falmer.

Driver, R. and Bell, B. (1986) 'Students' thinking and learning of science: a constructivist view', *School Science Review* 67: 443–456.

Driver, R., Asoko, H., Leach, J., Mortimer, E. and Scott, P. (1994) 'Constructing scientific knowledge in the classroom', *Educational Researcher* 23(7): 5–12.

Duffield, J., Allan, J., Turner, E. and Morris, B. (2000) 'Pupils' achievement: an alternative to the standards agenda', *Cambridge Journal of Education* 30(2): 263–274.

Duignan, P.A. and Macpherson, R.J.S. (1992) *Effective Leadership: A Practical Theory for New Educational Managers*, London: Falmer.

Duncan, D. (1999) 'School effectiveness and improvement', in M. Brundrett (ed.) *Principles of School Leadership*, Guildford: Peter Francis.

Edwards, R. (1993) 'A spanner in the works: Luddism and competence', *Adults Learning* 4(5): 124–125.

Elliott, J. (1996) 'School effectiveness research and its critics: alternative visions of schooling', *Cambridge Journal of Education* 26(2): 199–224.

Elliott, J. (1997) 'Quality assurance, the educational standards debate, and the commodification of educational research', *Curriculum Journal* 8(1): 63–83.

Engelund, G. (2000) 'Rethinking democracy and education: towards an education of deliberative citizens', *Journal of Curriculum Studies* 32(2): 305–313.

Eraut, M. (1994) *Developing Professional Knowledge and Competence*, London: Falmer.

Eskeland, K. (1996) 'Voice of the children: speaking truth to power', in M. John (ed.) *Children in Charge: The Child's Right to a Fair Hearing*, London: Jessica Kingsley.

Everard, K.B. (1990) 'A critique of the MCI TA NCVQ competency approach as applied to education management', *Education Change and Development* 11(1): 15–16.

Fang, Z. (1996) 'A review of research on teacher beliefs and practices', *Educational Research* 38(1): 47–65.

Fielding, M. (1997) 'Beyond school effectiveness and school improvement: lighting the slow fuse of possibility', *Curriculum Journal* 8(1): 7–27.

Fielding, M. (1999) 'Target setting, policy pathology and student perspectives: learning to labour in new times', *Cambridge Journal of Education* 29(2): 277–287.

Fisher, J. (1996) *Starting from the Child*, Buckingham: Open University Press.

Fisher, R. (2000) 'Developmentally appropriate practice and a national literacy strategy', *British Journal of Educational Studies* 48(1): 58–69.

Francis, L.J. and Grindle, Z. (1998) 'Whatever happened to progressive education? A comparison of primary school teachers' attitudes in 1982 and 1996', *Educational Studies* 24(3): 269–279.

Freudenthal, H. (1978) *Weeding and Sowing*, Dordrecht: Reidel.

Froebel, F. (1909) *Pedagogics of the Kindergarten*, New York: Appleton.

Frowe, I. (2001) 'Language and educational practice', *Cambridge Journal of Education* 31(1): 89–101.

Fullan, M. (1991) *The New Meaning of Educational Change*, London: Cassell.

Fullan, M. (1993) *Change Forces: Probing the Depths of Educational Reform*, London: Falmer.

Fullan, M. (1999) *Change Forces: The Sequel*, London: Falmer.

Galton, M. (1989) *Teaching in the Primary School*, London: David Fulton.

Galton, M. (1995) 'Do you really want to cope with thirty lively children and become an effective primary teacher?', in J. Moyles (ed.) *Beginning Teaching: Beginning Learning*, Buckingham: Open University Press.

Georghiades, P. (2000) 'Beyond conceptual change learning in science education: focusing on transfer, durability and metacognition', *Educational Research* 42(2): 119–139.

Gingell, J. and Brandon, E.P. (2000) 'In defence of high culture', *Journal of Philosophy of Education* 34(3), special issue.

Gipps, C. and MacGilchrist, B. (1999) 'Primary school learners', in P. Mortimore (ed.) *Understanding Pedagogy and its Impact on Learning*, London: Paul Chapman.

Gipps, C., McCallum, B. and Brown, M. (1999) 'Primary teachers' beliefs about teaching and learning', *Curriculum Journal* 10(1): 123–134.

Goldstein, H. and Woodhouse, G. (2000) 'School effectiveness research and educational policy', *Oxford Review of Education* 26(3–4): 353–363.

Graham, J. (1996) 'The Teacher Training Agency, continuing professional development policy and the definition of competences for serving teachers', *British Journal of In-Service Education* 22(2): 121–132.

Gray, J. and Wilcox, B. (1995) *Good School, Bad School*, Buckingham: Open University Press.

Gray, J. and Wilcox, B. (1996) 'The challenge of turning around ineffective schools', in P. Woods (ed.) *Contemporary Issues in Teaching and Learning*, London and New York: Routledge with the Open University.

Gray, J., Reynolds, D., Fitz-Gibbon, C. and Jesson, D. (1996) *Merging Traditions: The Future of Research on School Effectiveness and School Improvement*, London: Cassell.

Griffiths, M. and Tann, S. (1991) 'Ripples in the reflection', in P. Lomax (ed.) *BERA Dialogues* 5: 82–101.

Griffiths, M. and Tann, S. (1992) 'Using reflective practice to link personal and public theories', *Journal of Education for Teaching* 18(1): 69–84.

Gross, R.D. (1992) *Psychology: The Science of Mind and Behaviour*, 2nd edn, London: Hodder and Stoughton.

Hager, P. (1995) 'Competency standards – help or a hindrance? An Australian perspective', *Vocational Aspect of Education* 47(2): 141–151.

Hajnicz, W. (1998) 'The subjectivity of the teacher and the subjectivity of the children: negative or positive co-operation', *International Journal of Early Years Education* 6(2): 199–206.

Hall, T., Williamson, H. and Coffey, A. (1998) 'Conceptualising citizenship: young people and the transition to adulthood', *Education Policy* 13(3): 301–315.

Hallam, S. and Ireson, J. (1999) 'Pedagogy in the secondary school', in P. Mortimore (ed.) *Understanding Pedagogy and its Impact on Learning*, London: Paul Chapman.

Hamilton, D. (1999) 'The pedagogic paradox (or why no didactics in England?)', *Pedagogy, Culture and Society* 7(1): 135–152.

Hand, B. and Treagust, D.F. (1994) 'Teachers' thoughts about changing to constructivist teaching/learning approaches within junior and secondary science classrooms', *Journal of Education for Teaching* 20(1): 97–112.

Hargreaves, D. (1994) 'The new professionalism: the synthesis of professional and institutional development', *Teaching and Teacher Education* 10(4): 423–438.

Hargreaves, D. (1996) 'Diversity and choice in school education: a modified libertarian approach', *Oxford Review of Education* 22(2): 131–141.

Hargreaves, D. (1999) 'The knowledge-creating school', *British Journal of Educational Studies* 47(2): 122–144.

Hargreaves, D. and Hopkins, D. (1991) *The Empowered School*, London: Cassell.

Hatcher, R. (1996) 'The limitations of the new social democratic agendas: class, equality and agency', in R. Hatcher and K. Jones (eds) *Education after the Conservatives: The Response of the New Agenda of Reform*, Stoke-on-Trent: Trentham.

Hay McBer (2000) *Research into Teacher Effectiveness: A Model of Teacher Effectiveness*, London: Hay McBer.

Haydon, G. (1998) 'Between the common and the differentiated: reflections on the work of the School Curriculum and Assessment Authority on values education', *Curriculum Journal* 9(1): 5–21.

Hayes, D. (1997) 'Teaching competences for Qualified Primary Teacher Status in England', *Teacher Development* 1(2): 165–174.

Heath, A. and Clifford, P. (1980) 'The seventy thousand hours that Rutter left out', *Oxford Review of Education* 6(1): 3–19.

Hextall, I. and Mahony, P. (2000) 'Consultation and the management of consent: standards for qualified teacher status', *British Journal of Educational Research* 26(3): 323–342.

Hodge, M. (1998) 'A pragmatic ideology', *Times Educational Supplement* 20 June: 21.

Hopkins, D., Ainscow, M. and West, M. (1994) *School Improvement in an Era of Change*, London: Cassell.

Hopkins, D., West, M., Ainscow, M., Harris, A. and Beresford, S. (1997) *Creating the Conditions for Classroom Improvement*, London: David Fulton.

Horne, H.H. (1938) *The Democratic Philosophy of Education Companion to Dewey's Democracy and Education: Exposition and Comment*, New York: Macmillan.

Humphreys, K. and Susak, Z. (2000) 'Learning how to fish: issues for teachers engaging in self-evaluation and reflective enquiry in schools', *Research in Education* 64: 78–89.

Hyland, T. (1993a) 'Professional development and competence-based education', *Educational Studies* 19(1): 123–132.

Hyland, T. (1993b) 'Competence, knowledge and education', *Journal of Philosophy of Education* 27(1): 57–68.

Hyland, T. (1993c) 'Training, competence and expertise in teacher education', *Teacher Development* 2(7): 117–122.

Ingram, J. and Worrall, H. (1993) *Teacher–Child Partnership: The Negotiating Classroom*, London: David Fulton.

Jencks, C.S., Smith, M., Ackland, H., Bane, M.J., Cohen, D., Ginter, H., Hens, B. and Michelson, S. (1972) *Inequality: A Reassessment of the Effect of the Family and Schooling in America*, New York: Basic Books.

John, M. (ed.) (1996) *Children in Charge: The Child's Right to a Fair Hearing*, London: Jessica Kingsley.

Johnson, D.W. and Johnson, R.T. (1994) 'Constructive conflict in the school', *Journal of Social Issues* 50(1): 117–137.

Johnson, E.A., Thomas, D. and Krochak, D. (1998) 'Effects of peer mediation training in junior high school on mediators' conflict resolution attitudes and abilities in high school', *Alberta Journal of Educational Research* 44(3): 339–341.

Jonathan, R. (1997) 'Illusory freedoms: liberalism, education and the market', *Journal of the Philosophy of Education* 31(1), special issue.

Jones, K. (1983) *Beyond Progressive Education*, London: Methuen.

Kaplan, A. (2000) 'Teacher and student: designing a democratic relationship', *Journal of Curriculum Studies* 32(3): 377–402.

Kelly, A.V. (1989) *The Curriculum: Theory and Practice*, 3rd edn, London: Paul Chapman.

Kelly, A.V. (1994a) *The National Curriculum: A Critical Review*, London: Paul Chapman.

Kelly, A.V. (1994b) 'A high quality curriculum for the early years – some conceptual issues', *Early Years* 15(1): 6–12.

Kelly, A.V. (1995) *Education and Democracy*, London: Paul Chapman.

Kershner, R. and Pointon, P. (2000) 'Children's views of the primary classroom as an environment for working and learning', *Research in Education* 64: 64–77.

Kliebard, H.M. (1995) *The Struggle for the American Curriculum: 1893–1958*, 2nd edn, New York: Routledge.

Knuver, A.W.M. and Brandsma, H. (1993) 'Cognitive and affective outcomes in school effectiveness research', *School Effectiveness and School Improvement* 4(3): 189–204.

Konnor, M. (1991) *Childhood*, London: Little, Brown.

Korthagen, F. and Kessels, J. (1999) 'Linking theory and practice: changing the pedagogy of teacher education', *Educational Researcher* 28(4): 4–17.

Kuhn, D. (1999) 'A developmental model of critical thinking', *Educational Researcher* 28(2): 16–26.

Labercane, G.D., Last, S., Nichols, S. and Johnson, W. (1998) 'Critical moments and the art of teaching', *Teacher Development* 2(2): 191–204.

Labour Party (1996) *New Labour: New Life for Britain*, London: Labour Party.

Lawrence, J.A. and Valsiner, J. (1993) 'Conceptual roots of internalisation: from transmission to transformation', *Human Development* 36: 150–167.

Lawton, D. (1973) *Social Change, Curriculum Theory and Curriculum Planning*, London: Hodder and Stoughton.

Lawton, D. (1989) *Education, Culture and the National Curriculum*, London: Hodder and Stoughton.

Lazar, I., Hubbell, V., Murray, H., Rosche, M. and Royce, J. (1977) *The Persistence of Pre-School Effects: A Long Term Follow-Up of Fourteen Infant and Pre-School Experiments*, DEHW publication no. OHDS 78-30129, Washington, DC: US Government Printing Office.

Leat, D. (1993a) 'Competence, teaching, thinking and feeling', *Oxford Review of Education* 19(4): 499–510.

Leat, D. (1993b) 'A conceptual model of competence', *British Journal of In-Service Education* 19(2): 35–40.

Leithwood, K.A. and Stager, M. (1989) 'Expertise in principals' problem solving', *Educational Administration Quarterly* 25: 126–161.

Leithwood, K.A., Begley, P.T. and Cousins, J.B. (1992) *Developing Expert Leadership for Future Schools*, London: Falmer.

Lester, N. (1992) 'All reforms are not created equal: cooperative learning is not negotiating the curriculum', in C. Boomer, N. Lester, L. Lonore and J. Cook (eds) *Negotiating the Curriculum: Educating for the 21st Century*, London: Falmer.

Lings, P. and Desforges, C. (1999) 'On subject differences in applying knowledge to learn', *Research Papers in Education* 14(2): 199–221.

Lipman, M.A., Sharp, A.M. and Oscanyan, F.S. (1980) *Philosophy in the Classroom*, Philadelphia, PA: Temple University Press.

Littledyke, M. (1998) 'Teaching for constructive learning', in M. Littledyke and L. Huxford (eds) *Teaching the Primary Curriculum for Constructive Learning*, London: David Fulton.

Liverto-Sempio, O. and Marchetti, A. (1997) 'Cognitive development and theories of mind: towards a contextual approach', *European Journal of Psychology of Education* 12(1): 3–21.

Lonka, K., Hakkarainen, K. and Sintonen, M. (2000) 'Progressive inquiry learning in children: experiences, possibilities, limitations', *European Early Childhood Research Journal* 8(1): 7–23.

Lyle, S. (2000) 'Narrative understanding: developing a theoretical context for understanding how children make meaning in classroom settings', *Journal of Curriculum Studies* 32(1): 45–63.

Lyotard, J-F. (1979) *The Post-Modern Condition: A Report on Knowledge*, Manchester: Manchester University Press.

Mac an Ghaill, M. (1996) 'Sociology of education, state schooling and social class: beyond critiques of the New Right hegemony', *British Journal of Sociology of Education* 17(2): 163–176.

MacGilchrist, B., Myers, K. and Read, J. (1997) *The Intelligent School*, London: Paul Chapman.

Mackenzie, R. (1997) 'A cultural perspective on creative primary teaching and the arts in the 1990s', in D. Holt (ed.) *Primary Arts Education: Contemporary Issues*, Bristol: Falmer.

Maclure, S. (1993) 'Fight this tooth and nail', *Times Educational Supplement* 18 June.

Mahony, P. and Whitty, G. (1994) 'Teacher education and teacher competence', in S. Tomlinson (ed.) *Educational Reform*, London: Institute for Public Policy Research with Rivers Oram Press.

Mansell, W. and Kelly, A. (2000) 'Performance pay system "will not work"', *Times Educational Supplement* 29 December.

Marenbon, J. (1998) 'QCA values in education: a threat to academic education and morality', *Journal of Values Education* 2: 14–23.

Margerison, C.J. and McCann, D.J. (1992) *Types of Work Profile Handbook*, York: TMS Trust.

Marsden, D. (2000) 'Understanding the links between pay and performance', PMW Public Policy Seminar, 22 February.

Marshall, B. (2001) 'Including the socially excluded: league tables and Labour's schools policy', *Critical Quarterly* 43(1): 29–40.

Mason, M. (2000) 'Teachers as critical mediators of knowledge', *Journal of Philosophy of Education* 34(2): 343–352.

Mead, G.H. (1934) *Mind, Self and Society*, Chicago: University of Chicago Press.

Meiksins Wood, E. (1986) *The Retreat from Class: A New 'True' Socialism*, London: Verso.

Mercer, N. (1991) 'Accounting for what goes on in classrooms; what have Neo-Vygotskians got to offer?', *Journal of the British Psychological Society* 15(1): 61–67.

Merson, M. (2000) 'Teachers and the myth of modernisation', *British Journal of Educational Studies* 48(2): 155–169.

Moore, R. (2000) 'For knowledge, tradition, progressivism and progress in education: reconstructing the curriculum debate', *Cambridge Journal of Education* 30(1): 17–36.

Mortimore, P. (1998a) 'Can effective schools compensate for society', in A.H. Halsey, H. Lauder, P. Brown and A.S. Wells (eds) *Education: Culture, Economy, Society*, Oxford: Oxford University Press.

Mortimore, P. (1998b) *The Road to Improvement*, Lisse: Swets and Zeitlinger.

Mortimore, P. and Whitty, G. (1999) *Can School Improvement Overcome the Effects of Disadvantage?*, London: Institute of Education, University of London.

Mortimore, P., Sammons, P., Stoll, L., Lewis, D. and Ecob, R. (1988) *School Matters: The Junior Years*, London: Open Books.

Muijs, D. and Reynolds, D. (2001) *Effective Teaching: Evidence and Practice*, London: Paul Chapman.

Nash, R. (1999) 'Realism in the sociology of education: "explaining" social differences in attainment', *British Journal of Sociology of Education* 20(1): 107–125.

Nash, R. and Harker, R.K. (1998) *Making Progress: Adding Value in New Zealand*, Palmerston North, NZ: ERDC Press.

Nelson, K., Plea, D. and Henseler, S. (1998) 'Children's theory of mind: an experiential interpretation', *Human Development* 41: 7–29.

Nordhaug, O. (1990) 'Individual competences in firms', paper for the Centre for Human Resources, Wharton School, University of Pennsylvania, PA.

O'Cadiz, M. del-P., Wong, P.L. and Torres, C.A. (1998) *Education and Democracy: Paulo Freire, Social Movements, and Educational Reform in Sao Paulo*, Boulder, CO: Westview Press.

Ofsted (1995) *Guidance on the Inspection of Nursery and Primary Schools*, London: HMSO.

Ofsted (1996) *The Annual Report of Her Majesty's Chief Inspector of Schools*, London: HMSO.

O'Hagan, B. (1999) *Modern Educational Myths: The Future of Democratic Comprehensive Education*, London: Kogan Page.

O'Hear, A. (1987) 'The importance of traditional learning', *British Journal of Educational Studies* 35: 102–114.

Osborne, M.D. (1997) 'Balancing individual and the group: a dilemma for the constructivist teacher', *Journal of Curriculum Studies* 29(2): 183–196.

Osler, A. and Starkey, H. (1998) 'Children's rights and citizenship: some implications for the management of schools', *International Journal of Children's Rights* 6: 313–333.

Ouston, J. (1999) 'School effectiveness and school improvement: critique of a movement', in T. Bush, L. Bell, R. Bolam, R. Glatter and R. Ribbins (eds)

Educational Management: Redefining Theory, Policy and Practice, London: Paul Chapman.

Ouston, J., Maughan, B. and Mortimore, P. (1979) 'School influences on children's development', in M. Rutter (ed.) *Developmental Psychiatry*, London: Heinemann.

Ozga, J. (ed.) (1988) *Schoolwork: Approaches to the Labour Process of Teaching*, Milton Keynes: Open University Press.

Paechter, C. (1998) 'Schooling and the ownership of knowledge', *Curriculum Studies* 6(2): 161–176.

Pascal, C. and Bertram, A.D. (1993) 'The education of young children and their teachers in Europe', *European Early Childhood Education Research Journal* 1(2): 27–37.

Pearson, A.T. (1984) 'Competence: a normative analysis', in E.C. Short (ed.) *Competence: Inquiries into its Meaning and Acquisition in Educational Settings*, Lanham, MD: University Press of America.

Perkins, D.N. and Salomon, G. (1989) 'Are cognitive skills context-bound?', *Educational Researcher* 18(1): 16–25.

Peters, R.S. (1966) *Ethics and Education*, London: Allen and Unwin.

Peters, R.S. and Hirst, P. (1970) *The Logic of Education*, London: Routledge and Kegan Paul.

Philips, J. (2000) 'Agree to disagree', *Times Educational Supplement* 15 September.

Phillips, D.C. (1995) 'The good, the bad, and the ugly: the many faces of constructivism', *Educational Researcher* 24(7): 5–12.

Piaget, J. (1954) *The Construction of Reality in the Child*, New York: Basic Books.

Piaget, J. (1971) *Biology and Knowledge*, Edinburgh: University of Edinburgh Press.

Piaget, J. (1978) *Success and Understanding*, London: Routledge and Kegan Paul.

Polanyi, M. (1967) *The Tacit Dimension*, New York: Doubleday.

Pollard, A. (1997) *Reflective Teaching in the Primary School*, 3rd edn, London: Cassell.

Pollard, A. (1999) 'Towards a new perspective on children's learning?', *Education 3–13* 27(3): 6–60.

Pollard, A., Broadfoot, P., Croll, P., Osborn, M. and Abbott, D. (1994) *Changing English Primary Schools: The Impact of the Education Reform Act at Key Stage 1*, London: Cassell.

Popper, K.R. (1966) *The Open Society and Some of its Enemies*, 5th edn, vol. 2, London: Routledge.

Popper, K.R. and Eccles, J.C. (1977) *The Self and its Brain*, Berlin: Springer International.

Preece, P.F.W. (1994) '"Knowing that" and "knowing how": general pedagogic knowledge and teaching competence', *Research in Education* 52: 42–50.

Pring, R. (1986) 'Aims, problems and curriculum contexts', in P. Tomlinson and M. Quinton (eds) *Values across the Curriculum*, Lewes: Falmer.

Pring, R. (1995a) *Closing the Gap: Liberal Education and Vocational Preparation*, London: Hodder and Stoughton.

Pring, R. (1995b) 'The community of educated people', *British Journal of Educational Studies* 43: 125–145.

Pring, R. (2000) 'The "false dualism" of educational research', *Journal of Philosophy of Education* 34(2): 246–260.

Proudfoot, C. and Baker, R. (1995) 'Schools that make a difference: a sociological perspective on effective schooling', *British Journal of Sociology of Education* 16: 277–292.

Purkey, S. and Smith, M. (1983) 'Effective schools', *Elementary School Journal* 83: 427–452.

QCA (1999) *The National Curriculum in England and Wales*, London: Stationery Office.

QCA (2000) *Statement of Values by the National Forum for Values in Education and the Community*, York: QCA.

Quicke, J. (1998) 'Towards a new professionalism for "New Times": some problems and possibilities', *Teacher Development* 2(3): 323–338.

Reid, A. (1998) 'The value of education', *Journal of Philosophy of Education* 32(3): 319–331.

Reid, K., Hopkins, D. and Holly, P. (1987) *Towards the Effective School*, Oxford: Blackwell.

Reid, W.A. (1997) 'Principle and pragmatism in English curriculum making 1868–1918', *Journal of Curriculum Studies* 29(5): 667–682.

Resnick, L.B. (1985) *Education and Learning to Think*, Pittsburgh, PA: Learning, Research and Development Centre, University of Pittsburgh.

Resnick, L.B. (1987) 'Learning in school and out', *Educational Researcher* 16(9): 13-20.

Resnick, L.B. and Neches, R. (1984) 'Factors affecting individual differences in learning ability', in R.J. Sternberg (ed.) *Advances in the Psychology of Human Intelligence,* Hillsdale, NJ: Lawrence Erlbaum.

Resnick, L.B., Bill, V. and Lesgold, S. (1992) 'Developing thinking abilities in arithmetic class', in A. Demitriou, M. Shayer and A.E. Efklides (eds) *Neo-Piagetian Theories of Cognitive Development: Implications and Applications for Education*, London: Routledge.

Reynolds, D. (1992) 'School effectiveness and school improvement: an updated review of the British literature', in D. Reynolds and P. Cuttance (eds) *School Effectiveness Research, Policy and Practice*, London: Cassell.

Reynolds, D. and Farrell, S. (1996) *Worlds Apart? A Review of International Surveys of Educational Achievement Involving England*, London: Ofsted.

Reynolds, D. and Reid, K. (1985) 'The second stage: towards a reconceptualization of theory and methodology in school effectiveness', in D. Reynolds (ed.) *Studying School Effectiveness*, Lewes: Falmer.

Reynolds, M. (1999) 'Standards and professional practice: the TTA and Initial Teacher Training', *British Journal of Educational Studies* 47(3): 247–260.

Reynolds, M. and Salters, M. (1995) 'Models of competence and teacher training', *Cambridge Journal of Education* 25(3): 349–359.

Roche, J. (1999) 'Children: rights, participation and citizenship', *Childhood* 6(4): 475–493.

Rogers, C. (1954) *Client-Centred Therapy*, Boston, MA: Houghton-Mifflin.

Rogers, C. (1957) 'The necessary and sufficient conditions of therapeutic personality change', *Journal of Consulting Psychology* 21: 95–103.

Rogers, C. (1983) *Freedom to Learn for the '80s*, revised edn, Columbia, SC: Merrill.

Rogoff, B. (1990) *Apprenticeship in Thinking*, Oxford: Oxford University Press.

Rohrs, H. and Lenhart, V. (eds) (1995) *Progressive Education across the Continents*, Frankfurt am Main: Peter Lang.

Rosenholtz, S. (1985) 'Effective schools: interpreting the evidence', *American Journal of Education* 93: 353–387.

Rossbach, H-G. (2000) 'Life-long learning in the perspective of primary school education', *European Early Childhood Education Research Journal* 8(2): 73–87.

Rousseau, J-J. (1911 [1762]) *Emile*, New York: Everyman.

Rudduck, J. and Flutter, J. (2000) 'Pupil participation and pupil perspective: carving a new order of experience', *Cambridge Journal of Education* 30(1): 75–89.

Rutter, M., Maughan, B., Mortimore, P. and Ouston, J. (1979) *Fifteen Thousand Hours: Secondary Schools and their Effects on Children*, London: Open Books.

Ryle, G. (1949) *The Concept of Mind*, London: Hutchinson.

Sammons, P. (1999) *School Effectiveness: Coming of Age in the Twenty-First Century*, Lisse: Swets and Zeitlinger.

Sammons, P., Hillman, J. and Mortimore, P. (1995) *Key Characteristics of Effective Schools: A Review of School Effectiveness Research*, London: Institute of Education for Ofsted.

Sanday, A. (1990) *Making Schools More Effective*, Warwick: Centre for Educational Development, Warwick University.

Scheerens, J. (1992) *Effective Schooling: Research, Theory and Practice*, London: Cassell.

Scheerens, J. and Bosker, R. (1997) *The Foundations of Educational Effectiveness*, Oxford: Pergamon.

Scheerens, J. and Creemers, B.P.M. (1995) 'School effectiveness in the Netherlands: research, policy and practice', in B.P.M. Creemers and N. Osinga (eds) *ICSEI Country Reports*, Leeuwarden: ICSEI Secretariat.

Schon, D.A. (1983) *The Reflective Practitioner*, New York: Basic Books.

Schon, D.A. (1987) *Educating the Reflective Practitioner*, New York: Basic Books.

Senge, P. (1990) *The Fifth Discipline*, New York: Doubleday.

Sherman, A. (1988) 'Allowing children to be children: the message young children receive about school', *Education 3-13* 26(1): 57–63.

Sherwin, M. (1996) 'The law in relation to the wishes and feelings of the child', in R. Davie, G. Upton and V. Varma (eds) *The Voice of the Child*, London: Falmer.

Silcock, P.J. (1990) 'Implementing the National Curriculum: some teachers' dilemmas', *Education 3-13* 18(3): 3–9.

Silcock, P.J. (1993a) 'Can we teach effective teaching?', *Educational Review* 45(1): 13–19.

Silcock, P.J. (1993b) 'Towards a new progressivism in primary school education', *Education Studies* 19(1): 107–121.

Silcock, P.J. (1996) 'Three principles for a new progressivism', *Oxford Review of Education* 22(2): 199–215.

Silcock, P.J. (1999) *New Progressivism*, London: Falmer.

Silcock, P.J. and Duncan, D. (2001) 'Values acquisition and values education: some proposals', *British Journal of Educational Studies* 49(3): 242–259.

Silcock, P.J. and Stacey, H. (1997) 'Peer mediation and the cooperative school', *Education 3-13* 25(2): 3–8.

Silcock, P.J. and Wyness, M.G. (1997) 'Dilemma and resolution: primary school teachers look beyond Dearing', *Curriculum Journal* 8(1): 125–148.

Silcock, P.J. and Wyness, M.G. (1998) 'Strong in diversity: primary school inspectors' beliefs', *Curriculum Journal* 9(1): 105–127.

Silcock, P.J. and Wyness, M. (2000) 'Diligent and dedicated: primary school pupils talk about their reformed curriculum', *Curriculum* 21(1): 14–25.

Simon, B. (1981) 'The primary school revolution: myth or reality?', in B. Simon and J. Willcocks (eds) *Research and Practice in the Primary Classroom*, London: Routledge and Kegan Paul.

Smith, R. and Standish, P. (1997) 'Conclusion', in R. Smith and P. Standish (eds) *Teaching Right and Wrong*, Stoke-on-Trent: Trentham.

Smithers, A. and Robinson, P. (2000) *Coping with Teacher Shortages*, Liverpool: University of Liverpool for the National Union of Teachers.

Smolin, L. (1997) *The Life of the Cosmos*, London: Phoenix.

Smyth, J. and Dow, A. (1998) 'What's wrong with outcomes? Spotter planes, action plans, and steerage of the educational workplace', *British Journal of Sociology of Education* 19(3): 291–303.

Spark, M. (1965) *The Prime of Miss Jean Brodie*, Harmondsworth: Penguin.

Stahl, S.A. (1999) 'Why innovations come and go (and mostly go): the case of whole language', *Educational Researcher* 2(8): 13–22.

Standish, P. (1997) 'Absolutely fabulous', in P. Standish and R. Smith (eds) *Teaching Right and Wrong: Moral Education in the Balance*, Stoke-on-Trent: Trentham.

Starkey, H. (2000) 'Citizenship education in France and Britain: evolving theories and practices', *Curriculum Journal* 11(1): 39–54.

Stenhouse, L. (1975) *An Introduction to Research and Curriculum Development*, London: Heinemann.

Stephenson, J. (1994) 'Capability and competence', *Capability* 1(1): 3–4.

Stephenson, J. (1996) 'Beyond competence to capability and the learning society', *Capability* 2(1): 60–62.

Stewart, J. and Hamlin, R. (1992) 'Competence-based training: the case against change', *Journal of European Industrial Training* 16(7): 21–32.

Stoll, L. and Fink, D. (1996) *Changing our Schools: Linking School Effectiveness and School Improvement*, Buckingham: Open University Press.

Strike, K.A. and Posner, G.J. (1985) 'A conceptual change view of learning and understanding', in L.H.T. Pines and A.I. West (eds) *Cognitive Structure and Conceptual Change*, London: Academic Press.

Stringfield, S. and Herman, R. (1995) 'Assessment of the state of school effectiveness research in the United States of America', in B.P.M. Creemers and N. Osinga (eds) *ICSEI Country Reports*, Leeuwarden: ICSEI Secretariat.

Stringfield, S. and Herman, R. (1996) 'Assessment of the state of school effectiveness research in the Unites States of America', *School Effectiveness and School Research* 7(2): 173–189.

Sugrue, C. (1997) *Complexities of Teaching: Child-Centred Perspectives*, London: Falmer.

Sutherland, P. (1992) *Cognitive Development Today, Piaget and his Critics*, London: Paul Chapman.

Sutton, A., Wortley, A., Harrison, J. and Wise, C. (2000) 'Superteachers: from policy towards practice', *British Journal of Educational Studies* 48(4): 413–428.

Sylva, K., Harry, J., Mirelman, H., Brussell, A. and Riley, J. (1999) 'Evaluation of a focused literacy programme in Reception and Year 1 classes: classroom observations', *British Journal of Educational Research* 25(5): 617–636.

Talbot, M. and Tate, N. (1997) 'Shared values in a pluralist society?', in R. Smith and P. Standish (eds) *Teaching Right and Wrong: Moral Education in the Balance*, Stoke on Trent: Trentham.

Tamir, Y. (1995) 'Two concepts of multiculturalism', in Y. Tamir (ed.) *Democratic Education in a Multicultural State*, Oxford: Blackwell.

Teddlie, C. and Reynolds, D. (2000) *The International Handbook of School Effectiveness Research*, London: Falmer.

Teddlie, C. and Stringfield, S. (1993) *Schools do Make a Difference: Lessons Learned from a Ten Year Study of School Effects*, New York: Teachers College Press.

Thompson, M. (1999) 'Whose profession is it?', address to the Eleventh Annual Conference of the Association for the Study of Primary Education, Crowne Plaza Hotel, Liverpool.

Tomlinson, P. (1995a) 'Can competence profiling work for effective teacher preparation? Part 1: general issues', *Oxford Review of Education* 21(2): 179–194.

Tomlinson, P. (1995b) 'Can competence profiling work for effective teacher preparation? Part 2: pitfalls and principles', *Oxford Review of Education* 21(3): 299–314.

Townsend, T. (1997) (ed.) *Restructuring and Quality: Issues for Tomorrow's Schools*, London: Routledge.

Trevarthen, C. (1992) 'An infant's motives for speaking and thinking in the culture', in A.H. Wold (ed.) *The Dialogical Alternative*, Oxford: Oxford University Press.

Trigg, P. and Pollard, A. (1998) 'Pupil experience and curriculum for life-long learning', in C. Richards and P.H. Taylor (eds) *How Shall we School our Children? Primary Education and its Future*, London: Falmer.

Truelove, S. (1992) *Handbook of Training and Development*, Oxford: Blackwell.

TTA (1996) *TTA 11/ 96 National Standards for Teachers*, London: TTA.

TTA (1997a) *Standards for the Award of Qualified Teacher Status*, London: TTA.

TTA (1997b) *Career Entry Profile*, London: TTA.

TTA (1997c) *National Standards for Headteachers*, London: TTA.

TTA (1998) *National Standards for Headteachers*, London: TTA.

Turner-Bisset, R. (2000) 'Reconstructing the primary curriculum: integration revisited', *Education 3-13* 28(1): 3–8.

Vaill, P.B. (1991) *Managing as a Performing Art: New Ideas for a World of Chaotic Change*, San Francisco, CA: Jossey-Bass.

Van Manen, M. (1995) 'On the epistemology of reflective practice', *Teachers and Teaching: Theory and Practice* 1: 33–50.

Van Velzen, W., Miles, M., Ekhold, M., Hameyer, U. and Robin, D. (1985) *Making School Improvement Work: A Conceptual Guide to Practice*, Leuven: Acco.

Vartuli, S. (1999) 'How early childhood teacher beliefs vary across grade level', *Early Childhood Quarterly* 14(4): 489–514.

Verba, M. (1994) 'The beginnings of collaboration in peer interaction', *Human Development* 37: 125–139.

Von Glaserfeld, E. (1995) *Radical Constructivism: A Way of Knowing and Learning*, London: Falmer.

Vygotsky, L.S. (1962) *Thought and Language*, Cambridge, MA: MIT Press.

Vygotsky, L.S. (1978) *Mind in Society: The Development of Higher Psychological Processes*, Cambridge, MA: MIT Press.

Wain, K. (1996) 'Foucault, education, the self and modernity', *Journal of Philosophy of Education* 30(3): 345–360.

Walkerdine, V. (1992) 'Progressive pedagogy and political struggle', in C. Luke and J. Gore (eds) *Feminism and Critical Pedagogy*, London: Routledge.

Wallace, C. (1988) 'Towards a collegiate approach to curriculum management in primary and middle schools', *School Organisation* 8(1): 25–34.

Weale, A. (1995) 'From little England to democratic Europe?', *New Community* 21(2): 115–225.

Webb, R. (1993) *Eating the Elephant Bit by Bit*, London: Association of Teachers and Lecturers' Publications.

Weindling, D. (1997) Strategic planning in schools: some practical techniques, in M. Preedy, R. Gleitter and R. Levacic (eds) *Educational Management: Strategy, Quality and Resources,* Buckingham: Open University Press.

Wells, G. (1986) *The Meaning Makers*, London: Heinemann Educational.

Wertsch, J.V. (1991) *Voices of the Mind*, London: Harvester Wheatsheaf.

West, M. and Hopkins, D. (1995) 'Reconceptualizing school effectiveness and school improvement'. British Educational Research Association Annual Meeting and European Conference on Educational Research, Bath, 17 September.

Wharton, D.M. (1997) 'Learning about responsibility: lessons from homework', *British Journal of Educational Psychology* 45(1): 4–21.

White, J. (1997) 'Philosophical perspectives on school effectiveness and school improvement', *Curriculum Journal* 8(1): 29–44.

White, J. (1999) 'Thinking about assessment', *Journal of Philosophy of Education* 32(3): 201–211.

White, R. (1993) 'Autonomy as foundational', in H.J. Silverman (ed.) *Questioning Foundations*, New York: Routledge.

White, R.T. and Gunstone, R.F. (1989) 'Metalearning and conceptual change', *International Journal of Science Education* 11, special issue: 577–586.

Whitty, G. (1990) 'The New Right and the National Curriculum: state control or market forces?', in B. Moon (ed.) *New Curriculum – National Curriculum*, London: Hodder and Stoughton.

Williams, E. (2000) 'The price of perfection', *Times Educational Supplement* 28 January.

Willmott, R. (1999) 'School effectiveness research: an ideological commitment?', *Journal of Philosophy of Education* 33(2): 253–268.

Wilson, J. (1999) 'Accountability', in M. Brundrett (ed.) *Principles of School Leadership*, Guildford: Peter Francis.

Wilson, J. (2000a) 'Doing justice to inclusion', *European Journal of Special Needs Education* 15(3): 297–304.

Wilson, J. (2000b) *Key Issues in Education and Teaching*, London: Cassell.

Winch, C. (1998) 'Markets, educational opportunities and education: reply to Tooley', *Journal of Philosophy of Education* 32(3): 429–449.

Winch, C. and Gingell, J. (1996) 'Educational assessment: reply to Andrew Davis', *Journal of Philosophy of Education* 30(3): 377–388.

Woodhead, M. (1998) '"Quality" in early childhood programmes – a contextually appropriate approach', *International Journal of Early Years Education* 6(1): 5–17.

Woods, P. (1990) *The Happiest Days? How Pupils Cope with School*, London: Falmer.

Zeichner, K. and Liston, D. (1987) 'Teaching student teachers to reflect', *Harvard Educational Review* 57(1): 23–48.

Zeichner, K. and Tabachnick, B.R. (1981) 'Are the effects of teacher education washed out by school experience?', *Journal of Teacher Education* 32: 7–11.

Ziyal, L. (1996) 'Definition of critical performance demands: a new approach to competency', *Competency* 4(2): 25–31.

Index